Peter Filby

TVR

The Early Years

Peter Filby

AUTOCRAFT BOOKS
Reigate, Surrey

First published June 2010
© Peter Filby 2010

All rights reserved. No part of this publication may be reproduced in any form, or by any means, without prior permission in writing from the publisher.

ISBN 978 0 9545729 1 4

Published by Autocraft Books
1 Howard Road, Reigate
Surrey RH2 7JE

Tel: 01737 222336
Email: peterfilby@tvrbooks.com
Website: www.tvrbooks.com

Typeset by Sally Mitchell
Production by Grapevine Design and Print, Worthing
Page design by James Mansell

CONTENTS

Introduction		7
Chapter 1	Venture into the Unknown	9
Chapter 2	The Birth of a Tradition	23
Chapter 3	New car, New Problems	43
Chapter 4	Trouble Very Regular	65
Chapter 5	The Aitchison-Hopton Era	89
Chapter 6	Collapse in 1962	115
Chapter 7	Survival Time	143
Chapter 8	The Monster from America	167
Chapter 9	Collapse in 1965	197
Chapter 10	The Trident Dream	217
Chapter 11	1965 – Racing for Survival	227
Timeline 1956 - 1965		243
About the Author		253
Acknowledgements		254
Coming Next...		255

INTRODUCTION

It all started in such a simple, innocent way. Various luminaries of the TVR Car Club had been suggesting for several years that I should reprint my old book *Success Against The Odds*. This sounded very straightforward until I eventually relented and began work on the project. Time-wise, we must be talking here of 2004 or 2005, and it wasn't long before I realised I wouldn't be happy with anything less than a complete rewrite. Hmm... this sounded rather heavier.

But you know what? As soon as I began to concentrate on the book, I was reminded of what an incredibly fascinating, compelling and entertaining saga TVR history is. The longer I worked on it, the more I enjoyed it and the more involved I became. So I decided I would do a thoroughly proper job and avoid rushing towards some stress-inducing, pre-set deadline. Removing such a restriction on time meant I could relax, expand my research wider and wider, make more contacts and encourage more information to come flowing in. And that's exactly what happened. Marvellous!

All this fresh information, accompanied by endless double- and treble-checking of facts, meant the new book could be the real deal. Of course, there have been several TVR books published since I wrote the first one many moons ago in 1975 and '76. But it was clear that a marque as great and legendary as TVR deserved something more – a thoroughly in-depth effort that would give this formidable name its rightful place in motoring history. And the book simply *had* to include as many typical anecdotes as I could get people to recount. After all, the marque's founder Trevor Wilkinson was telling them at an early stage: "A friend bought the first Grantura, and driving home one night he passed a house with the curtains open. Noticing a woman undressing in her bedroom, he put the car straight into a ditch!"

There was only one problem with my project. I had such an enjoyable and fulfilling time being free of all constraints and writing 'the' book that I let it get out of hand

and produced far too many words – indeed, enough for a super-heavyweight and extremely impractical 500-600 page tome! The answer was to make it into two books, this first one finishing neatly at the end of 1965 when Grantura Engineering went bust. The Lilley era (late 1965 to late 1981) is covered in the second volume over fourteen chapters, which means it's an even more substantial job than *The Early Years*. This explains why everything took so long. Hopefully you'll find the wait for volume one has been worth it – and won't mind waiting a few more months for number two.

The story of TVR is a quite incredible one, even by the specialist motor car industry's own extraordinary standards. It was always a great struggle for the men of Blackpool, despite the cars themselves being highly entertaining to drive and mostly capable of decent performance and confident high speed cornering. The big problems were that the company management wasn't always as professional and organised as it should have been, while finances were generally seriously stretched. Thus fortunes fluctuated wildly, the outcome being a crazily chequered career for a remarkable sports car that somehow remained a born survivor.

THE EARLY YEARS

This book aims to describe in entertaining fashion the highs and lows of the marque's early years, charting the cars' evolution and giving due credit to the people who built them and backed them. And there's comprehensive pictorial coverage of all the different models produced before the end of 1965. I also felt it was important to show how well TVRs performed in motor sport – racing, hillclimbing, sprinting and autocross – so have included a brief competition section at the end of most chapters. Hopefully you'll agree it all adds up to a thoroughly complete record of the marque's first 15 years of existence. If my high-tech ballpoint pen doesn't break down, *The Early Years* is also the launching pad for a series of three, or potentially even four, volumes that will give TVR the solid historical standing such a great name thoroughly deserves.

I've had a wonderful time over the last few years meeting TVR people and hearing their stories. If I have one regret, it's that I didn't start the work at least ten years ago, for I would then have been able to renew my old acquaintances with TVR founders, Trevor Wilkinson and Jack Pickard, and their key associates, Bernard Williams and Stanley Kilcoyne, all of whom helped me so much with *Success Against The Odds*. Sadly, all these men have passed away in recent years and will never see the book that pays full tribute to their valiant efforts. So it is to them that I would like to dedicate *TVR The Early Years*.

Peter Filby

CHAPTER ONE

Venture into the Unknown

TVR founder Trevor Wilkinson built his first 'special' in a small Blackpool workshop in 1947, basing it on an old Alvis Firebird. Two years later he fabricated his own chassis for another 'special' and named it TVR. Two more very basic TVR one-offs were built before the end of 1951, and these were followed in 1953 by the first of a series of 'production' chassis for which customers could choose their own engines and fibreglass bodies. Built in 1954 using one of these chassis, the TVR Sports Saloon was the first of the marque to be sold as a kit car.

▼ Trevor Wilkinson pictured in 1984 at the premises of his company Trevini Plastics, which at the time was busy making roadsweepers' barrows. (Peter Filby)

The year was 1947, the location an old wheelwright's shop in Beverley Grove, South Shore, Blackpool. A young man called Trevor Wilkinson struggled to remove the tired old bodywork and rotten wooden body frame from his ancient four-cylinder Alvis Firebird. Once he'd got the job completed, Les Dale – a friend who shared Trevor's premises – took a long hard look at the bare rolling chassis. Very soon, thanks to Dale's skills, it was clothed with an all-aluminium, two-seater open sports body. The re-bodied Alvis never received a name of its own; it was never a priority to think of one. Like most other home-built machines of the time, it was a true 'special'.

Light engineering was the main business at the premises, but full of enthusiasm for his new project, a determined Trevor worked hard in his spare time to make it a runner. Late evenings and long weekends passed. In those early post-war years, materials, parts and resources were difficult to come by. Tools and equipment in the workshop were not all they might have been, to say the least, but one evening the unique machine was at last complete – one ambition realised, another in the most embryonic form. As the Wilkinson special rumbled off on test run number one, its cycle wings wobbling unsteadily, Trevor was unwittingly lighting the touch paper to one long, somewhat turbulent, always lively chapter in motoring history. Little did he know it but he was setting in

THE EARLY YEARS

motion an incredible roller-coaster sequence of highs and lows. The marque name he would soon create would, over the years, have a quite remarkably chequered career, even by the specialist sports car industry's extraordinary standards.

Born in May 1923 above the family grocer shop in Bond Street, Blackpool, Trevor was destined to become a creative, hands-on man. There was no family background in motor engineering or motor sport but Trevor felt he was born to be involved in those pursuits. Later, when the family was living in a large house in South Shore, Blackpool, he used its double garage for the reconditioning of used cars. As for his schooling, he was educated at the local Arnold School and shone at handiwork – until leaving in 1937, at fourteen and a half years old, to serve a mechanic's apprenticeship at the Excel Motor Company, the local Renault agent. Upon leaving, he was a fully qualified mechanic.

Much to his own surprise, and despite him enduring two medicals, the country declined Trevor's services for the heady years between 1939 and 1945. Mr Wilkinson Snr found plenty of uses for them however... helping out in one of the family's shops, which specialised in equipment for children. Four-wheeled devices were already Trevor's first love but it wasn't softly sprung prams that he really had in mind. There was seemingly no point in motorising such vehicles – walking pace was generally quite rapid enough for the occupants. Still, safe handling and decent pavement holding could be worked on, he mused, as he repaired wheels and made up some special bearings that were unavailable to the mass pram-buying public during the war.

His war effort over, a 23-year-old Trevor founded his own fledgling business, Trevcar Motors, in 1946. Such a venture had been very much against family advice but, recognising his son's grit and perseverance, Mr Wilkinson Snr relented and provided half of the £1200 needed to buy Trevor's first premises, the sadly neglected wheelwright's shop in Beverley Grove. A rather shy and modest chap, Trevor was absolutely single-minded concerning his future, so he was naturally happy to concrete, re-wire, paint and generally make ship-shape the whole place ready for business to begin. His philosophy was 'true happiness lies in achievement', and with £100 in his bank account he set out on the long, hard road towards a successful business. Although his own design of sports car was hovering at the back of his mind, simply designing and making things were really his main interests at this time.

With car repairs and a spot of second-hand car dealing was how it all got going, but the business quickly moved into handling more creative light engineering work. An extremely hard worker, Trevor's main focus during these early days would be developing his business... and trying to make a living. Working on the Alvis Firebird

▲ Built in 1951, this is TVR 'special' number three. In his late twenties, Trevor looks well pleased with his efforts. Finished in yellow, the car had 1200cc Austin A40 Sports power and could manage acceleration to 60mph in about 11-12 seconds.

special of 1947 certainly turned his early automotive aspirations into some form of raw reality, but moving a step further and building a self-designed sports car from the floor upwards would take time and tenacity. So the priority at this stage was to concentrate on work that created income.

One local man had been helping Trevor in his spare time over evenings and weekends to earn some extra cash. The two enthusiasts got on well and shared similar ideas, and during 1947 there was a new full-time employee at Beverley Grove, Jack Pickard. Born in July 1919 in Oldham, Lancashire, Jack had served a pre-war apprenticeship with a mechanical engineering company. He rapidly expanded and developed his talents, becoming proficient at repairing old cars and restoring bodywork. His first full-time job was with Gilmore and Daniels, a small Blackpool engineering company that made parts for aero engines, and he stayed there for about five years. But Jack's real passion was motor cars, and when he was faced with the opportunity to join Trevor, hear about his ambitions and become part of a tiny but potentially exciting operation, his future was sealed. A warm, quietly spoken and good humoured personality, he was to become dedicated to working with Trevor and ultimately creating sports cars.

Renamed TVR (TreVoR) Engineering, the business soon began to expand. One of Jack Pickard's skills was carpentry and he would often make wooden moulds with which to develop in fibreglass the various items customers had requested. This led to other moulding work, including larger jobs such as fairground bumper cars and buggies for the big dipper at Blackpool Pleasure Beach. On the engineering side came the manufacture of a wide variety of things – bakery equipment, amusement machines, devices for making Easter eggs and even a machine for coating ice-cream blocks with chocolate. Unlikely though it may sound, these light engineering jobs were the earliest roots

▼ It all started here. The first TVRs were built in this old wheelwright's workshop in Beverley Grove, Blackpool. Trevor (left) and Jack Pickard are pictured there in 1976. (John Bailie)

THE EARLY YEARS

of the TVR sports car legend, and for quite some time operations at Beverley Grove would continue in this way.

At this point in his career, Jack's weekly wage was £7, and, as boss, Trevor quite likely took less. The money clearly wasn't great, the hours were long and the work hard, yet the two men's dedication and enthusiasm were unwavering. With their shared vision of a unique sports car always at the back of their minds – and usually being discussed at lunch and tea times – they remained realistic about the situation: such dreams would have to wait. In any case, enough capital to build the first TVR (it would, by nature, be a special) would take time to save up. So throughout 1948 varied engineering work remained their staple trade and brought their weekly income. Amongst other projects, lorries were repaired and reconditioned, while more manufacturing jobs included golf caddy carts and even mouth organs!

At last, early in 1949 Trevor declared himself and TVR Engineering's bank balance ready to start developing the first TVR chassis. Forced to work on the new project over evenings and weekends simply to keep intact, and avoid draining, the company's steady bread-and-butter income, the two men doggedly logged extra hours. Gradually taking shape before them was a slightly primitive but strong multi-tubular steel chassis designed by Trevor to take independent trailing arm and coilspring front suspension and a Morris 8 live rear axle mounted on half-elliptic leaf springs. Also from the old Morris were the tall 22in diameter wheels and shock absorbers. The upper chassis frame members were of smaller and lighter tubes and they formed the body frame, so that when the body was fashioned it would be little more than a simple aluminium skin wrapped over the upper frame.

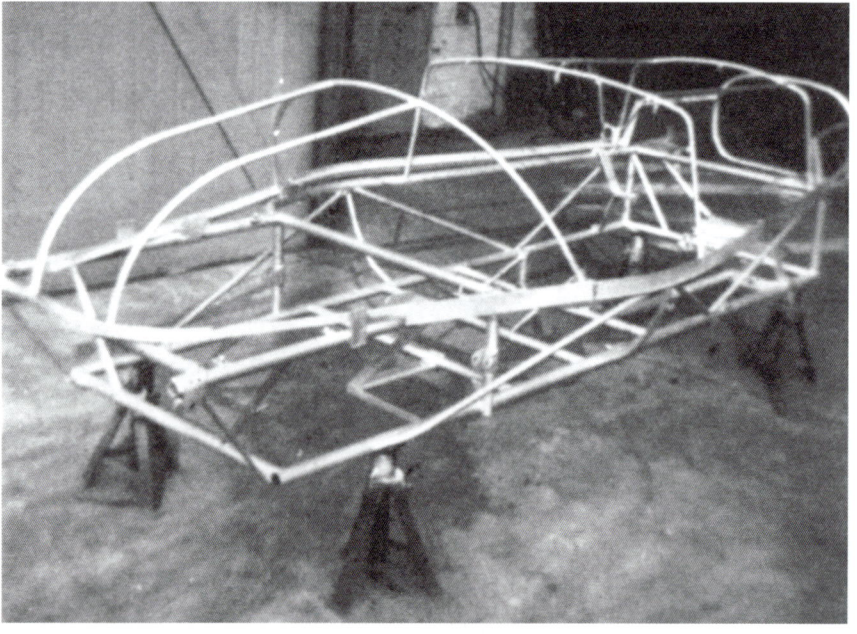

▼ TVR's first chassis, as used for the first three 'specials' built between 1949 and 1951. The lighter gauge upper tubes formed the body frame.

Without losing sight of the need to keep the wolves from the door, Trevor and Jack were naturally full of anticipation – the very first TVR, this was it! In truth, it was very much a typically basic post-war special, its chassis the work of inexperienced enthusiasts – in other words, partly educated guesswork and a real venture into the unknown. Trevor had never had any formal engineering design training and it showed. For parts, it was a matter of making do with whatever was available; there wasn't exactly a great choice. They had robbed an ancient Morris of its back axle, made use of the same car's brakes, fabricated their own cast alloy trailing arms for the front suspension, and managed to extract the 1172cc side-valve engine and three-speed gearbox from an even more ancient 1936 Ford 10hp van discovered in a scrapyard.

Jack remembered how they came across the coilsprings for the TVR's front suspension: "We used to make things and do maintenance work for this old Scotsman who ran the bumper cars down at the seafront pleasure beach. He used to hoard old bumper parts in a great pile. Well, one day we looked at this pile, saw a coilspring and thought 'that looks alright, we'll try it'. It turned out to be a humble fairground dodgem bumper spring! Worked well on the TVR though."

VENTURE INTO THE UNKNOWN

▲ The company's first business card included an early attempt at a corporate badge.

Indeed, those coilsprings, together with their bumper, should really have continued on the TVR in their original 'bumping' capacity, for the first thing the still naked but driveable chassis did was run headlong into a tree. Once again called in to make a body, Les Dale had started work on a simple, two-seat aluminium shape that would not necessarily revolutionise sports car design. Perhaps to get the feel of the machine in action, to enable his artistic instincts to transfer the TVR's character into shaped aluminium, Dale just could not wait to find out.

Trevor explained: "It was barely more than a rolling chassis with the drivetrain fitted. It would roll along well but not to a halt, certainly not in any kind of hurry! So we fixed up two handbrake cables, one either side of the seat. Les would have to pull like hell on these with his bare hands to stop the car. He shot off down Beverley Grove, naturally failed to stop at the junction with the main road, and disappeared round the corner, just avoiding a bus. Then the next thing we saw was a policeman cycling past. There had to be trouble, so we stayed where we were. After about fifteen minutes we thought we'd better have a look for Les, and we found him walking back along the main road looking rather guilty. He'd resorted to the best brake he could see, a tree!"

Les Dale's artistic abilities were temporarily restrained. Repairs were necessary. Test day number two was held at a more suitable venue after Trevor persuaded the authorities at Blackpool's Squires Gate aerodrome to loan him a section of runway, despite the slim chance (hopefully) of the TVR taking off. This time there were half-decent brakes, but no such luxuries as figure-hugging seats, a petrol tank or a proper radiator cap. The petrol 'system' was strapped on to the frame in the form of an old petrol can mated to a pipe leading to the fuel pump. Accommodation for the driver and anyone willing to be a passenger, whilst not being in the luxury class, was at least available. Well, let's just say that the basic Ford van seats had been bolted hastily to a piece of wooden board, which was in turn bolted to the chassis.

The whole point was that at seven o'clock in the morning on a windswept runway Trevor and Jack proved to themselves that it could be done. Touring around the barren

▶ The very first of the line. TVR 'special' number one was built in 1949. Power came from a tuned 1172cc Ford 100E engine producing a lusty 35bhp! Top speed was about 75mph.

THE EARLY YEARS

runway, the car reacting to every imperfection on the concrete surface, the brakes working adequately, they felt delighted. Their car worked – it was fantastic! Sensibly, though, they accepted there'd be tough times ahead if they were going to make any more cars. "I stuck with the company because I had faith in it," Jack said. "A lot of people would tell us we were foolishly wasting our time, but we were young, enthusiastic and a bit mad. It was nice to be doing something different."

Les Dale could now be given a free hand to finish the aluminium bodywork, fitting it over the light steel frame. That hand turned out to be rather too free, for Trevor was somewhat taken aback at the results. Jack was more forthright, feeling it was an understatement to say that the first body did not look attractive or modern enough. Painted British Racing Green, it did at least appear functional and wasn't badly proportioned. Even the 22in diameter wheels looked the part. The tuned 1172cc Ford engine was no snorting beast and provided only limited power (some 35bhp), while the TVR was no real lightweight at just under 11cwt, so maximum speed struggled to reach a lowly 75mph. It was lively enough performance by the standards of the time and the Morris drum brakes proved quite adequate all round.

Trevor had already removed three letters from his christian name to form his company's name, and this was kept for the car – a nice short title with a central V that lent itself perfectly to a bonnet badge. TVR number one was born and a new sports car marque was in embryonic form. Never forgetting their need to keep on top of their company's staple trade, Trevor and Jack were thinking at this point of building only a tiny number of cars – if there was the opportunity. Little could they have imagined where their sideline and hobby would ultimately lead to.

Despite all its quirks and idiosyncrasies, upon the strange machine's completion in 1949 Trevor's cousin agreed to buy the first TVR special. Perhaps even more surprisingly, he paid £325 for it – not a small amount of money at the time. Unfortunately, little could he have imagined that his new pride and joy would soon be written-off in a road crash or that Trevor would end up scrapping its remains and using some of its salvageable parts in TVR number two.

Both the sale and the demise of Trevor and Jack's first TVR were of some value at the company's Beverley Grove premises. Already in the early stages of construction, the second car's completion could be advanced as more parts were now in hand from the wrecked car. Improvements could be made, too. TVR number one had been lively enough in action but was seriously devoid of creative comforts – the simple van seats, a boot lid that opened to reveal a spare wheel and enough extra space to house a few rounds of sandwiches, this had been only just acceptable, and due to the lack of a hood, waterproofing was something of a problem when it rained. Doubtful cornering on very hard springs that sent the car

▼ Nothing wrong with the styling of TVR number one. Very well proportioned, its simple aluminium bodywork was painted British Racing Green. The wheels were of Morris 8 origin.

VENTURE INTO THE UNKNOWN

▶ Number one's front suspension was designed and made by Trevor. Like the wheels, the brakes and rear axle came from a Morris 8.

▼ Completed in 1950 with 1172cc Ford side-valve power, TVR number two was sold by the company as a rolling chassis minus engine and gearbox. It certainly seemed to have lost out in the styling stakes.

round in a series of hops and jumps, this had been rather alarming but great fun nonetheless. All in all, the first TVR had left plenty of scope for improvement with future efforts.

Trevor and Jack's delight about their car building progress was soon given added support when a customer appeared wanting to buy TVR number two as a rolling chassis minus engine, gearbox and bodywork. A local enthusiast, the man wanted the car for competition use and intended to finish it to his own specification. Having said that, as the car's build progressed its details were actually very similar to those of its earlier sister. The chassis design was unchanged and the rear axle, half-elliptic leaf springs, wheels, shock absorbers, brakes and worm and peg steering were all of Morris 8 origin. For the front suspension there was a change to a wishbone and transverse leaf spring arrangement using a combination of Austin/Morris, Ford and MG parts, all of them modified to suit.

The exact date of the second TVR's eventual completion was never recorded but it seems probable that it was in the first half of 1950. Les Dale was again the craftsman asked to fabricate the aluminium bodywork (over a light tubular steel frame) and the well-rounded end result was rather similar to the first car's appearance.

Eventually, finished in light blue paint and powered by another 1172cc Ford side-valve engine, TVR number two is believed to have started out in life competing in various sprint and hillclimb events. If it was used on the road, it's likely that it was driven illegally for short, local journeys, road traffic law enforcement being rather lax in those days. The car's first legal road registration would happen later in June 1952, after which it continued to be used in competition by several different owners through the rest of the 1950s.

At some point during this period extensive changes were made to TVR number two's bodywork, probably to enhance its racing performance. Most noticeable aspects of the revised styling were a much lower bonnet line and a more streamlined nosecone that improved the car's appearance and dragged more air into the

THE EARLY YEARS

radiator. A single aero screen, roll-over hoop and side exhaust completed the new, more purposeful, competitive image. Other special features incorporated were Marchal headlights from a French Delage tourer, a fire extinguisher said to be from a Royal family staff car, and a rev counter from a World War Two Spitfire fighter plane! Later, during the 1960s, the remarkable little machine would still be going strong racing regularly in the 750 Motor Club's 1172 Formula championships.

And so to the third TVR. Number two had left Beverley Grove and general engineering work remained the first consideration to keep TVR Engineering ticking over and the wages paid, but Trevor was determined to build a car of his own for road and competition use. After several months' work, 1951's TVR number three was again similar to the previous version but received a 1200cc Austin A40 Sports engine with matching gearbox and rear axle. As with car number two, the front suspension was by wishbones and a transverse leaf spring. At about 11cwt on the scales, number three out-performed number one by 5mph in top gear before the bodyshell's lack of aerodynamics caused wind resistance to interfere with progress.

Painted yellow, the latest machine's bodywork featured more detail styling changes

▲ Prior to restoration, TVR number two displays its extensively altered body frame. (Peter Filby)

▼ Restoration complete, number two's appearance was clearly influenced by the Lotus 7. (Peter Filby)

▲ Looking very different from its first body, number two's more aerodynamic aluminium shape was seen mostly on race tracks during the 1950s. The cockpit was suitably spartan. (Peter Filby)

by the hand of Les Dale, particularly in the nose area. With three vertical cut-outs in a somewhat crude looking and blunt nose panel, this seemed to be a backwards step from the first and second cars' pleasantly rounded noses. No question, TVR number three wasn't exactly beautiful. However, Trevor was a keen member of the local Blackpool and Fylde Car Club, and in competition events during 1952 and 1953 the yellow special soon answered its critics with its lively performance. Driven by its creator on its first hillclimb, it was second in class only to an Aston Martin. During more than twelve months' competition exploits in the north-west, mainly hillclimbs and sprints, Trevor notched up several awards in club events – enough to enhance TVR's local reputation and further encourage interest from potential customers.

One young man friendly with Trevor at this time was the locally based David Hives, a keen car enthusiast who occasionally visited Beverley Grove to buy fibreglass material and steel. David often drove his own special in sprints and driving tests competing against Trevor's TVR number three. The Hives car was a modified MG J2 which had received Ford E93A power after the original MG engine had blown-up. As fate would have it, some ten years later David would become a long-serving and key member of TVR's shop floor, development and managerial staff.

▶ With its strange looking nose, TVR number three took a faltering backwards step in the beauty stakes. As Trevor said: "It was a question of covering up the mechanicals somehow." The car was eventually written off in an accident.

THE EARLY YEARS

A major problem with the first three TVRs had been the expense of their aluminium bodies. Their confidence levels raised, the summer of 1953 saw Trevor and Jack setting to work on a new multi-tubular chassis, not unlike the first three but simpler (it had no upper body frame) and tougher looking – it used 16-gauge tubing of 1.5in diameter. Also, it was engineered specifically to accept more Austin A40 components such as the independent coil-sprung front suspension and rear axle – although the rack and pinion steering was from a Morris Minor. The two men had come to the conclusion that a simplified chassis using as many major components from one car as possible, and clothed with a low-cost, moulded fibreglass body made by any one of the growing numbers of special body makers of the time, could well be marketed in small numbers. It was an exciting thought for Blackpool's budding car makers.

Because the engineering trade still took precedence in the workshop, work on the new chassis was done in spare time and generally continued late into the evening – dedication and long hours were the name of the game. For power, Trevor transferred the Austin A40 Sports engine and gearbox from his own TVR number three to the redesigned chassis. The relief evident upon eventual completion of the new rolling assembly was, as ever, only overshadowed by the desire to trundle down the road in it to see how it went. With a rough, unmade central section, Beverley Grove had always proved suitable for giving cars a good pounding. The construction of some new houses was to blame for the test strip's most agricultural section...

"I went down there, hitting the rough stuff at a fair speed," Trevor recalled, "not giving a thought to the fact that the steering wheel had been left loose pending final adjustments and was only held in place by a key. Well, of course the wheel lifted, the key fell out and suddenly I had no steering. No problem, except I was heading straight for three workmen who were building the new properties. There they were, sitting on the pavement on a plank supported by two oil drums, eating sandwiches and drinking tea... and then they weren't there. The nearside front wheel of the car had brushed along the plank and, with sandwiches and mugs flying everywhere, they'd gone backwards over the plank and down into the foundations! Luckily no

▲ TVR's second chassis design was a simple affair engineered to accept predominantly Austin A40 running gear. It retailed at £50 in basic form.

▼ Customers could also buy this chassis in rolling form, as shown, and make their own choice of fibreglass body. Various engines could be fitted.

▲ Fitted with an RGS Atalanta fibreglass body, the first TVR to be offered as a full kit was known as the Sports Saloon. Introduced in 1954, the kit cost £650 plus tax. Only three were built.

▼ Trevor used GFV 866, the first Sports Saloon, for personal transport. Power was a 1200cc Austin A40 unit but a variety of other engines could be fitted. The interior was nothing if not functional.

further damage was done."

The workshop at Beverley Grove had already been enlarged. The extra shop floor area meant that one side could be used for general engineering and building chassis, while across the floor could be a bodywork and final completion area. All that was needed now was a fibreglass body for TVR number four. Looking for a 'stylish' shape to fit their latest chassis, Trevor and Jack soon discovered the modestly attractive RGS Atalanta body supplied from premises in Windsor by Richard G Shattock, a noted special builder who had been one of the first people in Britain to offer fibreglass bodies for sale.

"The Shattock body was well made but it wasn't ideal," recalled Trevor. "For about £40 - £50 you got a complete moulding comprising the front end with wings and bonnet, back section and long central section. This central part of the shell allowed for adjustment, as it could be cut and shortened according to the wheelbase it was to fit. Lastly, the door openings had to be cut out and the doors refitted. After much cutting and adjusting, Jack and I finally got all the panels to fit the TVR chassis, but it wasn't a satisfactory way of doing things."

The new TVR prototype initially shaped up in the body shop as a convertible. When the job was nearing completion, an RGS hardtop was acquired, modified to fit and bolted down with just four bolts, and so could very quickly be removed. Finished by spring 1954, registered GFV 866 and named the TVR Sports Saloon, it was the first TVR 'production' model officially to be marketed and looked ideal for what was a fast-growing hobby amongst car enthusiasts. Jack was excited and ambitious as always: "We could see thousands being sold. It was going to spread all over the world!"

A figure nearer twenty was probably more realistic. Indeed, over the next two years about twenty examples of the latest chassis would be sold to special builders, the customer always choosing which off-the-peg bodyshell and engine he or TVR would fit. In fact, the TVR Sports Saloon body was to grace only three of those chassis despite Trevor's efforts to publicize his product in competition events – sprints, rallies and hillclimbs – with the first of the trio. His first outing in the car was in that year's

Morecambe Rally over the weekend of 21st-23rd May. Finishing the event on the Saturday night, the car appeared in the Concours d'Elegance on the following Sunday morning after only a quick wash down. Trevor won no prizes that time out but the good looking car was admired by many of those present and the exposure had been useful.

In fact, Trevor was to do a lot more competition work in his Sports Saloon and several years later, in his last season of action with the car, it was still performing well enough for him to take six awards. One thing he didn't enjoy was circuit racing – he felt it was too costly and only worth doing if you had the right car with the right specification and, of course, the right financial backing. The Sports Saloon certainly didn't fit the bill but Trevor did enter one race, having been invited to compete as part of a Buckler team in the 750MC Birkett Six-hour Relay at Silverstone late in August 1954. Trevor completed his stint without incident and the team finished the race successfully, albeit without a notable placing. Apart from its competition exploits, the Sports Saloon was also pressed into action as an everyday road car, and Trevor was to use it for both purposes for something like eight years in all.

With the advent of a 'production' chassis, ambitious ideas of making more cars at Beverley Grove had prompted the need for a brochure. The TVR Sports Saloon, it proudly stated, was 4ft 4in high overall, weighed 14cwt, 'thundered' to 60mph in 13 seconds and could manage a respectable maximum speed of 90mph. With a partially leather trimmed interior, bucket seats and carpeted luggage compartment, the Sports Saloon was priced at £650 in kit form. It even had, in a first for TVR, a dedicated marque badge. This was designed by John Cookson, a young art student who was friendly with Trevor and had often competed in his Buckler Mk5 special against Trevor's yellow TVR special (number three).

The theory behind Cookson's badge design was to give the little TVR company some credibility and the impression of a pedigree. Explained John: "It came at a point when I felt we needed to present TVR as an established maker of cars rather than an operation making just one-off specials. Trevor gave me the go-ahead and my idea was to go a bit retro with a 'winged' design influenced by the sort of badges used by well-established marques such as Morgan, Invicta and Bentley. It was stamped out of steel and then chrome plated, but it was expensive to produce and easily collected dirt between the intricacies of its central TVR logo and extended wings. So some time later it was revised as a slightly modified version of the design but this time finished with a smooth surface."

Although he could find faults with the Sports Saloon, Trevor had quickly gained an affection for his latest machine. He wasn't surprised that advertisements in the motoring press in 1955 brought another order, this time for a fully finished Sports Saloon painted in two shades of green, and he managed to give his new customer's car much improved interior trim. A Lieutenant in the Army who was stationed in Germany, the gentleman was more than pleased. He later wrote from Greece to say how happy he was with the car and that it had done everything he had asked of it except climb Mount Olympus without boiling!

▲ Trevor pilots his personal Sports Saloon around a marker point during a seafront rally, probably at Morecambe. For several years this TVR was his daily road car.

▼ Designed by Trevor Wilkinson's friend John Cookson, this badge was fitted to TVRs from early 1954 onwards.

VENTURE INTO THE UNKNOWN

To the untiring TVR pioneers, what had previously been over-ambitious ideas of getting their car into regular production were now at least looking hopeful, especially after further orders were received for chassis and kits. Despite space limitations at Beverley Grove, there were sometimes two chassis under preparation at any one time, and at the hardest-stretched limits of the term this indeed meant some sort of 'series' production. Trevor and Jack's dreams were edging towards reality and they now employed a young apprentice to handle most of the company's simple engineering work. The more complicated stuff was being looked after by another recent addition to the team, the highly skilled John Ward.

A local man of delightful disposition who was already a clever and very thorough craftsman, John started at TVR as a lathe operator and was soon to become machine shop manager, a position he was to hold with the Blackpool marque for many years. He approached his work in 'old school' style and in terms of designing and making new parts there was really nothing he couldn't turn his hand to. He wasn't quite so skilled with his shotgun, though – at some stage he'd had a serious accident when it suddenly went off and blew away half of one hip, leaving John with a pronounced limp.

Keeping a supply of hungry motoring enthusiasts and special builders knocking on the workshop door wanting to discuss car construction and perhaps take test drives did have its drawbacks. Not everybody was happy with the Sports Saloon demonstrator's curvaceous but somewhat bulbous lines. Mind you, this did not necessarily signify a return to Les Dale's styling talents. There was another happy bunch of fibreglass moulders and bodywork specialists working in Hudson Street, Rochdale, Lancashire, under the collective title of Rochdale Motor Panels & Engineering Ltd. These chaps were selling a variety of fibreglass sports car bodies to special builders and

▼ Another shot of Trevor's Sports Saloon in seafront rally action at Morecambe. TVR's boss used his car regularly in club competition events.

THE EARLY YEARS

were probably the most successful of the many companies joining this fast-growing business. Trevor and Jack felt that a Rochdale body was worth offering with the TVR chassis and ultimately a handful were so fitted, at least two of them being Rochdale C-Type 'shells.

Apart from having individual tastes regarding body styling, each new customer at Beverley Grove had his own idea of how his car might compete performance-wise with the Austin-Healey or Jaguar he'd really like to be ordering. If it wasn't to be the lowly 1172cc Ford 10 four-banger in the engine bay, it might be the 1200cc Austin A40 unit or the rather superior 1489cc MGA unit. One notable man came along to discuss buying a chassis fitted with mounts for his 2½-litre, twin-camshaft Lea-Francis engine – his name was Bernard Williams, a well known local speedway rider with whom Trevor and Jack would soon come into much closer contact. Throughout 1955 and 1956 these were the sort of engines that were fitted to the basic TVR chassis, which did itself have one variation. This was an assembly built with a slightly lighter gauge tube, basically very similar in layout but incorporating Morris Minor based, torsion bar rear suspension with an A-bracket locating the differential. All done to satisfy the customer's specific requirements.

Obviously, no two TVRs were ever the same, for they were all specials. Over the 1954-56 period they left the factory in whatever form the customers demanded: complete do-it-yourself kits, unclothed rolling chassis, bare chassis frames and one or two ready-to-go cars. Two varieties of Rochdale bodies were offered and four chassis were given open Mistral fibreglass bodies moulded by Microplas, a Mitcham, Surrey, based company well known for making bodies and parts for specials. Each moulding still had to be chopped and modified to fit, the doors cut out and often the bonnets as well. Incisions were made with loving care: the company could not afford mistakes. Never losing sight of the need to take on light engineering work to keep the money coming in and pay the wages, Trevor and Jack worked as hard as ever, often from 8am to 11pm. Instinct now assured them that their efforts at car making would eventually prove worthwhile.

▲ This was just one of the Rochdale body styles that could be fitted to the TVR chassis.

▼ Chatting to a friend, Trevor, in light coloured coat with dark collar, stands beside his Sports Saloon at Barbon hillclimb in Cumbria. Car number 55 was the seventeenth TVR built and had an RG Shattock body.

CHAPTER TWO

The Birth of a Tradition

After eight years in existence, TVR Engineering was established with an all-independent production chassis and its first exports to the USA, the latter representing the beginning of a long and ultimately lucrative relationship with American enthusiasts. Early in 1956 the company moved to bigger premises and by summer had built its first open sports racer of in-house design. In August 1957 the birth of the first TVR coupé, with its notchback rear window, was cause for celebration, but behind the scenes there were worrying question marks...

With basic TVR specials leaving the Beverley Grove workshop in various guises (from bare chassis to full kit cars) on a regular basis, Trevor Wilkinson and Jack Pickard now sensed the seeds of success and felt it was time to move up a level. Accordingly, spring 1955 saw them hard at work designing and constructing an all-new multi-tubular chassis incorporating a substantial centre tunnel/backbone section. Although the existing chassis was

▼ Its body moulded in fibreglass, the TVR open sports (it had no 'proper' name) of 1956 clearly displayed the origins of the traditional 1960s TVR styling theme. Jack Pickard is the driver.

23

THE EARLY YEARS

proving itself sales-wise, Trevor felt the seats could do with being lower to allow more headroom and that full independent suspension at each wheel would have a greatly improved effect on handling. In other words, something more advanced was needed – a true sports car, a true TVR with better performance and its own individual appearance.

The new chassis was an uncomplicated semi-spaceframe design. Made of round section, 1.5in diameter, 16-gauge steel tubing, the four main longerons extended rearwards only as far as the gearbox. If they had continued through the proposed passenger compartment, they would have formed an uncomfortably high central tunnel. Trevor therefore reduced the upper and lower main tube vertical separation from about 12in in the engine area to less than half that through the cockpit area. The tubes then swept rearwards back up to the level of the upper transverse torsion bar housing. Explained Trevor: "The first chassis had gone round the seats, the second had gone under the seats, and I had come to the conclusion that the only place for it was between the seats – up to a sensible height."

Vertical and horizontal bracing tubes strengthened the structure, all joints being brazed with nickel bronze. Outriggers were incorporated and a vertical steel bulkhead was provided to carry the door hinges and mate up with the roof reinforcement. As intended, the seats were now mounted on much lower floors about six inches from ground level. Attempting to achieve the desired handling improvements, Trevor turned to the VW Beetle, taking its trailing arm and transverse torsion bar front suspension assembly and fitting it to the front *and* rear of the new TVR chassis. Telescopic shock absorbers were fitted all round, but Trevor had little idea of the reputation the chassis would soon create for having an exceptionally solid ride.

Designed for road use in standard form and racing in lightweight form, the new semi-spaceframe design was a significant one. It was to be used, complete with the same Beetle based suspension, for all future TVR chassis and cars built between spring 1956 and late 1962. It was to lift the company from constructing an ever-changing trickle of specials to manufacturing kit cars of more settled specifications. Finally, once a decision had been made on bodywork, it would carry for the first time the earliest elements of a distinct TVR shape that would evolve until the stage when, even more than twenty years later, it would still be possible to recognise the original design theme in the 'classic' TVR style.

◀ Trevor Wilkinson used this Sports Saloon both as a competition car and as his personal transport for several years. It was finished in metallic light blue with a dark blue roof.

THE BIRTH OF A TRADITION

▲ RGS body on a TVR chassis at Beverley Grove. RG Shattock was one of a growing number of fibreglass body makers for specials during the 1950s.

▼ Despite its bulbous rear bodywork, the Sports Saloon appeared low and purposeful beside any production car.

Unaware of the incredible story he was starting, Trevor found himself enjoying life immensely. TVR Engineering seemed to be on solid ground and regular car construction could gain impetus as rapidly as sales and constant improvement allowed. Extravagant dreams of small-series production had been toned down to reality by the limitations of the small premises, and the company was never exactly awash with money. Trevor also acknowledged that he had a severely restricted interest in financial management, office administration and business matters. Both he and Jack Pickard were strictly practical men who wanted to be on the shop floor developing the cars, making components and getting their hands dirty – they weren't very interested in money, accounts books and, indeed, any form of paperwork. The naivety of their approach to business naturally did not suppress the feeling that it would be particularly pleasant to have a backer to provide some extra funds with which to expand and build more cars.

Just such a situation came to fruition suddenly and rather unexpectedly via the customer who'd earlier discussed building a Lea-Francis powered TVR. Called Bernard Williams, he was a quietly spoken, assured, financially secure gentleman who lived in St Anne's, south of Blackpool, and had been a star rider in pre-World War Two dirt-track motorcycle racing in the north-west. Interestingly, during the war he'd played an extremely important role in the construction of Lancaster bombers built by AV Roe & Co at two factories south of Manchester. His job had been to organise and control the smooth supply of parts and components for the aircraft, and he was said to be able to quote the code numbers for every single part used! Now more enthusiastic about four-wheeled sporting cars, he was extremely interested in Trevor's efforts and keen to become involved. Indeed, over previous months it hadn't been unusual for him to turn up at Beverley Grove just to hang around, generally help out or even clean cars.

By July 1955 Trevor found himself with a new director of TVR Engineering who brought in a small amount of additional working capital. A charming man, Bernard Williams had persuasively talked his way into the quieter man's life and he soon showed his mettle as a versatile member of the team who could turn his hand to most things. In fact he was to prove in the long run an extremely competent hands-on worker, an excellent TVR salesman, an office manager and a very capable negotiator when it came to dealing with company affairs, especially organising financial backing,

◀ The first of Ray Saidel's Jomars were known as Mk1s and had aluminium bodywork over their British built Dellow chassis. Not really suitable for racing, these two cars were the only Mk1s built. (Alex Saidel)

which the car's various manufacturers were to need on a regular basis over the years! Anyway, the situation now was that Trevor had acquired his first Sales Director, an extremely confident and somewhat manipulative 'front' man who, in one role or another, was to remain with TVR for well over ten years and, with outstanding tenacity, play a key role in keeping the marque alive through thick and thin.

Not one to relish the limelight in any form whatsoever, the unassuming Trevor was initially content with the revised company set-up, but the arrival of Bernard Williams was to have a radical and frustrating effect on his (Trevor's) existence within a short time. "That was when it all started to go wrong," he reflected. "Bernard became aware of the fact that we were running short of sub-contract work and assured me that he could bring in plenty enough to keep us busy. He was extremely enthusiastic about TVR but he turned out to be a great teller of half-truths. He brought in some work, but a lot of it was of such a nature that we would have been better off without it! Half of it turned into losses for us, and he never took delivery of his much discussed kit, which was eventually sold to another customer."

TVR's first export order had been for the fully complete Sports Saloon that was shipped to Germany in 1955. The whole question of exports was to become hugely significant to TVR's future following the arrival of the mail one morning in August. One letter, dated 29th August 1955, was from the Merrimack Street Garage of Manchester, New Hampshire, in the USA. This was the largest car import dealership in all of New England, and its dynamic 36-year-old owner, successful racing driver Ray Saidel, had heard about TVR via an advertisement in the British motoring press. He wanted to know if Trevor would supply a lightweight competition chassis in rolling form fitted with the 1098cc Coventry Climax FWA light-alloy engine. Saidel planned to fit his own aluminium sports racing bodyshell.

Based on a very mobile, lightweight, wartime fire pump engine, the overhead camshaft Climax automotive engine was performing exceptionally well on racetracks, particularly in tuned stage two form. And gaining a lot of publicity too. Trevor jumped at the opportunity to deal with Saidel and received a confirmed order on 30th

THE BIRTH OF A TRADITION

▶ Designed in 1955, TVR's new multi-tubular backbone chassis was a landmark for the company, being used for production models until late 1962. (Alex Saidel)

December that year. TVR would be grateful for any promotion available through a pairing with an active racing team, albeit one from across the Atlantic.

This wasn't Saidel's first effort at building a sports racer based on a British chassis. Prior to his TVR connection, his racing concern, Saidel Sports Racing Cars, had built two cars based on the unlikely Dellow chassis and clothed them with aluminium bodywork similar to that being used on the forthcoming TVR chassis. Propelled by 1172cc Ford 100E engines, these cars were known as Jomar Mk1s, the name being derived from those of his children, Joanna and Marc. Despite their lack of power they were used mostly for racing – rather unsuccessfully, it should be added, because the Dellow was really a trials car and its chassis was far too heavy to be competitive on the track.

With a deal arranged, Trevor now put renewed effort into constructing the first chassis for Saidel, repeating his newest multi-tubular backbone design with VW Beetle based, all-independent suspension. Thanks to Saidel's enthusiasm, the American connection looked to have great potential and clearly could be a key element in TVR's growth through the late 1950s. The way things were going, it seemed as though more workshop space would soon be needed, especially as a higher voltage, three-phase electricity supply was now required for welding. It would be risky to expand, but with the expectation of regular orders coming from the USA, the TVR men were guardedly optimistic.

▶ The birth of TVR's important American connection. Trevor at the helm of the first TVR rolling chassis to be exported to Ray Saidel in the USA. Its all-independent suspension was another first for TVR.

THE EARLY YEARS

Selling his Beverley Grove premises, early in 1956 Trevor moved operations into a much bigger factory on the scruffy Hoo Hill industrial estate at Layton, a rather rough suburb of Blackpool. Almost the whole estate (its correct name was Fielding's Industrial Estate) had been a brick works, and TVR's 'new' premises were in the three large units that had been brick-drying sheds, with plenty enough room for chassis and component manufacturing, a machine shop, a separate area for moulding fibreglass bodies and some form of 'production' line for assembling kits. Most significantly, there was good potential to increase production – at least five cars or kits per week could be assembled there.

Still Managing Director of TVR Engineering, Trevor was cautiously impressed with the new set-up but later acknowledged a seed of doubt: "I remember I had £600 left from the sale of Beverley Grove and spent £200 of that

▼ The factory on Hoo Hill industrial estate was to be TVR's home for fifteen years. On the right are two of the three old brick drying sheds that formed the main workshops. (Drawing by John Bailie)

on wiring the new place. Suddenly the pennies had to be watched, because we were also now paying rent." The move to Hoo Hill took place during January and February 1956, mostly thanks to the company's Morris van, whose roadholding in the winter snow left something to be desired at anything over 7mph. The 'new' factory was rather dilapidated and it was a daunting prospect to see snow sometimes drifting through the broken roof glasses on to the earth floor below.

Gradually some form of order came from early confusion. With Jack Pickard now factory foreman and John Ward the machine shop manager, a new production layout was established and work on the first United States-bound chassis was soon completed. Early in May 1956 it was despatched to the docks for shipment to New York, eventually arriving at Ray Saidel's Merrimack Street Garage in Manchester, New Hampshire, in mid-June. With interest growing and sales of chassis and kits showing more promise at Hoo Hill (in fact, even before receiving his first chassis, Saidel had already ordered two more), now was the time to take on a new welder, a young fellow by the name of Stanley Kilcoyne, a local boy who was an instantly likeable rogue with a terrific sense of humour. Another important new member of the workforce was Josef Mleczek – soon to be nicknamed 'The Pole'.

▼ The engine in the first US export chassis was a 1098cc Coventry Climax FWA unit. The trailing arm and transverse torsion bar suspension was of VW Beetle origin.

THE BIRTH OF A TRADITION

▶ Like its front suspension, the new backbone chassis also used Beetle trailing arm and transverse torsion bar assemblies (taken from the *front* of the VW) at the rear. The driveshafts and cast-alloy uprights were specially made for TVR.

Little did he know it but Joe 'The Pole' was to become a loyal TVR man for close on the next thirty years. Originally a fisherman in his native Poland, he served in the Polish Navy during World War Two handling radar systems on destroyers. After the war he settled in the Blackpool area and worked on trawlers sailing from Fleetwood. Next, in his mid-thirties and fancying a change, he joined TVR Engineering as a general fitter, progressing on to fibreglass laminating work – at which he soon became an expert. Ultimately, Joe's skills were to lead him to taking charge of both the body shop and mould making. Needless to say, he was another TVR man blessed with a natural ability to see the funny side of life. The waggish Stanley Kilcoyne was also generally involved with any pranks or jokes that were doing the rounds, and his growing love of TVR and everything the marque would come to represent would ultimately see him become a factory institution and TVR fixture for more than forty years.

One character who wasn't to be involved with TVR Engineering for very long was a wealthy man called Fred Thomas. There had already been discussions between Trevor, Jack and Bernard about TVR's expansion requiring extra financial backing, and Bernard hadn't taken long to introduce Thomas to the scene. Not really a car enthusiast, Thomas was a sharp and manipulative businessman who was boss of a large engineering concern in Bolton, Lancashire. "It was Bernard's 'big idea'," recalled Trevor. "Having seen our set-up, Thomas took me over to his premises and presented me with rows of jig borers as far as I could see. It was amazing. He said his company was looking for products to finance and, if I was interested, my financial concerns would be over and I could concentrate on car production. I gave it much thought, but there was only one answer to that."

It appeared to be a hugely promising prospect for TVR. Had the unassuming Trevor known more about his new colleague he might have been more cautious, but his mind had always been full of the potential for giving up light engineering work and concentrating on the building of more chassis and more TVRs. Now a backer had been found and enough cash was supposedly available to do just that. It seemed that his dream could be fulfilled. Established in a decent sized factory and with the promise of substantial support from Fred Thomas, Trevor had no clue that he was heading slap bang into an undercurrent that was gradually to soak him of control and later wash him aside.

In the USA Ray Saidel was initially happy with his first TVR chassis. Once his skilled craftsmen at Merrimack Street Garage had fitted some open aluminium bodywork of their own design, the 1098cc Coventry Climax FWA powered sports racer was painted blue, given Jomar Mk2 designation and first track tested by Team Jomar (the drivers were Ray Saidel and Gus Ehrman) in August that year. Indeed, it was to be raced

▼ Most of the early TVR backbone chassis were bodied by Ray Saidel's craftsmen at his Manchester, New Hampshire, garage in the 'States and badged as Jomars.

regularly for nearly a year and, despite several mechanical failures, in 1956 alone it finished in the first three places in many of the races entered. But the season did reveal several serious flaws in the British built chassis, mainly concerning kingpin breakages and the inadequate drum brakes that were used all round. In one frank letter to TVR, a concerned Saidel wrote: 'We find we cannot even go out to practice without an extremely bad failure'. In fact, the American was alarmed enough to temporarily suspend his order for a third chassis.

◀ Underpinned by a TVR chassis, the Jomar gained Mk2 designation. Early tests of this first unpainted example took place early in August 1956. Ray Saidel is on the left. (Alex Saidel)

With the second Jomar/TVR chassis arriving in the USA in November 1956 (it was in full rolling form with a Stage Two 1098cc Climax engine and Alfin finned alloy brake drums), Blackpool's response to Saidel's complaints was to redesign the front suspension and improve quality with the next chassis. Replacement parts were sent to Saidel to update the first two chassis, the American reinstated his order and peace prevailed. But other niggling problems would still manifest themselves during the 1957 season, not the least of which was the total demise of Jomar/TVR chassis number one when disaster struck at Virginia International Speedway early in August that year. Following a bad crash, the car was a total wreck, its bent chassis, engine and transmission being the only salvageable parts.

Crashes and smashes were a predictable part of racing life, and despite the many

▼ The second Jomar racer to have a TVR chassis. With added head fairing, its aluminium bodywork was fabricated at Ray Saidel's workshop in Manchester, New Hampshire.
(Alex Saidel)

The practical, economical answer to cockpit entry with the Jomar Mk2 sports racer was a simple drop-down door. (Alex Saidel)

unfortunate incidents which occurred with his early TVR based racers, Ray Saidel was persistent enough to battle on, always being positive enough to remember the good times with his early Jomar Mk2. From TVR's point of view, this was merely the beginning of its long association with the USA, an affair that would of course go through rough times but would ultimately reap great rewards for the Blackpool car builders.

'Boot Hill', as the Hoo Hill factory was generally known, was certainly relieved to boot out the last Microplas and Rochdale bodied TVR specials during 1956. Early that year Trevor and Jack had grown tired of chopping up and modifying other people's body units and felt it was time for their first attempt at creating a pure and distinctive TVR design. This sounded fine but without even so much as Les Dale's artistic instincts for angular guidance, the birth of a TVR shape of in-house design proved difficult – until a simple answer was found. By mid-1956 two slightly sheepish faces were soon to be seen in a corner of the factory working up a shape that looked strangely similar no matter which end it was viewed from!

The men had built another of their current chassis and then, when the question of bodywork arose, had chosen the easy way out. Totally inexperienced when it came to creative body styling, Trevor and Jack were hastily making the best of an awkward job, having resorted to utilising some of the faithful Microplas Mistral body panels they'd thought were a thing of the past. For the front of the new TVR body they adapted a Mistral bonnet and nose cone with smoothly faired-in headlamps and the radiator air intake tucked low down and angled forwards. So far, so good. Some hesitation followed. Then, in a great rush of inspiration, they fashioned an uncannily similar rear end, using... yes, another modified Mistral nose cone. Work involved the

Trevor with the first TVR open sports at Hoo Hill in 1956. Styling the car wasn't difficult as both its front and rear body sections were taken from Microplas Mistral mouldings!

THE EARLY YEARS

headlamp apertures being filled in and the radiator air intake likewise, while the leading edge of the nose was cut back and given a defined edge.

Although the 'design' work took several weeks, Trevor and Jack's first efforts at front and rear body styling had therefore not been too demanding in terms of artistic endeavour! Of course, doors, lower body panels and a scuttle (all made from wooden and plaster patterns) were necessary to fill the spaces in between the Microplas front and rear sections but, all in all, the work required was nowhere near as expensive as creating an all-new car from scratch would have been. Once all the body panels were assembled on to the chassis, and the head fairing and low Perspex windscreen had been added, the little TVR open sports car looked surprisingly good – perhaps a little short but smooth, compact and purposeful in the typical style of a sports racer. Just right for the competition use for which the car was intended.

▲ Testing a revised open sports at Aintree circuit. Trevor is at the controls, Jack Pickard on the right.

Generally referred to simply as the TVR 'open sports', this car was never graced with any official model name, but Trevor got great satisfaction from getting the wind in his hair while testing the new prototype (it was finished in bright red) that summer. The little 1098cc Coventry Climax FWA engine he'd fitted gave the car lively performance, and while the VW Beetle-sourced trailing arm and torsion bar independent suspension matched up to most reasonable demands, the same could not be said of the drum brakes! Soon a second example of the new model was under construction, the prototype being sold to an eager British enthusiast who took it club racing, unfortunately with no great success. TVR Engineering's expansion into the Hoo Hill premises seemed to be paying off. Fred Thomas's promised support was most reassuring although, in the final analysis, all he was actually doing was guaranteeing the company's bank overdraft.

◀ With 1098cc Coventry Climax power, the sleek open sports heads out for another test lap at Aintree.

THE BIRTH OF A TRADITION

▲ Fitting a simple hardtop to an open sports body created the first TVR coupé. This is the unfinished prototype.

▼ TVR coupés under construction at Hoo Hill late in 1957. Just six examples were made.

As any young man would, Trevor looked to the future and gave little thought to the fact that no longer did he have complete control of the situation. Pressure of work saw to that. General engineering work had still to be attended to, more orders for chassis were coming in and the second TVR open sports was nearing completion. It resembled the first very closely, using the same chassis, running gear and body. The first car's outside door hinges were now situated inboard, while a smaller wrap-around screen, a detachable head fairing, a tonneau cover over the passenger seat, an opening boot lid and other detail changes all improved on the inaugural TVR design. The headlamps were again faired-in with Perspex moulded to shape by Jack Pickard in his own inimitable style – his tools had been one knobbly knee and the oven in Mrs Pickard's kitchen!

The TVR 'design' staff were proving adept at using whatever was closest to hand. After completing a third example of the TVR open sports model early in 1957 (it seems possible that a fourth example had also been built by mid-year), the company used Aintree circuit, near Liverpool, to allow the motoring press a chance to get behind the wheel. As the car was awaiting eventual shipment to Ray Saidel in the USA, *Autosport*'s writer Francis Penn was asked to go easy with the 1098cc Coventry Climax engine but still reached 90mph down the main straight. 'Superb' was his word to describe the roadholding and steering.

It was certainly early days but already the TVR marque was beginning to forge its fine reputation for high levels of performance and handling. But the open sports model wasn't exactly practical, so Trevor, Jack and Bernard decided that it was time to build a fixed-head TVR coupé. The boss felt that the market for affordably priced GT cars was wide open. The company's financial situation and the need for economy decreed use of readily available assets, so an open sports body was commandeered for the development of a simple notchback hardtop initially made as a wood and plaster pattern and then moulded in fibreglass. A Ford Consul/Zephyr windscreen seemed to be the best solution for a screen, and from there backwards the hardtop was of very functional design, finishing abruptly behind the two seats with a rather upright rear screen. It would certainly keep out the rain, but the downside was that the hardtop didn't exactly enhance the TVR's smoothly curved lower bodywork.

While much of mid-1957 was spent at Hoo Hill developing the

prototype fixed-head TVR, across the Atlantic Ray Saidel had clothed his second TVR chassis with Jomar Mk2 aluminium bodywork. First raced early in May 1957, the Stage Two Climax powered car was very successful in its class on almost every race appearance. Indeed, it was to enjoy some twenty-nine track appearances until July the next year when, while racing at Lime Rock Park, a big incident saw it hit by no less than seven other cars! Not surprisingly, the damage to both chassis and body was extensive and the wrecked racer was scrapped.

That same year, in February and March, Saidel had also taken delivery of his third and fourth TVR chassis, again with 1098cc Coventry Climax engines. As soon as their aluminium bodywork was finished, both cars were put to work on the racetracks. From amidst all the Jomar action at this time came a tale that Gus Ehrman, Saidel's co-driver in Team Jomar and a good friend who was keenly following developments, had previously achieved fame while racing an MG: he'd managed to overturn it and end up not far from the feet of a rather famous spectator – President Eisenhower!

For TVR Engineering, the export link with Saidel Sports Racing Cars of Manchester, New Hampshire, looked very promising indeed. In August 1957 the first (and only) export example of the TVR open sports model arrived at Saidel's premises for racetrack evaluation in right-hand-drive form, its fibreglass bodywork finished in red. But by this time Saidel knew all about the development of the hardtop that had been taking place at Hoo Hill. Agreeing with Bernard Williams that a fixed-head coupé would be more popular than the open car, the American had immediately ordered four of the new TVR coupés, two in fully complete form and two less engines.

▲ This coupé was the company's demonstrator for some time. It had 1098cc Coventry Climax power.

▼ From its beginnings with the open sports model, the classic TVR look became more apparent with the coupé. The windscreen was from a Ford Consul/Zephyr.

Already destined for the USA, the prototype TVR coupé was completed at Hoo Hill in August 1957. Although it was a simple conversion from the open sports model, for its year the new car's fibreglass bodywork had a certain

THE BIRTH OF A TRADITION

▲ Finished in bright red with white stripes, this was the first TVR coupé to be sold in the UK. The other car is an early 1930s Austin 12/4. (John Cookson)

attraction. With faired-in headlamps, the front-end styling was extremely smooth and there was minimal overhang at both front and rear. Although the small hardtop was of abbreviated, notchback style, the neat overall shape displayed the first signs of what was to become the classic TVR fixed-head style. A right-hand-drive car, the prototype was powered by a supercharged 1172cc Ford 100E engine driving through a three-speed gearbox and featured wire wheels to offset its two-tone red and grey paint.

By now intent on the full scale marketing of Blackpool-bodied TVRs in America under the Jomar name, Ray Saidel took delivery of that first notchback coupé early in October that year and it went on to be raced extensively by an American disc jockey. Assembled at Hoo Hill alongside the prototype, the second coupé was the first one to be sold in the UK, being delivered as a fairly basic body/chassis unit together with suspension and steering to Trevor Wilkinson's good friend John Cookson at the Cookson family business, an Esso service station at Cockerham, just south of Lancaster. As a young art student, some time earlier John had regularly visited the Beverley Grove and Hoo Hill factories to check on the latest developments and had become something of a TVR addict.

Driving his Buckler Mk5 special, John had also regularly competed against Trevor's yellow TVR special of 1951 (number three) in sprints and hillclimbs in the north-west. He'd been out many times as a passenger in that car, with Trevor at the wheel, and a few times in the first Sports Saloon. Indeed, it hadn't been unusual for TVR's boss to drive from Blackpool to Cockerham to meet John and chat about cars. On one visit, during the second half of 1956, Trevor had arrived in the prototype Climax powered TVR open sports, and a six-mile test drive in the sleek and purposeful looking machine instantly cemented John's unequivocal desire to own a TVR. Hence his order for the second notchback coupé.

Completed and on the road around February or March 1958, the Cookson coupé

▶ It was early days but this British registered coupé provides several clear indications of the way TVR styling would develop over the years. (Eric Pallant)

35

was powered by a 1500cc BMC block (from an Austin A50) with an MG head and manifolds, twin SU carbs and an MG gearbox. Being 6ft 4in tall, to give himself the maximum possible cockpit space John fitted simple padded seat bases and backrests that were trimmed foam sections fixed to the rear bulkhead. Finished in bright red, the bodywork featured twin white nose-to-tail stripes, each one to the exact width of the toilet rolls that had been used to mock them up! In action for sixty miles during the daily commute, and generally driven hard, the coupé not surprisingly suffered from several problems, but the factory always willingly rectified them (see panel on page 41).

▲ Waiting at Liverpool docks for shipment to the USA is the first TVR coupé ordered by Ray Saidel. Painted red with a grey roof, it was right-hand drive.

The third notchback coupé built at Hoo Hill in 1957 was completed in October with a 1098cc Climax engine and bodywork finished in off-white. For some months this car was kept as the factory demonstrator, and during this time it was driven for that purpose on a few occasions by racing driver Mike Hawthorn, who was to become Formula One World Champion in 1958. Bernard Williams had been friendly with Hawthorn for some time – friendly enough to suggest that Hawthorn might care to invest in TVR and become a director (the answer was no). The coupé was then sold to Wirral, Cheshire, garage owner Peter Jones, who pressed it into action as a racer during the 1958 season. At some point a heavy crash curtailed the car's racing career, leading to its rebuild with a new chassis late that year – and its subsequent use as a road car.

With three notchback coupés already made, and three more in the pipeline for export to Ray Saidel, the latest model from Hoo Hill was finally announced publicly to the British market early in January 1958. Venue for the small public launch was the prestige Manchester car showroom of Ford dealer H & J Quick Ltd, and by now it had been decided to call the car simply the TVR. But further moves were afloat. Clearly the decision had already been taken to press ahead with a revised final production version of the car, because the PR blurb stated that the display car was an interim stage in the development of the TVR – confirming that a restyled, fastback GT version was already close to completion. This would become known as the Mk1 and later as the Grantura Mk1.

◀ And here's the car above just after it had arrived in Manchester, New Hampshire. It's seen here in October 1957 in Veterans Park across the street from Ray Saidel's Merrimack St Garage. (Alex Saidel)

THE BIRTH OF A TRADITION

▶ This neatly restored 1098cc Coventry Climax FWA engine sits under the bonnet of the car pictured below. (Peter Filby)

▼ In lovely condition, this restored TVR coupé is believed to be the only example existing in Britain. Note the Jomar badge. (Peter Filby)

Although there was still some way to go before production of the fastback TVR could begin, the PR exercise in Manchester brought a shade more credibility to the marque. Under the display car's bonnet was an 1172cc side-valve Ford 100E engine with matching three-speed gearbox and a Shorrock supercharger, which raised power output to a lofty 54bhp at around 3000rpm. It was this engine, 'blown' or 'unblown', that would be offered in production versions of the car along with the 1098cc Coventry Climax FWA unit driving through a four-speed 'box. Drum brakes all-round were the order of the day and there were no changes to the existing chassis or its VW based all-independent suspension. Customers still had the option of ordering 'open sports' bodywork if they preferred it.

Its appearance marginally spoiled by the addition of a spare wheel mounted externally on the boot, the TVR notchback coupé looked good on its 15in diameter Dunlop 48-spoke wire wheels. Weighing about 12-13cwt depending on the engine

The boot-mounted spare wheel was an optional extra on the TVR price list. It didn't do any favours for the car's appearance. (Peter Filby)

fitted, it could manage entertaining performance and reach a maximum speed of well over 100mph – a rather hopeful 125mph was claimed for the Coventry Climax powered car. The tiny doors and large steering wheel didn't exactly help entry but, once inside, the driver was in a compact, cosy environment and was held firmly in place by the high transmission tunnel – with a good driving position, full instrumentation and all controls well within reach.

No question, here, in this very early TVR (which was also referred to as the Coupé with a capital 'C'), were the makings of an accomplished and rewarding sports car for the keen driver. Mind you, the prices weren't exactly cheap – £990 for the standard 1172cc Ford engined car, £1050 for the version with a supercharger, and a whopping £1450 for the Climax powered car. There was no news at this point on prices for kits, which was of course the form in which most TVRs would have to be sold.

With the US market showing strong interest and potentially offering greater scope

The simple dashboard, huge steering wheel and functional cabin of this restored coupé are as original except for the small centre console. (Peter Filby)

THE BIRTH OF A TRADITION

▲ Six of these neat little machines were completed, of which four were exported to the USA. A seventh example was converted into the first fastback Mk1. (Peter Filby)

▼ It's not difficult to see why this early TVR was known as the 'notchback' coupé. (Peter Filby)

than the home market, the obvious approach was for the Hoo Hill factory to concentrate on sales to Ray Saidel, who continued to be extremely optimistic about the car's future in the USA and was hopeful of importing between thirty and fifty TVRs a year. Following the arrival of his first fixed-head TVR in October 1957, the other three he'd ordered reached his Merrimack Street Garage in December '57 and January '58. All were right-hand-drive and, apart from the first one, were equipped with external, boot-mounted spare wheels and TVR's notably super-slim bumperettes.

Anticipation in the USA was apparently high and on the face of it things looked rosy. Painted blue, one of the cars even attended the New York auto show in April 1958 to give demonstrations (Ray Saidel later raced this car). But it transpired that there was one fundamental problem with the notchback Coupés in the 'States, and that was the difficulty Saidel had in trying to sell them! According to contemporary views, they were unattractive, cramped, poorly built, rode extremely harshly and had their steering on the wrong side. It seemed there was a need to improve matters...

The hopeful answer to this rather serious dilemma was waiting in the wings at Hoo Hill. After just six Coupés had been built (four had gone to Ray Saidel and two existed in the UK), another example, probably just a body/chassis unit, was retained at the factory to use as the basis for a further development on the now clearly emerging TVR body styling theme. The concept of another TVR model was again inspired by Ray Saidel. Despite the struggle, the US market was still believed to have great potential, so the men at Blackpool listened keenly when Saidel suggested that, after lukewarm American reaction to the notchback coupé, they should create a sleeker, fastback GT car with rear bodywork more like a Porsche or Aston Martin.

By now an expert fibreglass worker, late in 1957 Jack Pickard was given full responsibility for streamlining the existing bodyshell. There could be no copying: this was the real nitty-gritty! With help from Trevor and enthusiastic input from Bernard, the rear end of the last Coupé was now laden with plaster and plywood as a new, improved shape was fashioned, incorporating a Perspex wrap-around rear screen that was specially made for the job – not by Jack Pickard's knee, either!

The plan was to improve on both the appearance and the exceptionally limited interior space of the Coupé. Trevor would have liked to

THE EARLY YEARS

incorporate all manner of major changes but his company simply didn't have the financial resources that would be needed. He realised that even the incredibly small doors would have to stay with the new fastback TVR for the time being. An enthusiast working on a car for the enthusiast, he knew the specification would be acceptable, for customers were generally most concerned that their sports car should be characterful, lively to drive, capable around corners and affordable, not necessarily that it should be very beautiful. With its sleeker bodywork moulded in-house and assembled lovingly by a small band of workers, the new TVR would hopefully do all that was required of it – in the rather basic fashion common to that era.

▲ Following the coupé, the next model developed at TVR's Hoo Hill factory was the Mk1, the first examples of which were made early in 1958.

TVR Engineering had been formed in 1947. Now, over ten years later, what had been for Trevor a hobby and sideline had developed into a full-time occupation. Although the UK market had barely been touched, there seemed little doubt that the Blackpool sports car was set for a secure future. At this stage the Hoo Hill factory was ideally suited to the rather moderate output levels of which the company and its small workforce (about ten) were potentially capable (maybe about 20 cars a year), although one magazine report stated: 'It is hoped to produce some 150 cars this year'! Indeed, there was certainly plenty of room on the Hoo Hill estate for expansion – a second large building was adjacent to the brick drying sheds.

Bernard Williams, who was probably the source of that faintly ridiculous exaggeration about production numbers, had certainly proved very confident and persuasive with prospective customers and was a fine salesman – the sort of salesman who could charm the birds out of the trees. But while Bernard calmly talked, charmed customers and smoothly embellished everything, Trevor and his other colleagues kept their feet on the ground and quietly got on with the engineering and manufacturing sides of the business. Leaving Bernard to look after the promotion and administration sides of the company, Trevor remained a practical, hands-on man who was most content when dealing with mechanical problems. "I was so involved with building cars that I really wasn't too bothered with the business side. I was never interested in money – it only came in useful to build more cars with."

The American market was expected to become an important source of income and was creating the need to build more cars. Indeed, Ray Saidel had been incredibly supportive to TVR by carrying out much development work on the cars as a direct result of his racing experience, and then passing back to the factory all the lessons learnt. By all accounts the early TVR sports car had cemented the foundations of a solid transatlantic relationship, and naturally Saidel wanted the first examples of the new fastback model as soon as possible. If the new car (the Mk1) was built well enough, it would hopefully be capable of capitalising on the situation and achieving Trevor's growing dream of steady small-series production.

Reflecting its limited output so far, TVR Engineering was still severely stretched on the money front and debts were growing. Adequate support funds were believed to be available, but Trevor couldn't possibly have guessed that the company's so-called financial backer, Fred Thomas, was less than scrupulous and not intending to keep his promises.

Coupé Recalled

THRILLED BY A brief drive in Trevor Wilkinson's red 'open sports' prototype, John Cookson became the first British owner of a TVR notchback coupé in August 1957. Building it from a kit, he had the car road-ready early in 1958 with 1500cc BMC power under the bonnet and bright red paint, with white stripes, on the bodywork. It was used daily to commute from his home in Cockerham, Lancashire, to his job in Kendal.

Recalled John: "It was the concept of the chassis that really started me off. It was such an efficient design, so compact and businesslike with the main chassis tubes gathered closely around the engine, gearbox and rear axle. The torsion bar springing was fully enclosed within the chassis cross tubes. Driving the red 'open sports' prototype was everything I expected. The car had minimal overhang front and rear, and access to the engine and gearbox was superb. But I needed a slightly more practical machine so opted for the new coupé version, which at the time existed only as a mock-up."

Once it was completed, John's first impressions of his new TVR were positive. "It was a very striking little car that made a big impression and inspired enthusiasm in others. It gave me a great buzz to drive it and was very reliable, only letting me down once when the header tank sprung a leak while my girlfriend and I were on holiday in Scotland – we easily got it soldered up. The engine had ample power for road use but I always felt there was untapped potential if only I'd had the money to tune it further. The MG gearbox was excellent."

Driven hard over about sixty miles every day, John's coupé inevitably developed teething problems. "It was quite different from anything else on the road and I loved the look of it. I felt the roadholding was decent, but initially the harsh ride over rural roads was almost intolerable for daily transport. Rear end steering was also an immediate worry but the factory readily agreed to take the car back and fix those early problems. In fact, they took it back several times for repair or to make little improvements such as update the dashboard, and on a couple of occasions they lent me their light grey demonstrator to keep me on the move.

"Another serious problem was a cracked chassis tube.

▼ On the road early in 1958, this notchback coupé was used as daily transport by its builder John Cookson. (John Cookson)

Coupé Recalled cont'd

The failure occurred in one of the top tubes just forward of the front bulkhead and was possibly due to the engine's weight putting extra stress on the chassis. Either that or it was the high mileage and the way I drove the car! Willing as ever, the factory added some diagonal bracing tubes to strengthen that area of the chassis – one of several modifications that were carried through to the Grantura. In a way, my coupé was acting as a test and development car on behalf of the factory. Having been favoured with the first coupé, I was happy to play a part in its development.

"I entered just two competitive events with the TVR in 1959. A circuit race at Aintree was a disaster when overheating forced my retirement after a few laps, but a class win at Barbon Speed Hillclimb, when the car was easily fastest, was very satisfying and brought useful publicity for the marque. But the race experience also raised doubts about adhesion. When cornering hard, the coupé was well balanced but seemed to lose grip and start sliding earlier than had been my experience with other cars. I eventually sold the TVR in August that year."

▼ In only its second (and last) competitive event, John Cookson's 1500cc engined coupé crosses the line to win its class at Barbon hillclimb near Kirkby Lonsdale in Cumbria in 1959. (John Cookson)

CHAPTER THREE

New Car, New Problems

Aimed mainly at the American market, the new TVR Mk1 of spring 1958 heralded the birth of the classic TVR shape. But the car brought with it a whole new round of problems, both on the factory floor and in the company boardroom. By the end of the year the bubble had burst and TVR Engineering had collapsed. Yet, despite everything, the marque somehow managed to struggle on in the hands of a new company, Layton Sports Cars. Unfortunately, little else was to change.

Despite its semi-regular construction of chassis and cars for export to Ray Saidel, TVR Engineering sensibly still made a proportion of its income from light engineering work. But cars were much more exciting, so early in 1958 Trevor Wilkinson, Bernard Williams and Jack Pickard concentrated on final completion of their new fastback GT prototype, initially to be known as the TVR Mk1 (though it would later become the Grantura Mk1). "With the Mk1 we were

▶ Jack Pickard (left), Trevor Wilkinson (centre) and John Ward look rather proud of their efforts over the TVR Mk1. This was probably the very first example to be finished. It was destined for export to Ray Saidel in the USA.

THE EARLY YEARS

trying to improve the appearance of the Coupé, which I didn't think looked much good," said Trevor. "It needed to look longer and sleeker. Then again, when we'd finished the Mk1 I looked at it and thought, well, it still needs to look longer and sleeker!"

It was mid-March in 1958 when the first completed Mk1 fastback rolled out of the old Hoo Hill factory. Destined for Ray Saidel in the USA, it was certainly a distinctive looking machine. The front three-quarter view was arguably its best angle, the smoothly styled nose and bonnet being not unlike that of the Lotus Elite, which had been introduced in 1957 and was already hailed as one of the world's most beautiful cars. But from the bonnet rearwards things deteriorated somewhat for the TVR. The Ford Consul/Zephyr Mk2 windscreen was still used and the tail end was smoothly contoured but, viewed from the side, the shape was squat and stubby and the fastback dipped away from the short roof very sharply indeed. However, pretty or plain, the Mk1 had a chunky, purposeful stance and these aspects of its styling gelled together nicely, making a strong initial impression on the world of specialist sports cars. Just about the weakest aspect of the new model's overall appearance was its set of extremely frail looking bumperettes – clearly there for visual effect rather than serious protection!

Although the earlier notchback Coupé had hinted strongly at the first signs of what was ultimately to become the classic 'original' TVR shape, it was the Mk1 fastback that heralded the true birth of that shape. Years later, its utterly distinctive appearance would be confirmed as the clearly recognisable forerunner of a long, long, family line of internationally famous sports cars. However you looked at it, the Mk1 was a very important model on the TVR scale.

Under its individual styling, there was no change regarding the new TVR's use of Trevor's latest multi-tubular backbone chassis with a 7ft wheelbase, its independent suspension originating at both ends from the front of a VW Beetle by means of trailing arms with upper and lower laminated torsion bars. As always, this set-up threatened rather high roll angles, which were therefore limited by very stiff springs. These in turn gave an extremely firm ride. Indeed, in terms of noise, vibration and general harshness, it quickly became clear that the car badly needed refining. After some driving experience with the Mk1 Jack Pickard admitted it was a real boneshaker, while the double-acting, telescopic shock absorbers probably had similar feelings on the matter. With the short wheelbase, steering from Ford by worm-and-peg and a slight rearward weight bias, oversteer was the predominant characteristic of the new model's lively and highly capable cornering ability.

Eight fibreglass mouldings (including the main central section), each of up to three eighths inch thickness, made up the body, which was bonded to the chassis – as was the fibreglass floor. At a total weight of just under 13cwt, the car was easily stopped by 11in Girling drum brakes (as used on the Austin-Healey 100-Six) on each

▲ Pictured by the base of Hoo Hill's tall chimney, TVR's multi-tubular chassis was the backbone of the company's business between summer 1955 and autumn 1962.

NEW CAR, NEW PROBLEMS

15in diameter wheel – most cars would use 48-spoke Dunlop centre-lock wire wheels despite the fact that they were supposed to be options to the 'standard' bolt-on steel disc wheels. The spare was carried upright at the very rear of the cabin, behind the TVR-fabricated 8.75-gallon fuel tank. Needless to say, the wheel required awkward and time-consuming effort to pull out through the cabin and the tiny doors (a criticism that would be applied to TVRs for many years!). Exactly the opposite was the case with access to the engine and front suspension: this was superb thanks to the way the bonnet, including the complete nose section, was hinged at the front and tilted forwards.

The plan with the Mk1 was to stick with an unchanged range of power options, although the engine bay would accept, within reason, whichever engine the customer wanted to fit. Expected to be most popular were the Coventry Climax units, at first the 1098cc FWA, then later the 1216cc FWE engine (as fitted to the Lotus Elite), both of them available in various stages of tune. Others options would be the ancient 1172cc Ford 100E side-valve unit, with or without a Shorrock supercharger, and later the new 997cc Ford 105E overhead-valve unit or the 1489cc MGA unit. Performance would therefore vary a great deal but would always hold the promise of high entertainment. While the Ford powered car was to use a three-speed (100E) or a four-speed (105E) gearbox, the MG and Climax powered cars would employ four-speed BMC B-type (MGA) gearboxes. An MG differential in a TVR-designed, light alloy casing was used and a later option would be a close-ratio gearbox.

Opening the tiny doors revealed a cosy if rather tightly cramped interior dominated by a huge 17in diameter steering wheel, wide transmission tunnel and simple padded seats. Typically period fare, the saloon-type wheel featured a chrome horn ring with a direction indicator switch on the wheel centre. The somewhat high dashboard was well instrumented and covered in PVC trim, as was the rest of the interior (for Ford powered cars). Later on, more luxurious leather trim and deep pile carpet were to reflect the superior status of the Climax

▼ Called squat, stubby and many other things, the Mk1's styling was attractive from some angles. Note the super-slim bumperettes of this very early car. They were there for cosmetic reasons only.

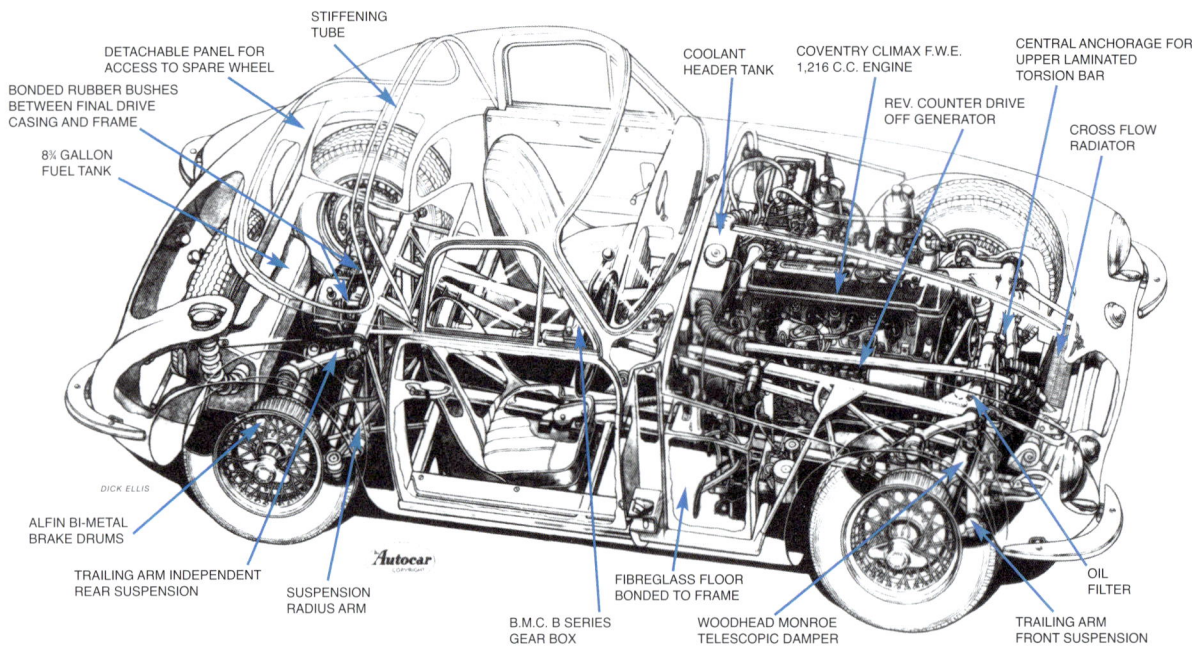

▲ Dick Ellis did this excellent cutaway drawing of the Mk1 for *The Autocar* magazine early in 1958. Note the VW Beetle trailing arm and transverse, laminated torsion bar suspension all round.

powered models. Perspex was used for the distinctive, wrap-around rear window that was made specially for TVR. One obvious problem was the lack of luggage accommodation in the rear (some of the space being taken by the spare wheel), and there wasn't an opening boot – a strange omission in view of TVR's stated intention that the car was designed not so much for competition but as a high-speed, economical tourer.

With the first batch of Mk1 fastbacks already booked for shipment across the Atlantic to Ray Saidel's Merrimack Street Garage, TVR planned initially to aim sales more or less exclusively at the US market. Depending on results, cars would be offered on the British market later. Despite the problems he'd encountered with chassis and cars already bought from Blackpool, Saidel was still optimistic about his future working with Bernard Williams, with whom he'd by now become a close friend. Better still, Saidel Sports Racing Cars had booked a stand at the 1958 New York International Automobile Show to launch the Mk1 fastback – Saidel called it the Jomar Coupé – before a huge audience.

▼ 1216cc Coventry Climax FWE engine in a Mk1.

Finished in light blue and fitted with a supercharged 1172cc Ford 100E engine, the first TVR Mk1/Jomar Coupé to be built at Hoo Hill (it was right-hand-drive) arrived at New York docks late in March 1958 and went on display at the motor show in April. It met with an amazing response. Ray Saidel was staggered to be inundated with dealer requests (thirteen were signed up) and promises of close on 200 orders! Back at the factory Trevor, Jack and Bernard felt much the same reaction. For such a small company, the figure was quite mind-boggling, but the men had learned in no uncertain terms where

NEW CAR, NEW PROBLEMS

▶ An option with the 1172cc Ford 100E engine, shown here in a MK1, was a Shorrock supercharger which boosted power to 56bhp at 4600rpm.

the future might lie. However, the reality was that the car builders of Hoo Hill could neither afford nor manage anything like the volume of output apparently required by the US market.

Once the initial euphoria of the New York show appearance had died down, Ray Saidel's main problem was going to be holding on to his dealers and maintaining their commitment to buy cars while the men at Blackpool figured out how to make them! The American's brochure proudly advertised the Jomar Coupé and the Jomar 'Gran Tourismo' Coupé, the latter with a top speed of up to 135mph depending on which engine was fitted. Prices varied from $2995 for a basic 1172cc Ford powered

▶ Known as the Jomar in the USA, the Mk1 made its public debut at the New York auto show in April 1958. Note both TVR and Jomar bonnet badges. (Alex Saidel)

Aiming to improve the Jomar breed via racing success, Ray Saidel was in action whenever possible. In this GT race at Montgomery track in 1958, he piloted his Jomar notchback coupé to first in class. (Alex Saidel)

car with steel disc wheels up to a pricey $4195 for a top-of-the-range car with wire wheels, Alfin drums and Stage Two Climax power – that price being uncomfortably close to that of a Porsche 356A! The same brochure proclaimed that the Jomar Mk2 sports racer was still available at $3995 with a TVR-made fibreglass body which was unchanged from 1956's TVR open sports, whose chassis it utilised.

While the Hoo Hill factory was being reorganised to try and inaugurate some semblance of semi-regular production, most of the early Jomar racers were in action extensively in the USA throughout the 1958 season, attempting to promote the brand and stir up interest in the road-going Jomar Coupé. But in truth production at Blackpool was moving desperately slowly and it was only after several months in build that the second Jomar Coupé arrived at Ray Saidel's premises late in May that year. Painted green, it was again right-hand-drive and again powered by a supercharged 1172cc Ford 100E engine.

Unfortunately, no records were kept by TVR Engineering for this period, but it seems very unlikely that any Mk1s slipped into British garages or race preparation workshops until at least the latter part of 1958. Yet although there wasn't really great cause for celebration, it could be argued that the company now had some form of series production car (extremely small series!) on its hands. Detail changes and minor developments were already in hand – the Perspex covers over the headlamps tended to steam up quickly so were deleted, and the headlamps themselves were found to be slightly below the legal height so were repositioned and decorated with chrome rings. The very earliest Mk1s could also be easily distinguished by their smoothly finished wheel arches, clean and uninterrupted body panels behind their front wheels and the absence of opening quarter-windows in their doors.

Despite its many faults and general lack of refinement, the TVR Mk1 was lively, individual and quite acceptable to the small number of motoring enthusiasts who were interested in it. True, it was noisy and harsh, but this in itself created excitement, and in terms of performance and handling it was something of a revelation. Almost ten years had passed since Trevor Wilkinson had built his very first TVR – now the marque was creeping on to the map. In its earliest production days of 1958, Bernard Williams claimed that the Mk1 was being made at the rate of one or two per month, but this seems rather improbable.

Staff numbers had grown to ten by now, all of them doing a bit of everything as and when required, including attending to the general engineering work that was still booked in. It remained a time for learning, a period when plenty of

NEW CAR, NEW PROBLEMS

mistakes would be made, as Jack Pickard knew: "We were still pretty green, and in truth those early Mk1s were real amateur jobs. I mean, we'd never trimmed anything to any reasonable standard before. We couldn't stitch, so we had to use glue on almost everything."

Both Jack and Trevor loved their work and felt great satisfaction from seeing the TVR operation grow from almost nothing. Although they were perpetually short of money, they quite naturally felt they'd started out on the road to success. In truth, though, the accountants' figures showed that building TVRs and Jomars was not proving profitable and that the company had over-stretched its finances to the point where it was dangerously short of operating capital. The two engineers knew very little of the worsening financial position and the worryingly unstable ground on which the company now stood. Unfortunately, it wasn't an area with which they cared to become too involved. Tedious stuff was bookwork and business administration, as any creative engineer would tell you, and Bernard Williams was apparently quite competent at looking after the accounts office.

The advent of TVR Engineering's first potentially successful car had unhappily coincided with the first alarm bells from the situation established by the financier Fred Thomas. For two and a half years things had rolled along reasonably smoothly from Trevor's point of view, but daily life in the company's accounts office had become increasingly difficult. None of the essentially hands-on men running the company had felt great concern over the deepening financial crisis, for they knew that the development of a car cost money. But as the bank overdraft grew, so did the danger, because Trevor had lost financial control to Fred Thomas, who had guaranteed the deficit but hadn't made any further contributions. And Thomas's first concern wasn't necessarily car manufacturing. Nor was he in any way emotional about TVR and its future. Indeed, his true plan was to make the company bankrupt.

▼ Mk1s in various stages of construction at the Hoo Hill factory. These pictures are from the 1959 period, by which time the Mk1 had acquired small flares running rearwards from its front arches.

THE EARLY YEARS

Though the manipulative Thomas allegedly planned to close TVR down earlier in 1958 to create a big tax loss against the profits of his own much larger company, for some reason he hadn't done so. It seems probable that an unforeseen change in tax laws made on Budget Day that year prevented him doing so. Whatever the reason, TVR Engineering held its ground and Thomas held off, but in the autumn of 1958 the company was perilously close to going out of business – and clearly needed a large injection of cash to keep the bank manager happy and avoid crashing into liquidation. Predictably enough, one man who didn't intend to put his hand in his pocket was Fred Thomas.

Trevor knew he was at fault. He'd left company administration in Bernard Williams' hands and had tended to avoid facing-up to what was going on behind the scenes – ridiculous, considering he'd started it all. But it had happened and now there was a fight for survival on his hands. Grave concern hung in the air as 'front' man and sales supremo Bernard again rooted round amongst a few of his more wealthy contacts and former TVR customers to see if they would be interested in investing. His manipulative charm and clever persuasion must have paid off, because several of those contacts were interested in joining the operation. On the face of it, the company appeared to have a future, particularly in the USA, so nobody was being asked to invest in a completely lame duck. Or were they?

The reality was that across the Atlantic Ray Saidel was also struggling to get his Jomar/TVR business running with any semblance of efficiency. Only two fastback Jomar Coupés, both of them right-hand-drive, had arrived from Blackpool so far in 1958 and Saidel still had in stock the two notchback coupés he'd accepted earlier. Some proposed dealers said they were willing to wait for left-hand-drive cars to arrive, but this didn't help Saidel, who wanted to shift his right-hand-drive cars! By the end of summer that year, the dealers' patience was wearing thin. Worse, there

▼ An American publicity photograph of the first TVR Mk1/Jomar to reach Ray Saidel's garage in Manchester, Long Island, New York. (Alex Saidel)

NEW CAR, NEW PROBLEMS

▲ Opening quarter-lights in its door windows and left-hand-drive identify this as the cabin of an export Mk1.

▼ Powered by a supercharged 1172cc Ford 100E engine, this is one of the two left-hand-drive Jomars that reached US importer Ray Saidel in September 1958.

were about to be more complaints about the quality of TVR Engineering's workmanship.

The first two left-hand-drive fastback Jomar Coupés finally reached Saidel's Merrimack Street Garage in September 1958, one a black car with supercharged Ford 100E power, the other a red Climax engined machine. Having already discovered that Jomar road cars were susceptible to overheating and needed bonnet vents to release hot air from their engine bays, Saidel was not happy with his latest cars. In a letter to TVR that month, he wrote: 'We have been running into stone wall after stone wall. I can't sell, trade or give away one of the rhd cars. We spent a week bringing the new lhd black car up to the best standards we could (including fitting a heater/defroster) and when we finally delivered it to the dealer he refused to accept it'.

The list of complaints was long. Included in it were the poor fit of doors, flimsy and completely inadequate window frames, window winders too fragile, interior detailing very poor, bad clunking in the drivetrain, some upholstery unglued, the lhd pedal arrangement poor with no room to get your feet on the clutch, and the heater and defroster set-up ridiculous. Not surprisingly, Saidel was so dejected about the situation that he was on the brink of suggesting that TVR should find a new US distributor. But, understanding the dealer's complaints, he resolved to tackle the situation and persuade TVR to make improvements. His timing was poor...

At an alarming £9995 – a huge amount by the standards of the day – was how TVR Engineering's bank overdraft stood by October 1958. Action was urgently needed. Eight men attended a meeting on the 30th of that month to discuss the dire financial situation, new funding and the possible formation of a new company to replace the existing one. Trevor, Bernard and Fred Thomas were there along with accountant Frank Lambert, David Hosking, solicitor Derek Harris and big car enthusiast Henry Moulds, who was a business associate of Thomas. Moulds' family had owned textile mills until his father had sold out, leaving an affluent Henry with nothing much to do other than indulge his love of cars. In turn, Henry had brought along a friend of his, a delightfully eccentric character by the name of David 'Bunty' Scott-Moncrieff.

Now well into his fifties and a real country gentleman who was a wealthy land owner, Scott-Moncrieff had been involved with vintage and prestige motor cars for many years. He had immense knowledge of the business and, as the possessor of a somewhat manic sense of humour, he was already one of the great characters of the old car movement. Having read engineering at Cambridge, he'd styled himself as 'Purveyor Of Horseless Carriages To The Nobility And Gentry Since 1927' and had run a successful car sales business dealing with many amazing and exotic machines, amongst them the vast aero-engined 'Chitty Two' and numerous Mercedes SS and SSKs.

In one extraordinary adventure, Bunty drove a Bugatti Type 46 to the Arctic Circle and wrote a brilliant book about it. Indeed, he was a skilled technical author. He also loved motor racing, was a good driver and didn't care too much about his appearance – yes, his tweeds were classic in style but gaping holes in his socks were commonplace! Engineering was in the blood, one of his ancestors being William Dundas Scott-Moncrieff, who was the senior partner of the firm that designed and started building the famous Cutty Sark tea clipper on Clydeside in the mid-1860s.

While TVR legend at one time had it that Bunty's family, who came from Edinburgh, were descended from a line of Scottish kings and that he sometimes took up residence in a castle north of the border, fact was that he and wife Averil now lived in the gamekeeper's cottage on the Basford Hall estate near Leek in Staffordshire. Indeed, Averil's ancestors had owned the Hall for several generations until it had been requisitioned by the Government to use as a base for British officers during World War Two. It then became a school while Bunty and Averil continued to reside in the estate cottage and store wonderful old cars in its outbuildings.

▼ The wonderfully eccentric David 'Bunty' Scott-Moncrieff joined TVR's board of directors at the end of 1958. He's seen here on the right chatting to famous motor racing journalist Dennis Jenkinson.

That informal board meeting at Hoo Hill late in October produced some shocking figures but at least revealed the situation for what it truly was – disastrous! Nowhere near enough cars had been built in 1958 (the actual figure could have been as low as ten or thereabouts), and although there were still orders in hand, the cash-flow crisis was digging deep. There was only one clear course of action to take, however harsh. Accordingly, TVR Engineering's directors dissolved the company, juggled around with various debts and money issues, and early in December 1958 began trading under a new name, Layton Sports Cars Ltd. The new company immediately benefited from a new injection of cash but was saddled with the unwelcome burden of an instant overdraft transferred by the bank from TVR Engineering's account. Also, believing that the little sports car had a good future, Bunty had invested £4000 into what he genuinely felt could be an exciting venture.

One can only imagine that the changeover procedure could just possibly

NEW CAR, NEW PROBLEMS

▲ In Britain it was the TVR Mk1; in the USA it was the Jomar Coupé or, if fitted with a high-performance engine, the Jomar Gran Turismo Coupé.

▼ Another shot of Mk1s in production at Hoo Hill.

have bent a few rules and been conducted in a slightly less than 'proper' way but, whatever, on the 16th of December the first Layton Sports Cars directors' meeting was held, attended by Trevor, Bernard, Hosking, Thomas, Moulds, Harris and Scott-Moncrieff. Derek Harris was duly appointed Chairman and it was agreed that no less than £15,000 should be spent straightaway to purchase stocks of components and to recruit the labour force needed to get production rolling on a hopefully profitable basis. After an extremely brief breakdown, TVR was on the road again.

Speaking later, Bunty Scott-Moncrieff was adamant about the TVR's potential after the reshuffle. "The TVR set-up," he said, "was short of money, tools, materials and, indeed, everything except brilliant ideas and an infinite capacity for long hours of hard work. It was all too distressingly familiar, but there was one priceless asset. The car, to my mind, was a potential world-beater, and I was by no means the only person to think so. In our innocence we believed the extra money invested would be amply sufficient for our needs. But nobody, not even Frank Lambert, who always looked on the blacker than black side of everything, had an inkling of the appalling, shattering calamities that were to befall this little band of commercial adventurers."

Having joined the company in 1956, welder and general factory entertainer Stan Kilcoyne was already a loyal TVR man who had a natural ability to brighten up the days at Hoo Hill. He never forgot his first meeting with Bunty: "He was a real boy. The first time I met him he was standing a chassis up in a corner. He was beautifully spoken. I remember him saying: 'I'm not feeling terribly well today, I've been up all night with a sick Climax'."

One alarming paragraph had appeared in the minutes of the December board meeting. It concerned production numbers and said: 'Messrs Wilkinson and Williams were requested to ensure that the minimum monthly output figure of four cars for the month of January 1959, rising by one car per month thereafter for twelve months, be at least met'. Considering that the previous output had probably been less than one or

THE EARLY YEARS

two cars and chassis per month, there seemed little hope of meeting the new target. In that one note there had already appeared the first hint of further heavy commercial and financial pressures that lay ahead, inevitably to undermine the TVR's stability once again.

For Trevor, the one gratifying result of the new set-up was that there was now a fresh supply of funds to keep the business afloat and get production moving. With full approval from the other directors, he now resolved to push general engineering work to the background and concentrate on development and building more TVRs. In some ways it was a questionable move, as he wouldn't be able to fall back on any handy income should the need arise. But, full of expectation for his car's newly established future, who would have spared a thought for the possibilities of another failure? Yet none of the new directors had ever been involved in motorcar manufacturing. They couldn't be expected to understand much about it. And here they were, mostly involved only on a part-time basis, talking about minimum monthly output figures for a TVR that obviously still needed much more development.

Not so long before, Trevor had owned the freehold of the Beverley Grove workshops and been in full control of his company. Now he was surrounded by six other directors, all with their own opinions, and working in a rented, rambling and rather grim old factory. His relationship with Bernard had often been strained – at times more than strained – but Trevor was grateful for his most recent efforts to

▲ Distinguishing features of MK1s from early 1959 onwards were the front wheel arch flares, engine bay vents just ahead of the doors, chunky cast aluminium bumpers and door window quarter-lights.

◀ The 1489cc MGA engine was one of several power options for the Mk1. It gave about 70bhp and was mated to a four-speed MG gearbox.

NEW CAR, NEW PROBLEMS

▲ At only 4ft high overall, the little Mk1 was dwarfed by the vast Bentley saloon. (Hugh James)

▼ All early TVRs had tiny doors. Production manager and company director Henry Moulds coined the phrase: 'Made by man with woman in mind!'

get the operation re-financed. On the shop floor, the future looked fair enough, Jack Pickard remembered: "On the formation of Layton Sports Cars it was again a happy shop full of enthusiasm. We were so involved with what we were doing that we never worried much about the great increase in directors. Having seen it go from nothing to the Mk1, we thought we were away, we were made."

Trevor elected to share Jack's optimistic feelings. He was naively unconcerned that a disturbingly intricate, messy pattern had already been laid down, one that would weave its disruptive way through the company's affairs for several years hence. And the hard-nosed Fred Thomas was still on the board of directors. Behind the scenes nothing looked like changing for the TVR marque. Even the American connection was weakening – by the end of 1958, orders from Ray Saidel had almost dried up. Four glassfibre bodied notchback coupés and four fastback Mk1/Jomar Coupés had already reached Saidel's garage in addition to seven racing chassis, which were bodied by local craftsmen. But the future for US sales couldn't be viewed with any optimism.

The new year, 1959, began as it meant to carry on – with a vengeance. In January the pattern was promptly woven a little thicker by accountant Frank Lambert's addition to the board of directors. He also became company secretary and was destined to spend the next few months attempting to sort out many worrying discrepancies in the books. He had quite a job on his hands. Trevor of course hesitated at this addition of yet another director but, as usual, was too deeply involved with day-to-day production problems to worry overmuch. Book-keeping was generally the last thing on his mind.

THE EARLY YEARS

In February the situation was further complicated with the formation of Grantura Engineering Ltd as an associate company of Layton Sports Cars. The directors felt it was now time to launch the Mk1 on the home market, and in order to sell the car in kit form – and thus save Purchase Tax – it was a legal requirement that kits and components should be bought from two different companies. Basically, the new company would exist for the purpose of supplying and selling parts and components to both Layton Sports Cars and its customers. The job of moulding sets of TVR fibreglass body panels (and retailing them) remained Layton's responsibility. Apart from being unpleasant, it was labour-intensive and time-consuming work, each assembly taking three men some twenty-three hours to produce.

Amazingly, curing of the panels was assisted only by placing an electric heater close to them! A further forty hours were then needed to give the panels their final finish, bond the main body sections together and prepare the full bodyshell for painting. There was a choice of eight colours that could be applied (by an outside contractor), after which the bodyshell was bonded to its chassis in the main assembly shop. Only a shade less onerous was the job of fabricating the chassis, which took about thirty hours. There were still ten shop-floor staff employed at this time, including a couple of young lads to do the most mundane work.

With a highly skilled upholsterer/trimmer and assistants in full-time employment at Hoo Hill early in 1959, the bucket seats were now made in-house, their frames being bent over a simple former. Much of the trim was still simply being glued into the cabin while the leather upholstery used in the Climax powered models (it was listed as optional for other cars) was sewn up on Singer sewing machines. Hides were bought either from the famous Connolly concern or from a tanner in Scotland. Leather or wood

▲ Production at Hoo Hill in 1959. The main section of the Mk1 bodyshell was bonded to its chassis.

▼ Mk1s were sold in Britain as kits with or without engines. For export they were usually fully completed.

NEW CAR, NEW PROBLEMS

▲ Having found a first class upholsterer, TVR's own trim department was set up at Hoo Hill early in 1959.

veneer facias could be supplied if requested. So fitted, the quirky little TVR enjoyed a quite classy interior, but there were downsides – not only was the cabin difficult to get into but the car wasn't well known for its ability to withstand water intrusion during bad weather, so the lovely deep pile carpet of the Climax powered models was in grave danger of becoming soggy when it rained.

As UK sales began to materialise, Layton Sports Cars' other key role would be to undertake the final assembly of kits and cars using components supplied by Grantura Engineering. The arrangement was that the latter would buy all the engines, carburettors, gearboxes and various castings necessary, whilst manufacturing wishbones and chassis, amongst many other things. Grantura would then carry out final assembly of the engines ready to lower them straight into chassis. Each of the few kit-form TVRs (UK market) or left-hand-drive turn-key cars (export) to leave the factory would go out with all trimming and electrical equipment bought and fitted by Layton. All a tad confusing but this at least was how the set-up was supposed to operate in principle – in reality Layton Sports Cars was the 'front' name, the only name that was ever publicised, and things no doubt would work however best they could.

Indeed, regardless of the substantial amount of money invested in the company, it might not be far from the truth to say that inefficiency and disorganisation generally reigned supreme at Hoo Hill. On the shop floor the year had immediately got off to a poor start with only a quarter of January's production target of four cars being reached. Actually selling TVRs wasn't the problem – making them at anything more than a snail's pace was proving to be the real challenge. Parts supplies, for instance, were proving difficult to obtain.

Due to the previously uncertain financial position, one thing the company hadn't needed until now was publicity (in fact, it had been being actively discouraged), but to the motoring world at large the TVR was certainly an exciting new sports car, and there were plenty of eager motoring journalists willing to provide publicity in print if only they could get behind the wheel and drive the thing!

Quite clearly, there was great concern about holding on to Ray Saidel's American sales outlet. Wrote Bernard Williams in a late January 1959 letter to Saidel: 'We have made tremendous progress during the last few months and the car has been improved out of all recognition, for we have tackled all the snags which

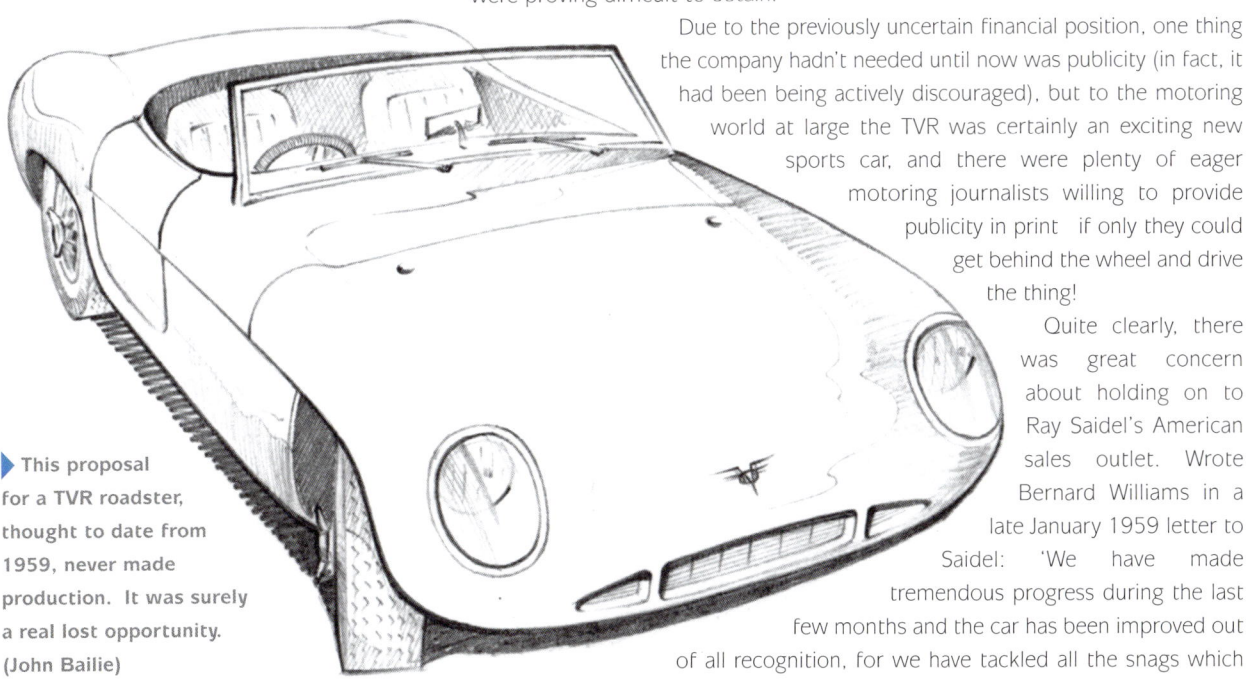

▶ This proposal for a TVR roadster, thought to date from 1959, never made production. It was surely a real lost opportunity. (John Bailie)

57

Trevor Wilkinson with a late model Mk1 for export. The twin air intakes at the front of the bonnet were initially intended for Ford powered cars, then made optional for any model.

you reported to us over a long period'. Exaggeration was clearly one of Bernard's strongest talents, but whether those familiar with the still raw Mk1 would have condoned his next claim is open to question. Said Bernard: 'I can honestly say that everyone will think it (the car) has been produced by a large manufacturer, for we have now got a really good professional finish'.

Despite Bernard's claims, no road-test car finished to an acceptable standard was available for the press at this stage. It was too early for the company to be able to afford such a luxury but, from the brief magazine news items that were published, occasional orders were trickling in, which certainly suited the factory's struggling production rate at the time. In fact, no major magazine publicity was to appear until March 1959, when *The Autocar* gave the TVR some respectability by devoting three pages to a detailed technical report on a car that at last had a model name – it was now called the Grantura Mk1. Stating that 'the car is now to be placed on the British market', it was excellent publicity and brought the TVR marque to a much greater audience. *The Autocar* also revealed that later in the year there would be an open roadster version (which, incidentally, was designed but never happened).

Further detail changes had been made to the Grantura's body before *The Autocar*'s story. The factory had found the development time to add several clear changes: there were now MGA-sourced swivelling quarter-lights in the door windows; to get more air into the engine bay, twin 'nostril' vents had appeared in the nose (initially only intended for the Ford powered car but fitted by customer request to other cars too); to release hot air that built up under the bonnet, particularly with the more powerful Climax engined cars, a vent had been inserted in each body side panel behind the front wheels and finished off with a horizontal chrome bar (much like the Aston Martin DB4 of the day); the bumpers were now more chunky cast aluminium units; and small horizontal flares now sat over the front wheel arches and tapered rearwards right to the back of the bonnet in Jensen 541 style. Work had also been done to improve the interior trim, reduce interior sound levels, improve the dashboard and change the pedals to pendant type.

As already mentioned, the Mk1 now at last had a proper identity – as the

NEW CAR, NEW PROBLEMS

Grantura. There'd been much discussion at Hoo Hill about the various suggestions from the team, but at least there was general agreement that calling the car the Trevor didn't have a lot of mileage! Bunty Scott-Moncrieff's lively wife Averil suggested 'Hoo Hill Hellcat' but, not surprisingly, that was turned down too. Grantura it was.

With the expectation of improved UK sales activity thanks to the magazine publicity and all the improvements made, the full Grantura Mk1 kit was priced from a starting point of £660 for the 1172cc Ford 100E version, moving up to a maximum of £950 for the 1216cc Climax FWE version. Prices for those cars in fully built form were £1003 and £1358 respectively. At Hoo Hill the general intention was now to push harder on the British market whilst continuing to ship cars to the USA if Ray Saidel was prepared to revive interest there. But amongst the many problems at the factory was the fact that, despite Bernard's enthusiasm and confident PR front, the staff were still learning – and struggling – to hand-build their fibreglass bodied sports cars in quantity and to the quality standards that customers expected.

With the TVR name gaining greater exposure, orders from British customers magically began to appear at the factory more regularly during 1959. Ironically, it wasn't long before the whole operation was showing the first signs of growing beyond its immediate resources. But unfortunately the slow production rate was still falling well behind demand, and whatever general engineering work came in was becoming a real nuisance (though financially still necessary) as everybody was much more interested in working on the cars.

As ever, development work was progressing slowly – indeed, production and development were really the same thing! The friendly nature of operations and the personal contact with customers meant that individual whims could be satisfied, so each Mk1 built tended to differ somewhat from its predecessor. Yet, in order to keep up with demand, construction needed to be simplified and made cheaper and more efficient wherever possible – not easy tasks amidst the generally disorganised scenario at Hoo Hill.

▼ TVR's involvement with club level motorsport grew steadily year on year. Supporters' cars at a Church Lawford airfield sprint meeting included these four Mk1s. The Grantura name had been adopted by now. (Roger Stanger)

THE EARLY YEARS

The hard fact was that fifteen cars were on order at the end of March 1959 at a point when production still wasn't managing significantly more than one car per month! Something needed to be done quickly to shake-up and reorganise the situation. But the action taken by the board thoroughly shocked one man: Trevor Wilkinson. The apparently harsh decision was to demote the rather passive Trevor and appoint the more energetic Henry Moulds in his place as production manager of Layton Sports Cars. It was a controversial move, indeed, but renewed life needed to be injected into the main assembly shop floor and production given the rocket. Although he would remain very much a hands-on, working director, Trevor was stunned. His position at TVR had again been undermined.

▲ Club competitor Dave Baldock's Grantura Mk1 road/race car in the 'pits' at Aintree in 1961. (Dave Baldock)

A quiet, well-meaning and much liked man, Henry Moulds was also blessed with a determined side to his character. Spurred on by the equally strong-willed Bernard Williams, he had a spirited bash at getting things moving in the factory. "When I first arrived it was rather a bare floor and the production layout needed proper organisation. It was also evident that the Grantura Mk1 still needed much more attention than myself and the other directors had been led to believe when we formed Layton Sports Cars. The main criticisms coming from customers were the rock-hard suspension, engine overheating and water leaking into the cockpit. We tried hard to improve the car in those, and many other, respects."

Energetic or not, Henry faced an uphill struggle. At the end of April 1959 a total of only five cars had been delivered in four months – less than a quarter of the target set earlier. One month later the delivery figure had risen to twelve, but this was still eighteen short of the planned figure. Things didn't promise well. There was little doubt that the current production rate meant a considerable loss was being made on each TVR sold.

And there was more bad news brewing across the Atlantic. In February 1959 Ray Saidel had taken delivery of his tenth (and last) racing chassis fitted with a 'blown'

◀ Early race action for ex-Squadron Leader James Boothby's Grantura Mk1 at Goodwood. Boothby was soon to become manager of a TVR dealership in Brighton, Sussex.

NEW CAR, NEW PROBLEMS

Climax 1500cc engine, and in April his fifth (and final) fastback Jomar Coupé, a red left-hand-drive car with 'blown' Ford engine, had arrived at New York docks. Indeed, he was still advertising the Jomar in US motor magazines in the hope that good competition results with the various TVR-chassised Jomar racers would ultimately encourage road car sales. Prior to the many changes and improvements made to the Jomar/TVR Mk1 between late 1958 and early 1959, he'd been unhappy with the standards of finish but had been constructive and helpful with his advice and recommendations. But his once excellent relationship with the factory – and in particular with Bernard Williams – was about to be badly damaged.

When Saidel visited Blackpool in May 1959 to see the factory set-up and finalise a more structured deal for his distribution of the cars, he was intending to sign an agreement based on sensible sales quotas that had already been verbally agreed upon – six cars in the first year and after that a guarantee of twenty-five cars per year minimum. But a seemingly reckless attempt was made by the TVR negotiators to pressure him into accepting a dramatically increased number: when the written contract arrived from TVR Chairman Derek Harris, it required Saidel to take fifty cars a year. No doubt such numbers were theoretically needed by the factory to raise production levels and keep everything afloat, but the truth was that Layton Sports Cars had scant hope of producing anything like that quantity for America alone. In any case, sales in the USA were now almost non-existent.

Saidel's response to the Blackpool company's ridiculous demands was simply to walk out on the negotiations and withdraw from the whole scenario. Even when Derek Harris backed down from his exaggerated proposal, Saidel was so angry he refused to discuss a return to the original terms. In his letter of June 18th 1959 to Harris, he explained in no uncertain measure: 'I frankly think that the directors (of Layton Sports Cars) must be entirely unfamiliar with the sales picture in this country

▼ US TVR importer Ray Saidel visited the Blackpool factory in May 1959 to sort out details of his contract with the company. Negotiations didn't go well. Ray is pictured leaning on the Grantura Mk1. (Alex Saidel)

THE EARLY YEARS

for specialised type machines. People in the trade have for years considered us lunatics for even attempting to sell one car a month! I would now not be interested if they gave me the entire USA for a guarantee of only five cars a year'.

After three years battling away trying to develop the TVR chassis and establish his Jomar marque, Saidel had abruptly terminated his association with Layton Sports Cars. That's how angry he was. The persuasive Bernard Williams had toiled tirelessly to keep the American involved with TVR after many, many setbacks over three years, and it was a very untidy end to what had at the outset seemed an extremely promising relationship. The big loser was the British company – it had lost its only American distributor.

What Layton's directors hadn't accepted was that Saidel didn't *need* the TVR. His Merrimack Street Garage already had franchises for many prestige, professionally developed sports cars, including Austin-Healey, Morgan, Jaguar, MG, Triumph and Alfa Romeo. With that kind of choice, enthusiasts in the USA could do without the little Blackpool bomber. The question was, how badly would Layton Sports Cars suffer from the consequent serious loss of income?

And so the struggle at Blackpool ground on. Excluding directors, the number of staff in the two TVR manufacturing operations (Layton Sports Cars and Grantura Engineering) rose to eighteen in May. But they weren't all ideally talented. The area had always had a high proportion of unskilled, nigh-unemployable labour. Wrongly, too many of the trainees at Hoo Hill were recruited from this type of person, young men who were trained and then quickly proved to be incompetent and were fired. This all cost a great deal of time and money and only further retarded the crawling production line. In other words, some decidedly sub-standard cars were still slipping out of the factory.

One of them was the Mk1 kit bought in spring 1959 from one of TVR's earliest dealers, David Buxton Ltd of Derby, by Cheshire farmer Keith Aitchison, who was to become more closely involved with the TVR factory in 1961/1962 (*see chapter six*). Keith built the car himself intending to use it as an everyday machine and weekend racer. He was essentially happy with the end product but had problems with its fibreglass bodywork. "I took my car back to the factory three times just to get the sub-standard paintwork sorted. Due to the totally inadequate curing process, TVR bodies were often not cured properly at that time. Indeed, it was still early days for

◀ Built in 1959, this Grantura Mk1 had 1489cc MGA power. TVR's 'front' man Bernard Williams used a Mk1, finished in metalic blue, as his daily runaround for about two years. (Hugh James)

NEW CAR, NEW PROBLEMS

▲ Typical late 1950s scene at a racing circuit. The TVR on the left is the well known 'Coffee Bean', while on the right is a Lotus Elite with another TVR behind it. (Humphrey Scott-Moncrieff)

fibreglass and few people really understood the material. Companies like ICI, who supplied the paints, weren't properly clued-up either. But one beneficial consequence of hanging around Hoo Hill waiting for my car was that I got to know a few of the staff quite well, particularly that great character, Stan Kilcoyne."

A directors' report on the subject of quality control made interesting reading. It said: 'When we increased the labour force in 1959, production did not rise as it was only possible to recruit unskilled labour in the fibreglass body moulding section. We then decided to train more labour over a six-to-nine month period to achieve greater output and higher standards of finish. During this period no less than twenty-four operatives were engaged, partly trained and then found to be below the required standard and subsequently left our employ'.

It was of no help to the situation that low wages were being paid, short hours were being worked, a general lack of urgency was being displayed and little management co-ordination was apparent. Things were distinctly unsettled in the boardroom too. While Henry Moulds was promoted to Managing Director, few lamented the quiet exit at this stage of Fred Thomas. But, tendered in June 1959, accountant Frank Lambert's resignation came as a surprise. He cited major concerns over the tax situation, a continuous breakdown in supplies of components, the state of the cash-flow, incomplete financial records and, ominously, many serious discrepancies in the books. Basically, there wasn't much to be optimistic about! The next bombshell followed closely in July with Lambert's recommendation that Layton Sports Cars should be wound up as soon as possible. "Offer it as a going concern," he said, though exactly where it was going was anybody's guess.

Lambert's reasoning was not far from correct. The minutes of the July board meeting reported the books being hopelessly muddled… the company in incapable hands… a serious shortage of materials… failure by staff to improvise during shortages… a bad shortage of skilled employees… cars sold at different prices to different people…cars allowed to leave the premises without payment… and so it went on. Things were dire and it was crisis time again. Yet nobody took much notice of Frank Lambert's views. His departure represented the third management casualty within a very short time. The Grantura Mk1 was barely surviving in an extremely unstable household. Worse, the household's head man, the marque's founder, was no longer Managing Director and now very much a background figure.

▶ Introduced in 1954, John Cookson's badge was still appearing on TVR bonnets in 1959.

Competition in 1958 and '59

MOST EARLY TVRS, from the first independently sprung chassis to the initial batch of Mk1 fastback coupés, were shipped to Ray Saidel in New York to become Jomars. Many of these cars were used for racing, but the TVR competition scene in Britain didn't really get under way until 1958 – and only in a very small way. Trevor Wilkinson had always seen his creation first and foremost as a road car, but thanks to its light weight and good handling it would inevitably become competitive for racing.

Very few pre-Mk1 examples of the TVR could be found on British circuits in 1958. Probably the first TVR to reach Scotland that year was the Climax powered 'open sports' of ex-speedway rider Ollie Hart and his son Stan, the car being in action several times at Charterhall circuit. Stan's success with the 'open sports' soon saw him graduating to a Formula Two Cooper single-seater with which he enjoyed a string of good results.

Early in 1959 a competition committee was formed at TVR's Hoo Hill factory by those directors interested in racing, the intention being to encourage more TVR competition appearances and thus generate publicity, hopefully of the positive sort! Accordingly, racetrack activity was soon on the increase with the first Grantura Mk1 racers coming to notice – the cars driven by Colin Escott, Keith Aitchison, and Bunty and Averil Scott-Moncrieff ('The Coffee Bean'). All these machines were built during the first few months of the year, Escott's Mk1 being a semi-works car while Aitchison's was initially a private entry until his excellent results gained him factory assistance.

Two other drivers racing Mk1s in 1959 were brothers Tony and Derek Bracegirdle. Supplied in kit form, Tony's car was finished in light blue and powered by a supercharged 1172cc Ford 100E side-valve engine, and its first outing was in July at Silverstone with Derek behind the wheel. Derek's own kit was assembled slightly later and first raced early in October at Oulton Park. With 1216cc Climax power, it was painted in a rather outrageous salmon pink – mainly because Derek felt it was safer to be seen clearly on the road! Both Mk1s were driven on the road to race events and not fully race prepared, so for both brothers it was a case of enjoying the action rather than gaining much success.

◀ Seen at an MG Car Club meeting at Silverstone in May 1959 is the yellow factory entered Mk1 driven by Colin Escott.

CHAPTER FOUR

Trouble Very Regular

The two years from mid-1959 to mid-1961 saw the rather substandard Grantura Mk1 evolve into improved Mk2 and Mk2A versions. But, as ever, it was a period fraught with difficulties: slow production rates, lack of proper jigs, an abundance of unskilled labour, poorly finished cars, unreliable parts supplies, financial problems and management disputes. As if this wasn't bad enough, sales in 1961 were extremely disappointing and a further injection of cash was desperately needed.

Despite all the management changes and general turbulence surrounding it, the squat little Grantura Mk1 gradually acquired more detail improvements during 1959. There had been continual customer complaints: things such as unsatisfactory suspension, the torsion bar locators, the bonnet fasteners, water leaks, poor steering geometry and, an old bugbear, body finish. Work was constantly in hand to sort out problems such as these and

▶ The Grantura Mk1 was offered on the UK market from early 1959 to mid-1960. Dave Baldock built his example over the winter of 1959/1960 and used it both as a road car and a racer. (Dave Baldock)

tackle the need to make production jigs and improve body panel mouldings, while at the same time raising the car's specification. Paintwork was always done by an outside contractor. Unfortunately, customer gripes in this department remained regular, despite the application by specialist paint sprayers of half a dozen undercoats and five top coats.

Performance was one thing few people complained about. The Mk1's acceleration was always brisk and its top speed good for the era. While the smaller 1098cc Climax engined car could charge up to about 100mph maximum, the smaller Ford side-valve engined cars could only manage about 85mph and the MG powered cars about 95mph. Prices at this time were quite stable and very reasonable: the 1172cc Ford 100E powered car was still only £660 in complete kit form, its supercharged equivalent was £725, while the popular 1098cc Climax engined kit was £950. The 1489cc MG version slotted in at around the £800 mark.

All the American bound, Ford powered cars of 1958 had been fitted with the Shorrock C75B supercharger. For the 1172cc 100E engine this pushed power output from a lowly 35bhp at 4600rpm to something around 56bhp. Best bet for decent performance was the much more entertaining Climax FWE 1216cc engine with 83bhp, as fitted to the Lotus Elite. A further option coming on stream early in 1959 was the 997cc Ford 105E unit.

With the Frank Lambert resignation crisis of mid-1959 blown over, Henry Moulds was proving quite a ball of fire on the Hoo Hill shop floor, without necessarily having a greatly beneficial effect on the actual output of cars. It wasn't really his fault – the usual financial constraints, poor workmanship and severe component delivery delays were affecting stability as menacingly as ever. Reflected Henry: "My first twelve months at the company were happy times, but when it was realised we weren't making any headway there seemed to be lots of problems."

Indeed there were. Only four orders existed at the end of June 1959 and there

▲ Grantura Mk1 performance was always pretty lively for the time. Best bet was the 1216cc Climax FWE (top) giving 83bhp. With supercharger fitted, the 1172cc Ford 100E engine (above) gained a rise in power from 35bhp to 56bhp @ 4600rpm.

were no less than twenty-six workers to handle them! Yet only two TVRs were completed during July. It was a disastrous situation, especially considering the earlier demands of Layton Sports Cars' new directors: that production should rise to twelve cars per month by September. Amusingly, one rather over-optimistic TVR spokesman (probably Bernard Williams) had fed the press a little white lie saying that output was planned to reach about five units a week by the end of 1959!

Despite all, and no doubt assisted by the small number of racing Mk1s gaining good results on the tracks, the sales scene was looking brighter again by September. Bunty Scott-Moncrieff had by now appointed another important UK distributor, St James Motors of Brighton, its brief being the distribution of TVRs in the south of England from Kent to Dorset. The general sales manager there was ex-Squadron Leader Jim Boothby (*of whom more later – in chapter seven*). Also, an export order had come in from AB Motors of Sweden in the form of a 'blown' Ford engined car, and there was a strong possibility of new life for the TVR in the USA, where two American companies were interested in plugging the gap left by Ray Saidel. They were Houston Continental Motors of Houston, Texas, and Continental Motors of Washington DC, both companies signing as distributors and ordering Climax powered Mk1s for use as demonstrators. Whether these export deals ever fully materialised was another matter...

The story behind the Washington distributor just about typified the sort of bad luck saga with which TVR so often became involved. By the time two Mk1s had been built, shipped and delivered to the Washington company, it had gone bust and its boss

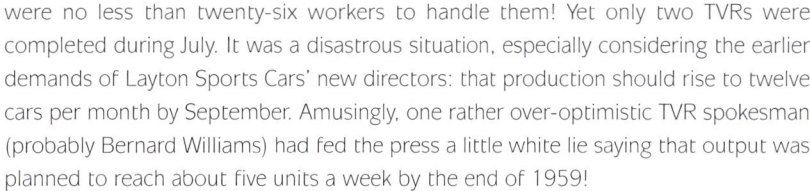

▼ One of only a tiny handful of Grantura Mk1s believed to remain in road use, this is an early 1959 example. (Peter Filby)

THE EARLY YEARS

◀ At TVR's Hoo Hill factory the Grantura Mk1 suffered from unstable and under-financed production conditions. The result was that the cars simply could not be built quickly enough. (Peter Filby)

Walter Dickson had been charged for the fraud which set in motion the collapse of Elva Cars. The result was that Dickson was thrown in jail and the two TVRs were stranded! Only after much hassle did Layton Sports Cars have the cars returned to the UK.

Regardless of demand for the Grantura Mk1, the company's abundance of unskilled labour and unreliable parts supplies (there was never enough money to pay for them) all meant that output remained poor. Worse, the condition in which cars and kits were being completed and delivered continued to be decidedly sub-standard. Said the minutes of an October board meeting: 'The present staff, and in particular Mr Wilkinson, should be made free to proceed on rectification work with the utmost urgency'. One other paragraph warned of financial danger ahead: 'A minimum of eleven cars are required for invoicing each month and even this figure does not quite cover our wages and general overheads'.

Bernard Williams was, as ever, busily engaged in turning on the charm and asking each new contact he made whether the man wished to invest in an exciting and fascinating but generally ailing company. Indeed, with the company constantly short of money, almost everybody who came through the door was a prospect for Bernard! By the end of November 1959 yet another name had been added to the conglomerate running things at Hoo Hill – that of skilled engineer John Thurner.

A quiet, academic and very clever man, Thurner had served an engineering apprenticeship at Rolls-Royce and, not

▼ Unusual and individual in appearance, though by no means beautiful, there was still a certain appeal about the Grantura Mk1's styling. (Peter Filby)

Competition in 1959

WHILE THE RAISING of TVR's image was a constant struggle, publicity from competition and hopefully the occasional racing success were of true value in a world where performance and roadholding mattered. At this stage of its career, the marque was still a rarity on the racetracks and was thus little known in British competition circles. But three drivers were trying hard to put TVR on the club racing map in 1959: Keith Aitchison, Colin Escott and Bunty Scott-Moncrieff's wife Averil. A great motor racing enthusiast, Averil was showing real spirit in her driving style with her Climax 1098cc powered early Mk1 nicknamed 'The Coffee Bean'.

Following their investment in Layton Sports Cars at the end of 1958, the Scott-Moncrieffs had ordered their Mk1 as something of a gesture to help boost production at Hoo Hill – and also because Averil had great faith in the car and wanted to race it. Assembled at the factory, the car looked smart with its dark brown paintwork and light beige interior, but it wasn't long before disaster struck. After only three or four races, so the story goes, Averil lent the 'The Coffee Bean' to a friend, the wonderfully named Balfour Rombach, at the Rest And Be Thankful hillclimb north of Glasgow and watched him shoot off up the hill.

Unfortunately Rombach didn't come back: out of Averil's sight he smashed-up the car so badly that it was almost unrecognisable! Remarkably, Averil and Bunty were quite philosophical about their total loss and simply ordered from the factory another identical machine, which used the same 1098cc Climax engine – it had been salvaged from the wreck. Painted the same brown as the first car, it was also named 'The Coffee Bean' and pressed into action by Averil as soon as possible at various racing circuits and hillclimbs around the country.

A quick and reliable driver, Colin Escott had originally been introduced to the TVR experience when he met Bernard Williams at a race meeting and agreed to pilot a works prepared Grantura Mk1 fitted with a 1098cc Climax engine. Already well known for his race-winning exploits in a Lotus Eleven during 1958, Escott first raced the cream coloured Mk1 at Oulton Park early in 1959. Although he wasn't happy with the car's handling, he went on to achieve several good results during the season, typical of which was his first place in class in a race at Oulton on 6th June that year. Another Mk1 he sampled was 'The Coffee Bean', which he felt was a much better car to drive.

Cheshire man Keith Aitchison, who was later to play a managerial role in TVR's fortunes for some four years from autumn 1961 onwards, built his steel grey painted Mk1 with 1600cc MGA power early in 1959 and used it as both a road and race car, doing most of his first season's racing at Oulton Park and Aintree circuits. Both his and Escott's exploits boosted TVR's reputation somewhat that year. Recalled Keith: "My Mk1 was a bit like a go-kart with no 'give' in the suspension at all. It was

▼ A late 1950s starting grid with Averil Scott-Moncrieff ready to go at the wheel of 'The Coffee Bean'.

THE EARLY YEARS

Competition in 1959 cont'd

surprisingly good to drive but it felt heavy and wasn't really quick enough. Its performance was not up to Lotus Elite standards and nor were the braking and worm-and-peg steering, and I also had some problems with overheating. Yet although I never won a race with it, I did OK and was well placed several times."

In mid-August 1959 a full team of Mk1s (one of them a factory entered car finished in yellow and driven by Colin Escott) joined in the fun and antics for the 750MC Birkett Six-hour relay race at Silverstone, but the cars suffered overheating problems and the team retired after 112 laps. By September, Trevor Wilkinson would be working on a special lightweight car which would prove more suitable for the many racing drivers who were now showing lots of interest in campaigning a TVR. But it wouldn't be ready until the start of the 1960 season.

surprisingly, he had originally been a TVR customer. The owner of an early Mk1, which he occasionally raced, and a man blessed with a great ability to see the funny side of life (he would need it over the next few years!), the extremely well qualified Thurner decided to invest in Layton Sports Cars after leaving his position at Rolls-Royce. His new title was Layton's Technical Director in charge of design and development, and his intention was to uprate the TVR via the design of more sophisticated, bespoke parts.

Losing ground steadily, Trevor was beginning to regret every new twist in the company's affairs. Not exactly the progressive type, he wished everybody would slow down, get the Mk1 right and consolidate. "I seemed to disagree with the others at

▼ Believed to be only the 20th example made, this Grantura Mk1 left the TVR factory with a Shorrock supercharged 1172cc Ford 100E engine. (Peter Filby)

TROUBLE VERY REGULAR

▲ As with all TVRs to date, there was nothing fancy about the 1959 Grantura Mk1's cabin. The layout was very simple and functional. The wood rim wheel was an optional extra.
(Peter Filby)

▼ By mid-1959 the original TVR badge had retained its basic design but had been filled in and made to appear more substantial.

every board meeting. It was always more and more production they wanted, while I said the car just wasn't ready. I felt there would be even worse disasters if the car was pushed beyond its capabilities, both in sales and production. It desperately needed big improvements and really good money spent on it.

"Naturally, there were also great gaps with deliveries of parts supplies because we had to rely on suppliers who weren't interested in supplying us. I'm sure they would have preferred us to go away! They'd only serve us under protest. Even though orders had started coming in again, our production methods were at fault. The orders weren't really of much use to us at a stage when we needed to sort out professional jigging and tooling, plus bring in much more finance."

Trevor was probably right. His old buddy Jack, who was still shop foreman, agreed with him. The trouble was that the matter was now well and truly out of their hands. One year before, Trevor had been running the operation. Relegated to a position of no real power or standing, he now had to make do with tending to development and improving cars whenever he could, mostly alongside John Thurner. Understandably, Trevor soon became aware that Thurner was an experienced, professional engineer with the ability to take the TVR further than he (Trevor) could ever take it, and some bitterness now crept in. "Initially I had felt shocking about my demotion from Managing Director – I was sick. Later I was just angry, realising that I'd been taken for a ride. I seemed to be doing all sorts of odd jobs at that time."

For the man who had created the first TVRs it was a sad position. 1959 had been a hell of a year – one crisis after another. People coming and going. Constant talk of one thing at board meetings while another actually happened on the shop floor. A year upon which he could reflect with great regret. His creation had been virtually prised from him by a band of hungry businessmen who knew precious little about engineering and were only interested in seeing some return from their investments. Before all this mayhem and disruption, Trevor had never been to a board meeting in his life.

Those meetings were peppered with unreasonable demands and general disagreement. The inexperienced directors of Layton Sports Cars never related their oft-repeated production needs to the actual output figures, which were generally quite dismal. Between mid-1958 and December 1959 only fifty-four Grantura Mk1s were produced and, much more alarmingly, each one was reported to have cost the company 'an excess labour cost, over economic level, of £90'.

A Government loan of £15,000 was secured during November and the company's overdraft was increased to £7500, but the board were once again wildly optimistic in setting a production figure of at

THE EARLY YEARS

least twenty cars per month for 1960. They were pushing ahead much too fast for the shop floor. The Mk1 desperately needed further sorting, although the situation would hopefully look rosier with the expected appearance in mid-1960 of an improved TVR body, the Grantura Mk2, now at the master 'plug' stage prior to production moulds of much improved quality being made.

Somehow, everything stumbled onwards. Though the last Grantura Mk1s were still sitting around the factory much later in the year, the first half of 1960 saw a flurry of production activity. Henry Moulds' efforts were at last paying dividends and over forty cars were built during this period, many being delayed for some time at the final completion stage due to the usual shortages of components. Yet there were many positive signs for the months ahead.

By the end of its production run (approximately mid-1960), exactly 100 examples of the Grantura Mk1 had been constructed. About twenty-five of them were exported, most of these going to the USA, while the rest found homes with mostly British enthusiasts. The model was the first TVR to be produced in any volume and it was really quite a commendable effort considering that its life had been surrounded by an astounding series of near-terminal problems. The boneshaker, as Jack Pickard had called it, had certainly been graced with some talents and a good helping of real character despite all its faults. Squat, short, stubby, stumpy – it had been called all these things. Yet, as the first of a long line of descendants, it was an exciting little car and had a certain individual and appealing style that TVRs, even many years later, would still display.

The Grantura name had now stuck but it wasn't the one Bunty Scott-Moncrieff had selected for it... he'd wanted to call it the Virgin. "Bloody difficult to get into but bloody comfortable once you were there!" Bunty's extrovert character was much loved by all. A remarkable, warm and delightful person, his relations with the shop floor lads at TVR were always good. Too good at times. One day he sent a boy out for some cigarettes; along

▲ Averil Scott-Moncrieff's spirited piloting of 'The Coffee Bean' in club racing events did a fine job promoting the TVR name from 1959 onwards.

▼ It's thought that exactly 100 Grantura Mk1s had been made by the time the model was replaced by the Mk2 in 1960. (Peter Filby)

TROUBLE VERY REGULAR

with the change, they'd been left on a bench nearby while Bunty discussed some production detail. When he turned round to pocket the cash it wouldn't budge – some joker had welded it up!

Possibly overshadowed by his wife Averil's hard-charging exploits in the two 'Coffee Beans' during 1959 and 1960, Bunty also competed occasionally in the second car during 1960. Self-deprecating as ever, he recalled: "I was given the job of driving the car at a few important race meetings because I was the only one with an international driving licence. Oh, and also because I was expendable. They obviously felt they could live very well without me."

Bernard Williams was generally landed with the task of sorting out engine delivery delays. After one of his visits to the Climax company in Coventry, on the way back to Blackpool he decided to call at Bunty's cottage on the Basford Hall estate and have a social chat. Evening was approaching as he drove on to the estate and followed the

▶ The charming and determined Bernard Williams played a hugely important role in establishing the TVR marque from 1955 onwards. He's on the right in this photograph with the wonderfully eccentric Bunty Scott-Moncrieff, another member of the TVR board.

THE EARLY YEARS

lane past the large but slightly decaying hall towards the cottage. Bunty soon noticed Bernard's weariness: "You look hungry, old chap. I'll get my man to rustle up some food for you."

Bernard was grateful. He wondered whether it would be roast lamb, chicken casserole or possibly a lovely piece of duck. The two men sat there discussing their company's ever-twisting fortunes, Bernard growing hungrier by the minute. At last the food arrived, and Bernard was full of anticipation. With great respect for the guest, an immaculate silver tray had been prepared, its accessories naturally also being of silver. Bernard licked his lips, until he saw the meal – one stark looking boiled egg and a piece of toast!

By spring 1960 staff numbers at the TVR empire had swelled to forty-three. The atmosphere in the factory was still good, if slightly chaotic. It was that sort of company. The workers got very involved with their product and there was a fine spirit amongst them. If only they could have produced the cars faster! Despite higher targets, more often than not only ten cars were completed, or almost completed, each month. This was, in fact, way below the company's break-even figure. And most of them were being sold as kits, which wasn't ideal if the company was to be recognised as a fully fledged motor car manufacturer – as the directors wanted, always remembering the need to reach the much higher standards of finish that would be required.

Things were certainly looking lively at Hoo Hill. As a result of factory support, Colin Escott and Keith Aitchison were providing good publicity with their racing exploits during 1960, while new names behind TVR wheels were Peter Bolton, John Thurner, James Boothby and Mrs Mary Wheeler. The marque's reputation was certainly spreading its wings and generating wider interest. At one stage, possibly thanks to all this publicity, a rush of orders appeared and there was talk of potential export agencies in such unlikely places as Australia, Italy and Malaya.

In the UK the net was also widening with more dealers and distributors. One of the

◀ While Ford and Coventry Climax engines were available, the 1489cc MGA engine was a popular fitment for the Grantura Mk1 and was also used in some early Mk2s. Power was around 70bhp and allowed a maximum speed of 95mph. (Peter Filby)

▲ Main visual changes for the new Grantura Mk2 introduced in mid-1960 were its rear wheel arch flares and extended rear fins carrying the tail lights. (Peter Filby)

▼ The Grantura Mk2's front bodywork was unchanged from the Mk1. (Peter Filby)

first was Dennis Wolstenholm, who ran a garage called Sports Motors in Ashton-under-Lyne, Manchester. He kept in close contact with the factory and looked after a semi-works Grantura Mk1 racer finished in a steel grey colour and driven occasionally by both himself and Colin Escott.

Back in the first month or two of 1959 sports car specialist David Buxton Ltd of Derby had been signed-up as a distributor and was now selling TVRs regularly. Another dealer was doing well at his garage in Woodbridge, Suffolk, selling TVRs to American servicemen stationed at the many USAF air bases in East Anglia. His name was Bill Last, a temperamental but sharp thinking wheeler-dealer who was soon to become the most successful TVR distributor. Indeed, he was to do a fine job for several years, but he would ultimately figure more prominently in TVR history than some people may have wished.

Clearly and somewhat surprisingly, for the moment the TVR was once again in growing demand. Amazingly, the influx of orders that had suddenly appeared – probably thanks to new distributors and dealers – nudged the 'orders outstanding' figure at one point to a stunning 277! There was certainly no way Layton Sports Cars could quickly raise its monthly output to cope with such extraordinarily high demand, so a decision was made to search for a new factory. Yet, although nobody felt the scruffy Hoo Hill premises were entirely suitable, it was eventually resolved that it would be easier in the short term to expand by taking over a second building on the old brickworks estate.

Chassis tubes were already being cut and welded-up in two of the eight brick kilns on the ground floor of the large building

With production numbers in the hundreds, the Mk2 easily outsold its earlier sister. This was a factory publicity shot.

alongside the main workshops. A further spacious area (some 10,000 sq ft) was now rented on the first floor above the kilns, and the body moulding side of TVR operations moved here, the advantage being that the building's timber roof generated ideal operating temperatures for fibreglass work. The disadvantage was that there was no easy way to get bodies, moulds, cars or any other large items in and out of the new workshop. So the lads were given a bulldozer one day and asked to build a sharply curved ramp that started in the yard and climbed up and around to a large door at the back of the workshop.

Layton's associate company, Grantura Engineering, still handling the supply of parts and components, shared the main ground floor workshops, with the working arrangements between the two companies (as decreed by the Government for the sale of kit cars) remaining much as before. Although the additional first-floor workshop space immediately proved worthwhile, the possibility of moving to much larger premises, preferably still in the Blackpool area, would not be dismissed. It was certainly a time for ambition, even if it was misguided. Complete, turn-key cars represented greater profit than kit-form cars, and the board level decision was to encourage dealers and distributors to push sales in that direction. To help manufacture the cars in the first place, a second request for a £15,000 loan was made to HM Government's Treasury. As ever, Layton Sports Cars was hungry for money.

The strange thing was that no sooner had the expanded Hoo Hill premises been activated, and staff increased to more than fifty, than new orders dropped off – alarmingly. Customers had possibly tired of waiting. Cars (mainly kits) on order on 30th April 1960 had numbered 234, while June saw that figure drastically pruned to sixty-four. This was a matter worthy of great consternation, for the production rate was at last going in the opposite direction; it was actually improving!

As ever, the Mk2 interior was neat and well laid out. The steering wheel was a rather bulky 17 inches in diameter. (LAT)

▶ This Grantura Mk2 was one of the early examples built with 1489cc MG power during the second half of 1960. (Peter Filby)

▼ Assembled from a kit made in 1960, this Mk2 was registered in June 1961. (Derek Hutchings)

Whatever the irregularities and fluctuating figures at the business end of things, after many delays the new, improved TVR was at last ready. Entering the fray in June 1960, the Grantura Mk2 was effectively a mildly modified Mk1 with its dimensions unchanged and retaining its earlier sister's tubular chassis and VW Beetle based trailing arm independent suspension. Apart from detail changes to the chassis and interior, the only obvious modifications were to the bodywork.

The new model's main visual distinguishing features were its raised and extended rear wings (they were almost small fins) upon which were now mounted the rear lights, and the near-horizontal flares that had been added over the rear wheel arches in an attempt to match those at the front. TVR's founder wasn't over-enamoured with the changes. "Had I been responsible for it, the Mk2 would have had a slightly lengthened and raised rear body section featuring an external boot, while the chassis would have had wishbone front suspension with trailing arms and coil springs at the rear."

It was perhaps a missed opportunity, but the TVR sports car remained otherwise unchanged and unrefined, its harsh ride still shaking Jack Pickard's bones, its suspension still displaying its strange idiosyncrasies. Although some of the first Mk2s received the now-obsolete 1489cc MG engine, the standard power unit was now the latest 1588cc MGA unit with matching gearbox. With 79bhp available at 5600rpm, it propelled the new car along in typically exhilarating TVR fashion. Earlier engine options remained on the list – the 997cc Ford 105E and the 1216cc Coventry Climax FWE units – but not the now ancient and underpowered Ford 100E side-valve unit. In the workshops there had also been a fruitless attempt to persuade a Daimler SP250 V8 engine into a development chassis. The Mk2's wheels remained 15in Dunlop 48-spoke wires, while braking was still by Girling 11in drums all round – the promised front disc brakes hadn't yet materialised.

Bearing in mind the way the company had been juggling its wildly fluctuating sales and production figures with the Mk1, *The Motor* began its July 1960 news story on the Mk2 with an intriguing comment. It said: 'After having produced cars on a more or less individual basis for some time past, Layton Sports Cars Ltd is now going into regular production with a gran turismo design'. So perhaps it was no surprise that despite dwindling orders, production of the first Mk2s had set off in June 1960 at a higher rate than ever before – about twenty per month. Fitting in amongst them at around this time of the year were three special lightweight racers. General organisation, parts supplies and flow systems had obviously been much improved.

One of the earliest customers for a Mk2 at this time was Arnold Burton, who was a director of his father Montague's well known national retail tailoring concern. Arnold's family were rather wealthy. He'd long been a great car enthusiast and had always found the money to indulge in the more desirable examples. Just before the war he'd owned an early Morgan 4/4 and had entered a few Yorkshire trials near his home in Leeds. The famous rally driver, Ian Appleyard, became a neighbour after the war, encouraging Arnold's renewed interest in motor sport via an Aston Martin DB2 which he regularly used for local and international rallies, including the Tulip, Monte Carlo and Alpine events. Next into the Burton stable was a Jaguar XK120, followed by an XK140 and an AC Ace-Bristol, all these cars being shown no mercy whilst competing in Europe's major rallies. Even Arnold's daily transport, a Mk6 Bentley, was occasionally pressed into competitive action.

Interestingly, the Burton name was connected with motor sport in an unusual way. In July 1956 the family company had inaugurated a unique event – a half-mile sprint around its factory in Hudson Road, Leeds, known as the Montague Burton Sprint and organised by the BARC's Yorkshire division. Its memory made Arnold smile: "You'd never be able to do it today. It was very hairy, what with the factory walls, but we never had any problems and certainly no serious accidents. It was very successful and we had three such events each year for seven years. None of the local people complained about the noise; they thought it was good entertainment. Then, in 1961, I bought Stockton Farm, near Wetherby, and set up Harewood hillclimb there. It's still an extremely successful event today."

As for the Grantura Mk2, Arnold was caught by enthusiasm for individuality, he recalled: "I'd heard about this car being made in Blackpool and thought it might be my

▲ Magazine ads by TVR dealers Aitchison-Hopton of Chester were always informative and entertaining. This was a late 1960 effort.

▲ Once in through the small door aperture, the Mk2 driver was well located! (Chris Overton)

▼ Arnold Burton's first involvement with TVR came via this Grantura Mk2.

sort of thing. I had a great liking for small cars and thought I could enjoy competing in the TVR. Then I saw a Grantura in action at Croft circuit – I think Peter Bolton was driving it – so I took some photographs and went along to the factory to present them to Trevor Wilkinson as some sort of introduction. I wanted to see whether I really fancied a TVR, whether I could handle building a kit. I certainly wasn't going to pay purchase tax!

"At the factory there seemed to be directors all over the place, one of the few people who really knew about engineering being John Thurner. Soon after, I had a bash in 'The Coffee Bean' at Rufforth circuit. That somehow convinced me … er, of something! Peter Bolton was a very good friend and encouraged me to go ahead, so I ordered a 1588cc MG powered Grantura Mk2 with British Racing Green paintwork. Going backwards and forwards keeping in contact with the factory while the car was being built (I have to admit with a considerable amount of help from others), I was soon made aware that they needed more capital. Despite some appalling faults, like the harsh ride and too much noise in the cockpit, I felt the TVR had the makings of something and I loaned the company an initial £3000."

There was now a new director to add to the list. And a new model to hopefully boost the company's fortunes once more. But the dwindling order figures weren't very encouraging, and they were worsening. From sixty-four on the books at the end of June 1960, orders stood nearly halved at thirty-four by the end of August. Maybe the T of TVR stood for trouble? Regardless of the improved Grantura Mk2's introduction, it seemed a serious slump was happening again. To deepen yet another crisis, a provisional audit of the books showed that Layton Sports Cars had been making large losses throughout the year. The directors shuddered. Prices of all models of full cars and kits were increased by £50 as from 1st September, but during that month the board of directors admitted that they again had a critical situation on their hands – in terms of both sales and cash. It looked like another ugly scenario.

This slump hit firmly home

within a very short time of Arnold Burton's first investment. It was followed by more discussions and disagreement about how to economise TVR production. One person took little part in the wrangles. Bad-tempered rows, he would have called them. Poor Trevor Wilkinson had already been slipping further and further into the background but he wasn't quite prepared for the result of the board's latest sessions. One startling and utterly frustrating decision for him was that John Thurner was to be given *full* charge of development and improvement of the Grantura.

For Trevor it was another step towards the brink of despair. Subconsciously he'd long been aware of trouble approaching but had kept pushing it to the back of his mind. Now he was very upset at being ousted by the highly skilled Thurner, whom he'd always regarded as an opponent of sorts whilst being happy to have such expertise available for development. There was naturally some professional jealousy, and Thurner's statement of his intention to design a completely new chassis (this wouldn't appear until spring 1962) only darkened the relationship. Trevor knew high costs would be involved and, unlike the other directors, was not in favour of further borrowing.

As ever, money was leaking from Hoo Hill in bucketfuls. While Grantura Engineering's business involved the much more straightforward buying and selling of parts and components used by Layton Sports Cars in its building of TVRs, Layton's business was altogether more complicated. An internal report dated August 1960 explained one reason for Layton's now shocking situation. It said: 'During the whole of the training period (for unskilled labour over nine months of 1959 and 1960) production has lagged sadly behind the economic level expected. During the first ten months of the company's existence, it is estimated that untrained labour has cost the

▲ Externally the Mk2A, first revealed in late 1960, was identical to the Mk2. Under the skin the major change involved fitting disc brakes at the front. (Peter Filby)

company much of its subscribed capital (£15,000 in November 1959)!'

Towards the end of 1960 the company's slide steepened. A big cash loss was confirmed – many thousands of pounds. Realising that things had reached almost rock bottom, and knowing nobody else was willing to invest further for the moment, Arnold Burton cast a few more thousand pounds into the coffers. This was a business investment, no question, but he was proving very generous towards the ailing firm. Yet was it enough? The trend was downwards still… only nine TVRs were on order at the

▲ Early in 1961 the 1622cc MGA engine was made available to TVR customers. It produced around 90bhp and lowered the Grantura's 60mph acceleration time to just under ten seconds.

▼ OK, it *is* a London bus, but this shot of a Mk2 confirms just how small the TVR was.

end of November. The latest factory demonstrator, a bright yellow Grantura Mk2, looked very special, but clearly the problem was enticing potential customers to the factory to see and appreciate it.

Inexplicably, the helter-skelter production rate was still moving smoothly – twenty-five chassis and twenty-five sets of body panels completed during November. Such figures were hopelessly out of balance with both the sales figures and staff numbers (over fifty). Then appeared the inevitable conclusion. 'Due to inadequate working capital, differences of opinion amongst directors, too rapid production and excessive wastage,' said the auditor in his report, 'I cannot view the company's future with any optimism'.

Trouble always seemed to strike towards the end of each year. Yet, generally clouded with gloom, December terminated with some very murky rays of light. A Mr Dick Monnich of Racemasters Inc, New York, USA, visited Hoo Hill and stated that he was interested in starting a TVR import business (to be called RM Imports) and was extremely hopeful of excellent sales in America. He'd first discovered TVR while stationed in the UK working as a fitter in the USAF and had bought an early Grantura from Bill Last. Then, in January 1961, a very ambitious young man, Bryan Hopton, of successful Lotus and TVR dealers, Aitchison-Hopton (Engineers) Ltd of Chester, made it known that he could be interested in investing in the Blackpool company. Time would obviously be needed to make the necessary arrangements, but was there hope again?

Layton Sports Cars had entered 1959 with eight directors. Due to two resignations and only one new appointment, the figure had been reduced to seven by the beginning of 1960. But after one addition during 1960, plus two new signings-on over the new year period, 1961 broke out with no less than ten directors at the helm! All to run a company that couldn't make its product at an economical rate, couldn't sell it at a profitable price and was sorely short of cash, yet had over fifty staff knocking out the product as fast as they could go. The two new men were Arnold and Reginald Hill, who ran their own finance company in Lancaster, had funds to spare and fancied a dabble in something more exciting. They would get some action at TVR sure enough!

Although in only its second year, the Racing Car Show at London's Horticultural Halls in January 1961 was already an important annual event for the world of race cars, specialist cars, tuning equipment and international competition. The fact that two TVRs were on display at this extremely popular show was impressive. The car on the Layton Sports Cars stand – managed by a three-man team from Aitchison-Hopton (Engineers) Ltd – was a lightly revised version of the Grantura labelled the Mk2A. The 'A' designation signified the now standard fitment of front disc brakes, and the show model was powered by the latest 1622cc version of the MGA engine, uprated with a light alloy HRG crossflow head and 40DCOE Weber carburettors. The second Grantura on display was a superb looking metallic red example sharing space on the WJ Last Ltd stand with an Elva Courier, which also used MGA power.

▲ The Mk2A's public launch came at the January 1961 Racing Car Show in London. (John Bailie)

▼ An early 1961 *Autosport* ad from the Brighton dealership run by TVR racer, ex-Squadron Leader James Boothby.

The Racing Car Show displays were quite a success with the TVRs grabbing great interest despite the considerable number of competitors vying for attention – cars such as the Gilbern GT, Turner, gullwing-doored Marcos GT, Ginetta G4 and the elegant Falcon Caribbean. But that strong interest unfortunately had only a mildly positive effect on sales, which for the time being would hover at around the fifteen per month mark – while Hoo Hill's laminators and welders were likely to make about twenty sets of body panels and chassis in the same period. By the end of January about twenty unsold TVR kits were cluttering up the factory, seven of them being unsold examples of the now superseded Mk1. After receiving a small investment from the Hill brothers, another unfortunate move was made by the fumbling management when they obtained stocking finance on half of those kits from another finance company. This just pushed Layton Sports Cars further into debt.

Amongst the ten directors, not all of whom gave more than part of their time to the management and direction of Layton Sports Cars, there seemed now to be no single strong character, no true leadership. They still couldn't agree on many points, as Bunty Scott-Moncrieff remembered: "There seemed to be at least one crisis board meeting every week! Everybody arguing like mad. It was always a pretty good ding-dong. I managed to disagree with Bernard on absolutely every point, though we did remain the greatest of friends. Trevor was just plain bloody awkward and several of us found him rather difficult to get on with."

In fact, the rather unambitious Trevor was extremely frustrated by events and simply wished he could just get on with building cars at his own pace, as in TVR's early days. He had no time for constant production efficiency investigations and business discussions. "Every board meeting was just a load of talk and suggestions, while nothing ever happened as a result. Everything just carried on in the same old way afterwards."

Arnold Burton shared in the general naivety: "All the board discussions revolved entirely around profit making, yet it took us years to realise that the more cars we sold, the more money we lost! We

always believed that prosperity was just around the corner, that we were going to make a lot of money to pay off our debts. Then it was always found that there was something wrong with the last batch of cars, so a change would be made on the next batch while they were actually going through. Having never stopped to evaluate the change properly, the next fault would be thrown up very quickly. We should have stopped production altogether for a year and spent at least £10-20,000 getting the car right. That would have been nothing compared to what we later spent. Yes, we were a bunch of amateurs with a car that customers generally found was never really what we had said it was – each one had so many problems and faults."

Here was the crux of the matter. Despite all attempts at sorting it, the hand-built TVR was still not an instantly saleable, well finished, high quality product. It was not a properly developed car. It had never had time to become such a thing. Consequently, many of the examples sold had damaged both car and company's reputations via unwelcome publicity from dissatisfied owners. In one area of the workshop at Hoo Hill, customer service manager Bob Hallett was always busy checking over and rectifying faults on cars built from kits by customers. Only the most skilled customers would get their cars right first time. What TVR desperately needed, after some two and a half years of haphazard production and a stream of mostly sub-standard cars, was an air of order and authority in the factory and a top quality car to be truly proud of. Could the newly revised model, the Grantura Mk2A, be that car?

In full production early in 1961, the Mk2A was in fact little more than a lightly improved Mk2 using unchanged fibreglass bodywork and fitted with better front brakes. While the first few kit-form cars left the factory with 1588cc MGA engines, the enlarged 1622cc MGA unit (now with about 90bhp) now became the standard fitment – although power could be raised (to 108bhp) if the optional HRG crossflow head and 40DCOE Weber carburettors were specified. Another option was the stalwart 1216cc Climax FWE engine and, though it was unlikely to prove of much interest at this time, the 997cc Ford 105E engine was still a possibility. Providing a small increase in ground clearance – always a TVR necessity – was a new exhaust system.

To haul the Mk2A back from speed, its braking system was upgraded with 11in Girling front discs as standard equipment – although, ironically, a number of early examples went out still fitted with the old all-drum system. While the Ford-type worm-and-peg steering was unchanged on MG powered cars, more precise rack-and-pinion steering was offered for the higher performance, Climax propelled models. The only other changes involved better seats, improved interior trim, more sound insulation and the loss on each door of the opening facility for the quarter-light windows.

Despite the Mk2A's limited improvements, somebody at Hoo Hill was apparently confident of its reception from one of the country's leading car magazines, because an arrangement was made for a private customer to loan his car to *The Motor* for a full road test.

▼ Motor sport and club competition were always an integral part of the TVR experience – and always would be. This Mk2 is taking part in a sprint event. (Derek Hutchings)

THE EARLY YEARS

Built by the customer from what must have been one of the first Mk2A kits, the car was 1588cc MGA powered and had a set of close-ratio gears in its gearbox. Strangely, it wasn't fitted with the front disc brakes it should have had, instead using drums all round, so was it in fact the earlier Mk2? In its nose, just above the radiator air intake, were the two 'nostril' vents originally intended only for Ford engined models.

Contrary to expectations, TVR's first-ever national magazine road test report, which appeared in March 1961, was full of compliments. Here are some of them: 'The MGA engine fitted to the test car can take the hardiest of driving. Cornering is far faster than at first imagined. Noise level is commendably low and so driver and passenger arrive less tired by, and far more pleased with, the car than when they set off in it. Should the driver wish really to make the best of the car, using the 'box fully gives very impressive acceleration in the higher speed range. The independent suspension was very hard, and yet the car did not give half as bumpy a ride as expected, and it improved as speed rose. There was a mild degree of oversteer but this was not progressive, becoming less noticeable as cornering speed rose. There was plenty of feel as regards how near the limit the car was, and the driver always felt completely the master of the machine'.

Turning to the cabin, the magazine's view was: 'The interior layout and minor controls are on the whole excellent. There is a luxurious air and the seats are comfortable. As a road car it has a very individualistic charm of its own that makes it remarkably good fun to drive. The glassfibre bodywork had an exceptionally good surface finish and, externally, such items as corner bumpers gave the whole car a properly finished look'.

Despite earlier reports, *The Motor*'s opinion of the test car was remarkably enthusiastic. There were a few criticisms – namely about the small doors, the lack of interior space, the position of the handbrake lever and the absence of an opening boot – but, generally speaking, this inaugural national report made the TVR sound quite appealing. Prices were still quite tempting, too. A fully complete MG engined car was now £1253 while just over £1500 got you the 1216cc Climax FWE powered model. In fact, most cars being sold in Britain were going out as kits for home assembly at a saving of about £400.

▲ Another entertaining ad from Aitchison-Hopton, this one dated September 1961.

◀ A shot from *The Motor*'s road test of a Mk2 printed in March 1961. It was TVR's first ever full test report, and very complimentary it was too.

If it seemed as though the apparently much improved TVR was going to turn around the company's fortunes and finances, hold on! Despite those attractive prices and despite such welcome magazine publicity, there was a surprising lack of effect upon sales. At the end of April there were no less than forty-four kits in stock, most of them MG powered, three-quarters of them now on stocking finance. It had been the only way to drag in cash. The bank had refused to increase the company's overdraft and, having already supplied an initial £15,000, the Treasury of Her Majesty's Government had not felt so generous upon receiving the second application from Layton Sports Cars. And so the relentless search for funding would have to continue.

Ace welder and principal factory joker Stan Kilcoyne was now in charge of the parts store, his knowledge of TVR parts and their origins already unparalleled. Stan was a natural born wheeler-dealer who claimed to have friends in the Blackpool Mafia! With a wicked glint in his eye, he got involved with high finance one day: "We had all these cars in stock and this guy rolled up to check that thirty cars were present before he OK'd the stocking finance. Well, there were actually only twenty-nine, because we'd sold one a few days earlier."

Continued Stan: "The finance man was looking for this last car and it was getting late for my lunchtime. I knew where the bloody thing was, like: it was gone. But I said, 'I know, it's down at the paint shop on Marton Moss, just outside town. I'll get it back for you while you go and have lunch'. So after he'd gone I whipped one out of the line of twenty-nine, same colour as the missing one, stamped a new chassis plate with the missing number, screwed it on, washed the car down and showed it to him when he came back. He just marked it down and buggered off – and there were still only twenty-nine cars there!"

During May 1961, at a time when staff numbers had reached a record sixty, Derek Harris became the latest Layton Sports Cars director to resign, though he intended to remain as the company's solicitor. The men on the shop floor had no difficulty making

▼ Having joined TVR as a welder in 1956, Stanley Kilcoyne soon became the company's parts manager. He was also the factory's principal joker and became much loved by TVR staff and customers alike. (Peter Filby)

fifteen chassis and eighteen sets of body panels during this month, but even allowing for a few sales, such output simply boosted stock to some thirty-five body chassis units – whereas June began with only five orders in hand!

While English agents had produced depressingly variable results, at least things had gently come back to life in the USA thanks to the agency deal signed with Dick Monnich of New York. Working out of the garage at his Long Island home, Monnich's company, RM Imports, was making some headway, slowly getting his fledgling American sales campaign under way, importing the occasional TVR here and there. But he had no service facility or parts department, and overall sales still needed a far greater boost than this: they were currently worse than disappointing.

At a point when Layton Sports Cars remained in a serious financial position, it was at last decided to cut staff numbers – by thirteen during June. One dismissal was painless enough after some energetic action in the first floor body moulding shop, which also doubled as the repair shop. Between the cars sitting about and the steel posts positioned at regular intervals, one apprentice decided that he had enough room to practise his driving. He fired up a customer's repaired Climax powered car and moved off. He was trying to get smarter between the posts, whipping it just a tad sideways as necessary. And then he misjudged it… and hit one car, which rolled into another, which rolled into the next one, and so on until several TVRs displayed modified styling both front and rear. "What a bloody mess," said Henry Moulds. "Have you anything to say before I fire you?"

As ever, daily life at Layton Sports Cars was rarely dull. The sad thing was that TVRs had now been manufactured at the Hoo Hill industrial estate for just over five years, yet the process was still as much of a struggle as ever. Indeed, keeping the company afloat was still a major struggle, too. As events moved into the second half of 1961 little was to change in that respect. But, with the impending arrival of TVR racer Keith Aitchison and his business partner Bryan Hopton as new shareholders, things at TVR head office were about to liven up considerably.

▲ After Ray Saidel stopped dealing with TVR, Dick Monnich's company RM Imports took on the mantle.

◀ Dick Monnich at the wheel of his early Grantura Mk2 alongside a friend's V8 powered 1961 Chevy Corvette. It seems there was no point in doing any street racing! (Keith Aitchison)

Competition in 1960

THE TVR RACING scene was developing healthily in 1960, Keith Aitchison, Peter Bolton and Colin Escott being amongst the names most notable for track exploits in their early Granturas. Other enthusiastic TVR pilots this year were Averil Scott-Moncrieff, James Boothby, Mary Wheeler, Dave Baldock, Norman Barclay and John Thurner, all of them in regular action with their Mk1s (mostly Climax powered). Two more such machines were regular competitors in Scotland, their drivers being David Hodgeton and Gordon Crozier. In fact, Crozier competed in the Highland Rally in his car, another early Climax engined Grantura.

After the demise of their first 'Coffee Bean' in 1959, Averil and Bunty Scott-Moncrieff were now campaigning its replacement, 'Coffee Bean' number two. Still 1098cc Climax powered, the dark brown Mk1 was piloted with great verve by Averil at circuits and hillclimbs nationwide during 1960 but without anything special in the way of results. Only occasionally was Bunty to be seen behind the wheel; he was more than happy to let his highly spirited wife entertain the fans and promote the TVR name. Colin Escott also raced 'The Coffee Bean' just once, getting a class win at Oulton Park in June.

Over the second half of 1959 and the first of 1960, Keith Aitchison had gained decent results in his 1600 MGA powered Grantura Mk1, but he was keen to go quicker. By mid-1960 he'd received factory assistance with the build of a white Mk2, which retained his 'old' engine in tuned form. Sure enough, the Mk2, a lighter car than the Mk1, performed much better and, still concentrating on northern circuits, Aitchison enjoyed another season of excellent class placings, doing another fine job of bringing the Blackpool brand to a wider audience.

A significant new name joining the TVR competition scene this year was that of Brighton garage proprietor Mrs Mary Wheeler. A charismatic, strong and determined character, Mary came from a wealthy, aristocratic background, but though she'd led an interesting and colourful life, financially she suffered more than her fair share of bad luck. However, she had a great ability to overcome difficulties and never lost her sense of humour.

Before moving to Brighton, Mary and her husband ran Wheeler's Service Station in Hickstead, Sussex. She was already a youthful forty-six years old when, in 1957, she started her competition career, driving her Triumph TR2 in the Brighton Speed Trials. It didn't take her long to become known as a notoriously good starter in motor sport, no doubt because she made a point of practicing racing starts in her TR2 during quiet spells on the main A23 road running past the garage!

Mary's first circuit race came at Goodwood in July 1958, and she switched to her first TVR for the 1960 season. Early in the year she bought a Grantura Mk1 kit which had an early Mk2 chassis and a stage three tuned 1216cc Coventry Climax FWE engine. The kit's supplier was TVR's main distributor for the south of England, St James' Autos of Brighton, as managed by Squadron Leader James Boothby. By this time the Wheeler garage had been relocated to Brighton, and it was there that Mary took her usual hands-on approach helping her chief mechanic Arthur Bonwick to assemble the TVR.

Little time was wasted building the car, and on May 29th 1960 Mary was behind her Mk1's wheel on the start line at Firle hillclimb near Lewes, East Sussex. Running in the Special Touring and GT

◀ Mary Wheeler storms up Firle hillclimb in May 1960 during her first ever event with her Mk1. She finished 11th in class that day.

Competition in 1960 cont'd

cars class (up to 1300cc), she achieved a creditable 12th overall that day, also receiving the Ladies' Award. It was a good start to her TVR competition career.

Finished in dark green, the Wheeler Mk1 made its racetrack debut at Goodwood in June in a five-lap handicap race in which Mary pitted her skills against a trio of Mk1s – James Boothby's 1216cc Climax powered lightweight, Averil Scott-Moncrieff's 1098cc Climax powered 'Coffee Bean' and John Thurner's dark green machine with 1489cc MGA power. Mary was placed an excellent third in an entertaining race. Brands Hatch came next, early in July, and the competition was rather heavier – two Elva Couriers, Bob Linwood's Fairthorpe Zeta, a Tornado Thunderbolt and no less than four Lotus Elites.

From that point on, Mary's TVR was a regular at Goodwood (her favourite circuit), Lydden Hill, Brands and Thruxton. Although she never achieved many race wins, largely due to having to operate on a shoestring, she was to prove very quick at hillclimbs and rarely missed an event at Firle. She also loved to compete at the Brighton Speed Trials. Thanks to their common interest in TVRs, Mary was very friendly with James Boothby, and the latter was also an enthusiastic TVR racer during 1960 with his Climax powered Grantura Mk1 lightweight. Indeed, his dark blue car was often seen at both Goodwood circuit and Firle hillclimb during the year.

As for the 'official' factory effort this year, proving just how ambitious the Blackpool company was to make its mark on the international racing scene were the boardroom discussions that had taken place in December 1959 regarding entering for Le Mans in 1960. The proposal was for a team of three TVRs to do battle in the 24-hour event but, perhaps thankfully, the directors saw common sense and dropped any such wild ideas. There simply weren't the funds or experience to compete in such a prestigious international race.

▶ James Boothby's Mk1 chases a big Jaguar saloon at Goodwood in 1960.

▼ The first circuit race for Mary Wheeler's Mk1 was at Goodwood in June 1960, when she came 3rd.

CHAPTER FIVE

The Aitchison – Hopton Era

In September 1961 successful, Chester based TVR distributors, Aitchison-Hopton (Engineers) Ltd, bought a controlling interest in TVR, Bryan Hopton becoming the new Chairman and Managing Director. Hugely ambitious and full of energy, Hopton succeeded in reviving the company's fortunes for a while, with excellent sales of the Mk2 and 2A Granturas. But his scheme to take TVR into prestigious international racing, starting with the Sebring 12-hour event in March 1962, was ill-judged and expensive.

Despite the competence of the Granturas Mk2 and Mk2A, 1961 was another remarkably unsettled year for the TVR. Thanks to insufficient sales, lack of funds and generally poor management, the company's survival was under constant threat. One answer to the situation was to find and encourage more home-market dealerships.

Due to the pressures of running his own Rolls-Royce restoration and sales business, Bunty Scott-Moncrieff had only ever been able to devote part of his time to Layton

▶ Although it was manufactured in 1960, this lovely Grantura Mk2 wasn't registered until May '61. It had chassis number 52 and 1622cc MGA power.
(Hugh James)

THE EARLY YEARS

Sports Cars, appearing at the factory perhaps once a week. But he had always been active in finding and establishing TVR dealers. This had become something of a headache because, when the production rate had been impossibly slow, there had hardly been enough cars to send out to customers, let alone dealers. More recently, when the line had been stirred into action, many of the dealers had failed to sell enough cars – at least, that's how the factory saw it.

Enthusiastic and professionally run dealers and distributors were extremely important to a company producing hand-built sports cars on an impossibly tight budget. By mid-1961 the number of garages distributing and selling TVRs around the country had considerably expanded. A notable name now trying to promote the TVR brand via his Weybridge, Surrey, garage was Tony Brooks, who had come to fame in Formula One racing in 1955 with a Connaught. After a season with BRM, Brooks signed as number two to Stirling Moss in the Vanwall team for 1957, and by 1959 was behind the wheel of a front-engined Dino 246 driving for Ferrari. Rated extremely highly as a driver, he was also a fully qualified dentist and was known in racing circles as 'The Flying Dentist'. In 1961 he rejoined BRM alongside Graham Hill but by the end of that season he had retired to concentrate on growing his garage business – and his TVR distributorship, which looked after London and the home counties.

Understandably, Brooks' attentions in 1961 were not wholly devoted to selling TVRs. Somewhat ambitiously, both Brooks' garage and Lotus and Maserati dealer, David Buxton Ltd of Derby (now also an agent for Piper aircraft), had agreed to take 100 cars each during 1961, but unfortunately their salesmen weren't performing anywhere near well enough to keep to the deals. Layton Sports Cars' directors weren't overly impressed, either, with the poor results being achieved by Sports Motors of Manchester and St James Autos of Brighton.

Other firms trying to spread the TVR word were Aitchison-Hopton (Engineers) Ltd of Chester, the Yorkshire distributors, The White Garage of Pool in Wharfedale, Cheshire Sports Cars of Cheadle, Bell's Cars of Kensington, London, Peter Bolton's garage in Leeds, Speedrite of Hull, Fisher's Garage of Edinburgh, Griffin Mill Garages of Pontypridd, Glamorgan, and Formula Junior race-car maker, Kieft Sports Car Company of South Birmingham. The latter hadn't been having an easy time selling TVRs, but when questioned on this Kieft's sales manager reminded Layton's directors that when they (Kieft) had secured many orders in summer 1961, the factory had been unable to deliver!

One of the best-established dealers was now

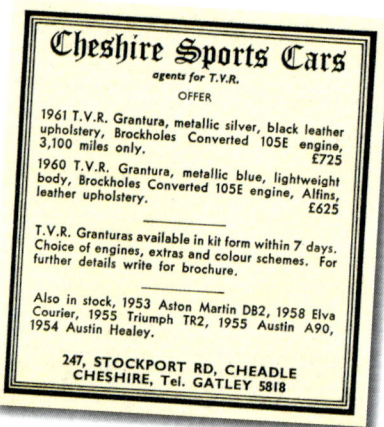

▲▼ Amongst the many agents and distributors joining the TVR throng in 1961 were Cheshire Sports Cars and Lotus and Maserati dealer David Buxton Ltd.

THE AITCHISON - HOPTON ERA

WJ Last Ltd of Woodbridge, Suffolk (looking after East Anglia), and Last made a rather ironic claim in his advertising: 'Only we offer complete written instructions on assembling your TVR' – which makes one wonder what the factory did to help customers building its kits (there still wasn't an official assembly manual at this time). Nuneaton's Research Garage tempted sales by offering free delivery anywhere in the country, but by far the best dealer offer was yet to reach the boardroom at Hoo Hill...

Earlier on, Bunty's untiring search for dealers had struck most significantly in autumn 1960 with the appointment of the aforementioned Aitchison-Hopton (Engineers Ltd) as distributors for the South-West Lancashire, West Cheshire, Wales and Shropshire areas. The company was a thriving specialist sports car dealer in Chester, and by 1961 its salesmen had become extremely adept at shifting TVRs. Furthermore, the company was soon to become deeply involved in TVR itself and see its Managing Director, Bryan Hopton, play an extraordinary (and ultimately disastrous) role in its history. Another TVR tragedy was about to be set in motion ...

Born into a farming family from Crewe in Cheshire, Keith Aitchison loved both agriculture and engineering. While his horses could gallop at reasonable pace, Keith ached for the turn of speed that motor racing offered, and at the tender age of twenty-one he managed to buy an ex-works, aluminium bodied Austin-Healey 100M. He raced this quite successfully in 1958 and early 1959 but, like all competitive drivers, found himself wanting something quicker. Ideally, his choice would have been a Lotus Elite but that would have been a big and expensive step up, so an £850 TVR Grantura Mk1 kit it had to be. Bought from David Buxton Ltd early in 1959 and built by Keith in his workshop at the family farm, the car was finished with an MGA 1600cc engine, a red interior and several coats of classy looking steel grey paint.

Raced mainly at local circuits such as Oulton Park and Aintree, the Aitchison Mk1 was moderately successful in 1959 and the first half of the 1960 season, and was then replaced with a semi-works Grantura Mk2. Using the same 1600 engine, thanks to its lighter weight this car was considerably livelier, getting the Aitchison name on to the results sheets on a regular basis. A friend who often supported Keith's TVR exploits was Bryan Hopton, successful restauranteur, MG TD driver and enthusiastic racing spectator.

At twenty-nine years old, Hopton was one of those men who thought big and already had grandiose schemes at the back of his mind. Anything was going to be an improvement on the ten shillings a week he'd earned as a 16-year-old farm labourer before moving on to work for his parents on their

▲ More TVR dealers in this *Autosport* classified ad from November 1961.

▼ A typical club racing scene with a trio of Mk1 racers on the grid at Aintree circuit in 1961. (Dave Baldock)

THE EARLY YEARS

As with so many race drivers of the time, Keith Aitchison used his 1622cc MG powered Mk1 for both road and track. (Keith Aitchison)

farm at Little Budworth, just an exhaust blast away from Oulton Park circuit. He spent some time as a calf dealer and then opened a chain of restaurants, but it was the sight of sports cars in close-fought action that really lit his fire. In particular, the noise and excitement of stubby little TVRs tearing around the Cheshire track was to have a lasting effect.

It was through Bryan Hopton's regular attendances at Keith Aitchison's races that the two men became close and eventually started to discuss ideas for a business. Recalled Keith: "In effect, I woke up one day and realised I was getting fed-up with paying out money all the time to keep my TVR racer going. Starting my own business seemed to be the answer, and Bryan agreed. We launched Aitchison-Hopton (Engineers) Ltd in July 1960 and began trading in what we called 'wire wheels'. 12 KMA, my steel grey Mk1 road racer, was the first TVR on the premises – which was a small, not particularly smart establishment alongside a canal in Chester."

Concentrating on interesting sports and kit cars, the business developed steadily until later in the year when it signed-up as a distributor for TVR and two of its fiercest competitors, the Warwick GT and the Lotus Elite – not forgetting the famous Seven. Thanks to his own racing success, Keith Aitchison was already a regular visitor to Layton Sports Cars' Blackpool factory and had become very friendly with Bernard Williams. The relationship was to have its benefits, as Keith explained: "Bernard realised I was doing well but said 'You've got to have a quicker car if you want to be really competitive'. He was anxious for TVR to get more results on the circuits and thus receive good publicity, and that's how I came to be given a new Mk2 by the factory. When I'd finished the new car, a lighter package than the Mk1, I went racing and was immediately much quicker."

During 1961 the Aitchison-Hopton garage often sold between four and six TVRs a month alongside its other business selling a range of Derrington performance accessories and Crypton tuning equipment. "We were the first company in the north-west to handle Crypton gear," said Keith, "and it attracted a lot of people to our workshops and showroom. At the time TVR didn't have the greatest reputation for an up-to-date or

Keith Aitchison was successful both at racing TVRs and selling them. In September 1961 he became a director of Layton Sports Cars.

▲ At Silverstone, Keith Aitchison's white Grantura Mk2 is about to start the 750MC's Birkett 6-hour relay.

▼ Climax powered Mk2 factory car during a test trip to Italy in summer 1961. (Keith Aitchison)

well made product, and I don't think there were many companies in the UK who wanted to be involved in the kit car business. But we were doing well with the marque and becoming more and more involved with the factory."

The close working relationship between the country's most active TVR distributorship and Hoo Hill's 'front' man, Bernard Williams, soon led to some interesting adventures. The shrewd Bernard realised the tie-up with Aitchison and Hopton could easily lead to the two men becoming well and truly 'hooked' into TVR. When, during summer 1961, they were asked by Bernard to evaluate the current Climax powered Grantura Mk2 by thrashing it down to Monza in Italy, they readily agreed. The trip coincided with a race meeting at the famous Monza circuit, which was a handy bonus.

"Sharing the driving," described Keith, "we went via France, Belgium and Germany, where we had a serious potential sales contact to see. We gave the TVR a thorough thrashing, one result being that the exhaust fell off twice. We arrived in Monza without any exhaust silencing at all; it was in the back of the car, all of which created a bit of a stir! While we were there, Bernard had arranged for us to meet Count Giovani 'Johnny' Lurani, an old racing pal of his from pre-war days.

While we were with him, he said 'Come on, we'll give the TVR Climax a go around the track' and I had a glorious hour letting the car loose in the company of Ferraris, Alfas and other exotic machines. The Count and others were much impressed with my lap times achieved with a standard road car."

As a result of the Monza trip there was talk at Hoo Hill of exporting body/chassis units to Italy, where agents could fit Alfa Romeo engines. Nothing came of that but a handful of cars *were* sold to the German contact. A further by-product of the European thrash was a Mk2 bonnet so badly damaged by all the stones thrown up into the engine bay by the front tyres that bulky inner wheel arches (moulded in fibreglass) were placed on the development agenda for the next new TVR, the Mk3 due in spring 1962.

While Italian-built, Alfa Romeo powered TVRs weren't going to happen, the ambitious Bryan Hopton rightly convinced Layton Sports Cars' nine directors that there was great scope for the expansion of exports to the USA and Canada. He also talked about the great benefits to be gained from possible racing success, particularly in international events during 1962. More pressing was a sales promotion trip, suggested by Bernard and funded by Layton, for both Hopton and Aitchison to visit small-time TVR importer Dick Monnich in New York and help develop the RM Imports business relationship. A genuine guy in his early 30s, Monnich was a great lover of English sports cars and had already imported a small number of Granturas. Particularly keen on the Blackpool machine, he felt he could sell at least 100 left-hand-drive examples in 1962. TVR's enthusiastic sales promoters also got potentially worthwhile results from other would-be agents on the American west coast and in Canada. There was certainly a buzz about the way they operated.

It was no secret that the whole TVR operation in Blackpool was struggling at this time – as ever! But Bryan Hopton and Keith Aitchison's involvement with Layton Sports Cars was becoming ever closer due to the factory's increasing reliance on sales by the Chester dealership, so it was perhaps inevitable that the relationship would move up to another level. While Aitchison's racing was well supported by Bernard Williams, who realised the excellent promotional value of track success, the dynamic and ambitious Hopton was toying with the idea of buying the whole company. Indeed, he was in a hurry to make it big-time. Such ambition certainly didn't escape the notice of Mr Williams.

When Hopton eventually proposed a bold takeover bid for the entire TVR set-up, Managing Director Henry Moulds, Bernard and the other directors listened intently – anything was interesting if it could relax the generally desperate shortage of cash and continuing hunger for more sales. The stark fact was that Layton

▼ During Keith Aitchison and Bryan Hopton's trip to Italy in 1961, their Grantura's exhaust system fell off twice! Here's Keith trying to fix it. (Keith Aitchison)

Dick Monnich was TVR's US importer in 1961. He's on the right here with his Grantura Mk2 ahead of an early Chevy Corvette. (Keith Aitchison)

Sports Cars was insolvent and, of course, trading at a loss. And so it was that in September 1961 the names of Bryan Hopton and Keith Aitchison cemented their arrival on the TVR map in no uncertain terms and boosted even further the total of Layton's directors. In a deal fairly dictated by themselves, they took a controlling interest in the company and provided fresh operating funds via their Chester garage business. It wasn't the huge six-figure sum mentioned in the press but at least it was enough to launch another TVR era in seemingly positive and promising style.

Keith Aitchison explained the logic behind the takeover: "We were more active with TVR sales than anybody else in the country. At the time our Lotus business was drying up while the Warwick GT, with which we'd done well, was in danger of going bust. We went into TVR because our sales of the car were strong, and if we hadn't acted and the company had gone bump as a result, then our own garage would probably have got into trouble too, because we didn't have much else other than our workshops and tuning operation."

Appointing himself Chairman and Managing Director, Bryan Hopton wasn't short of ideas and schemes for the dramatic revival of TVR. He set off as he meant to continue and promptly brought in yet another director, his brother-in-law Tony Clarke (said to be a brilliant salesman), and gave him the position of Sales Director. At the same time Hopton decreed that board meetings would henceforth be held in a comfortable Blackpool hotel, The Imperial, rather than in the less auspicious Hoo Hill factory. He also resolved to introduce as soon as possible John Thurner's eagerly anticipated new chassis with all-wishbone suspension, and made it plain that an entirely new model of sleek Italian design would be considered for eventual production – this would be the Trident proposal of 1962. And it was time, he felt, to start planning an international racing programme: the company needed more impressive race results if it was to do well through motorsport. Finally, while he was overturning the previous regime, he felt it would be worth changing Layton Sports Cars' name to TVR

Dynamic and ambitious, Bryan Hopton was Keith Aitchison's partner in a Chester garage and car sales business. Following on from being successful TVR dealers, the two men took over Layton Sports Cars in September 1961.

Cars Ltd – this was done before the end of 1961.

From now on, Keith Aitchison's most pressing responsibility would be to look after the Aitchison-Hopton car sales business in Chester, which suited him nicely because he was a steadier and more modest man than his dynamic, flamboyant partner, who would now concentrate his attentions on the Blackpool factory. "Bryan had big ideas," Keith explained. "He wanted to do it all and was at times a bit reckless, but he insisted on giving TVR a shot. Now spending most of his time at the factory, Hopton got on well with Bernard, recognising his many varied talents and versatility: anything from engineering to creative thinking in the sorting of problems. But he couldn't get on with Trevor, finding it difficult to tolerate his negative attitude to so many things, including progress."

A mild, introvert man, TVR's founder reeled back from Hopton's forceful impact on happenings at Hoo Hill and the remarkable sequence of events he was inspiring. Trevor certainly didn't agree that any new car should be designed in Italy, feeling the necessary design skills and perfectly adequate engineering facilities lay in Blackpool. And the now ridiculous number of directors! He'd already considered leaving the company on more than one occasion, but everything had been his when they'd first moved into Hoo Hill and now there seemed to be nothing to fall back on. Sadly, Trevor's presence in the factory now faded further into the background along with the enthusiasm of Arnold Burton and Bunty Scott-Moncrieff.

Indeed, enthusiasm was generally lacking amongst *most* of TVR Cars' directors at this time. They mostly only visited the factory on a weekly or occasional basis and many of the goings-on there simply went over their heads. This tended to leave Bernard Williams in a more influential position than ever, including largely having control over the accounts department, where he worked very closely with an old-timer called Alf Thomas, the resident accountant and wages clerk. As such, Bernard was the key person in the link between sourcing component parts supplies, making invoice payments and overseeing shop-floor production.

▲ A late 1961 factory ad for the Grantura Mk2A.

▼ Early TVRs will always be renowned for their tiny doors. A high transmission tunnel and high dashboard were also part of the package. (Hugh James)

THE AITCHISON - HOPTON ERA

Not long after Aitchison-Hopton (Engineers) Ltd had invested in TVR, Keith Aitchison expressed some doubts about the deal's handling. "It was only when we became involved in the day-to-day running of the company that we realised what was actually happening. Clearly our accountants had only been shown the paperwork that Bernard wanted them to see, and they hadn't been meticulous enough in their preparation because there was so much information *not* shown in the accounts books." Continued Keith: "Bernard courted our funding very smoothly. His great enthusiasm for TVR helped him manipulate people and influence them towards the company's potential. But it wasn't long before I was questioning the wisdom of our actions."

Rapier thin and bristling with boundless energy, Bryan Hopton was trying his best to inject life into TVR's existence. As ever, the car needed improvement, sales efforts needed endless attention, and competition activities needed planning in the hope of giving the car a racing pedigree. And the skill standard of the workforce needed developing.

Bringing much needed fresh talent into the company at this stage was a new staff member, an experienced and highly skilled mechanic called David Hives who had been born into the motor industry thanks to his father's large garage in St Anne's, just south of Blackpool. A significant part of that business was a fleet of vehicles comprising twenty-two taxis, two fire engines and four ambulances so, as a teenager, David was never short of subjects on which to learn all the basics of motor engineering. Because automotive parts were so difficult to obtain after World War Two, d.i.y. was often the only answer and the skills David acquired in this fashion included welding, panel beating, woodwork and virtually any other treatment a vehicle might need. For friends and customers he even built at least eight kit cars, including three early Grantura Mk1s and a couple of Rochdales.

▼ This immaculate 1622cc MGA powered Mk2A was originally painted brown and UK registered in March 1962 but ended up in Holland, where it was restored. Wire wheels were a must for most TVRs. (Brigit van Steijn)

THE EARLY YEARS

Having joined TVR after the family business hit trouble, David's initial role was as a mechanic in the assembly shop, and one of his first jobs was to sort out a decent heating system for the car's cabin. "To start with they gave me all the dirty jobs," he said ruefully. "Designing and fitting a heater *after* the engine and gearbox were in the car was a bloody impossible job! Something that should have taken an hour would take two days. Soon they gave me more responsibility and I went right through the whole car, sorting things out and making small jigs where needed to ensure that parts were always fitted in exactly the right place.

▲ Keith Aitchison squeezes himself into the 1588cc MGA powered works Grantura Mk2A at the start of the international RAC Tourist Trophy race at Goodwood in August 1961. His co-driver that day was Colin Escott.

"Despite the development already done, there was an awful lot more that needed improving," continued David. "My view was that those Mk2s and 2As were bloody horrible, bumpy things. If they'd been fitted with proper VW torsion bars they could have been alright, but the company made its own bars from a cheaper material and they didn't work anywhere near as well. The TVR was a typical kit car – put together by the right man it could be quite good, but otherwise it could be terrible!"

David's involvement in the TVR story and the roles he was to play in building and developing the cars over coming years were to be greater than he could ever have imagined. His great natural ability as a versatile engineer soon came to the fore and, blessed with a fine sense of humour, he was immediately a contributor to the generally happy atmosphere on the shop floor. Keen on anything TVR, he was also to become heavily involved in forthcoming works competition activities.

While competition results to date were gaining publicity but not exactly giving the TVR a fearsome reputation, the marque's name was at least spreading slowly but surely. Keith Aitchison, John Thurner, Peter Bolton and Mary Wheeler were all active

◀ Having joined TVR in 1961 as a mechanic, the extremely skilled and versatile David Hives was to become a key member of the workforce for several years. In his later time at Hoo Hill he was general manager and responsible for all new model development.

THE AITCHISON - HOPTON ERA

in club racing, while a promising newcomer was ex-World War Two fighter pilot, Tommy Entwistle. Yet for the moment the ever-improving image was still not encouraging sales fast enough. The successes of Lotus with its Elite coupé and Seven roadster, and Elva Cars with its Courier roadster, were surely pinching business from TVR, and then there was the up-and-coming breed of mass-production sports cars from the likes of Austin-Healey, MG and Triumph. In 1961 these were all convertibles and they must have been having an adverse effect on demand for the fixed-head Blackpool bombers.

While there was always cause for concern amongst the directors, the lads on the shop floor could normally find some reason to lighten the atmosphere. David Hives remembered one such incident: "There was this chap working inside a car on the line glueing in the carpets and underfelt, while another was drilling holes in the same car to fit the door hinges. It was a horrible job, that glueing, so we'd put some right tatty little lads on it. Well, suddenly a spark from the drill ignited the adhesive and the whole car shot up in flames. This little chap got blew straight out of the car!"

More rather smelly work at Hoo Hill was the moulding of fibreglass bodies up in the first floor workshop above the brick kilns where the chassis were made. When a chassis reached the first floor ready for its body sections to be bonded on, the next stage of assembly always needed plenty of components, which came from the stores down in the main workshops. With great wisdom and commendable economy, somebody had acquired a beaten-up old van for £5 to help transport all these components. But at one stage the van's electrical system refused to recharge its

▼ Keith Aitchison in the works Mk2A at speed in the international RAC Tourist Trophy at Goodwood in 1961. With co-driver Colin Escott at the wheel, the car was lying second in class with only half an hour left when its crankshaft broke. Note the reshaped nose aperture, a factory modification to allow more air to reach the radiator.

99

THE EARLY YEARS

battery. No problems there, thought the tatty little apprentices – just go to the stores every other day, put the old battery back and get a new one out. Simple as that.

The van had to be filled with components downstairs, then driven round to the back of the brick kiln building and up the U-shaped earth ramp to the first floor. This route had its dangers, mind you. To the left of the ramp there was a sheer drop that ended with the solid concrete foundations of some half-built lavatories. Too much speed up the ramp and the apprentices took their chances... but naturally each one of them loved the job, and there would always be a full-scale battle to sort out each day's driver.

David Hives again saw the funny side of things: "This little chap got into the van, and he'd never had a drive before. It was a terrible old crate with a bum clutch. Well, once he'd got going – a bit too fast – he just couldn't stop it. He came up the ramp, shot right off the top and nose-dived twelve or fourteen feet down into the concrete. Poor little bloke thought he were dead! Actually there was hardly a mark on him, but he couldn't move an inch: he was frightened as hell. We couldn't open the van's doors, either, and all the parts and spares he had in there were all collapsed on top of him – the poor little fellow was pinned to the wheel! And all we could see was a little face inside this van wedged into the concrete foundations. Not a word came from his lips. And there was somebody shouting 'They've buggered it, a bloody good van, they've ruined it'. Everybody had to come and help get the lad and the parts out. Hell, it was an absolute riot!"

The directors could generate laughs as well, particularly the wonderfully extrovert Bunty Scott-Moncrieff. The story goes that Bunty hobbled into the Hoo Hill works one day wearing his usual country tweeds but needing crutches to assist forward motion. He'd apparently parked his car on the hill outside a pub near the Basford Hall estate and had failed to apply the handbrake properly. Walking round to the back of the empty car, he'd not noticed it rolling backwards until it ran over his foot! (Mind you, there was also a tale that something very similar happened a few years later in the central square in Leek town, so either Bunty was very prone to accidents or the story was more of a legend!).

A wonderfully engaging and entertaining personality, Bunty was a much loved character with many global friends from the motoring world, but he also had a highly volatile side to his nature. Explained David Hives: "When he came to the factory we all had to be on our best behaviour. If he was in an angry mood you certainly knew about it. Luckily there was an early warning sign – if he was brushing his moustache upwards it meant everything was fine, but if he was pulling it down the message was 'get out of my way sharpish!' But we all had a great respect for him."

A magazine road test was always good for livening things up at Hoo Hill and in November 1961 *Autocar* did the business with a hot 1220cc Climax powered Grantura Mk2A. In stage two tune and with twin Weber carburettors, its engine was claimed to have 83bhp (at 6300rpm), drove through a German ZF gearbox, which was a much valued option on the Climax engined cars, and was hauled back

AITCHISON-HOPTON
(ENGINEERS) LTD.
CHESTER

RVT ARUTNARG

Backslang? Arabic? Cantonese? No, just plain English with a slight flavour of Italian for great Sporting Machinery. T.V.R. Grantura is written backwards for it is probably only the back view you have had of these wonderful cars whilst travelling along the open road. Fast, effortless driving in limousine comfort make the miles disappear. Be an overtaker not the overtaken, nor undertaken by an undertaker in the safe T.V.R. Be admired not an admirer in this beautifully styled car.

It's a road car used for racing not a racing car used for roads. There is such a subtle difference, it makes the T.V.R. today's finest production sports car.

GO
BUY
T.V.R.
for fast, safe travel

Classic Engine £795
MGA Engine £880
Climax Engine £1,045

DISTRIBUTORS
LOTUS T.V.R. WARWICK
16, CANAL SIDE,
SELLER STREET, CHESTER
Telephone: CHESTER 26100

▲ A special effort was always made to spice up the Aitchison-Hopton TVR dealership ads. This one is from October 1961.

THE AITCHISON - HOPTON ERA

▲ Racing Granturas in the paddock at Brands Hatch. On the left is ex-WW2 fighter pilot Tommy Entwistle's first TVR, a Mk2.

▼ Sorting out the grid at Goodwood in 1961. Four TVR's are ready for action.

from speed by front disc and rear drum brakes. Strangely enough, the writer wasn't particularly impressed by the car's performance. 'Low speed torque is not good and real pulling power is only available from about 4000rpm. 0-60mph takes 10.8 seconds, while the maximum speed of 101mph is well below what was expected of this car'.

However, the Mk2A's personality emerged as one of its strong points. 'It is a car for the person who drives for the sheer fun of it. Considerable liberties can be taken when cornering, since the quick and accurate steering allows any over-exuberance to be brought in check easily. The ride is harsh and directional stability is not one of its strong points; there's a tendency to wander at high speeds'. Practicality didn't get high marks, either. 'Total luggage space consists of a narrow shelf behind the seats and curtails the Mk2A's use as a touring car. But its compact dimensions, good manoeuvrability and high performance in the middle ranges make it a very fast cross-country car'.

Enjoying the TVR's driving pleasures in Britain inevitably meant the owner was most likely to assemble the car himself. To save that person paying purchase tax, the Grantura was a kit car and unfortunately came with all the stigma that kit cars suffered

101

Life with a Mk2

CIVIL ENGINEER HENRY Webber bought his Grantura Mk2 second-hand for about £550 from a doctor at a West London hospital. Powered by a 1588cc MGA engine and finished in metallic gold paint, it was an outstanding machine for its day. "I'd been looking forward to owning a TVR for several years; I really lusted after one," said Henry. "I still remember it with huge affection. It had splendid lines and I thoroughly enjoyed driving it. Its acceleration was fine but it ran out of steam at about 100mph. The ride was very firm but the handling was tremendous."

But life with a Mk2 had its pitfalls too. "It was rather like owning a helicopter – it needed as many maintenance hours as it provided flying hours. You definitely needed access to a good set of tools. I did my own maintenance work on the car but was regularly on the 'phone to Blackpool getting parts, and I got to know the stores people extremely well! 'Delicate' was how I'd describe the car. The fibreglass body wasn't that tough and suffered a certain amount of flex, and the doors were limited in how they opened.

"I used the TVR as often as possible but it wasn't at all practical. Ventilation wasn't good and there was always heat in the cockpit. There was no way you could get a suitcase in the back under that sweeping great window – there was only space for a squashy bag or two. If you went down a rough road or one with a steep camber, there'd always be a shower of sparks coming out of the back as the exhaust system scraped along the crown of the road! But the most unfortunate thing was that because the seats were so low, the transmission tunnel so high and the gearstick even higher, it was extremely difficult to kiss my fiancée Gwalia goodnight!"

When Henry finally came to sell the Grantura, he placed an advert in *Motor Sport* and was somewhat taken aback at the response. "The ad appeared on a Thursday or Friday, and when I arrived home from work at about 3.30pm on the Saturday there was one potential purchaser sitting in his car outside, my mother was entertaining a second to tea, and a third was walking around the TVR, which was parked at the back of the house. I drew up alongside in another car and he did the deal on the spot!"

THE AITCHISON - HOPTON ERA

◀ A December 1961 ad from one of TVR's long-time dealers.

▼ *Autocar*'s road testers rated the Grantura Mk2A as an excellent driver's car in the magazine's late 1961 report.
(Brigit van Steijn)

from, although it *was* an up-market kit car. In return for £888, the fibreglass bodywork came ready bonded to its chassis with rear suspension and wheels in place but the driveshafts still to be coupled up. The engine, radiator and front suspension still needed to be fitted, and although the wiring loom was in place behind the facia, the wires needed to be routed and connected up. Trimming and painting had already been done but many detail assembly jobs awaited attention.

At this time sales chief Bernard Williams' official (but no doubt exaggerated) line was that the company's output was one TVR built per day by forty-six employees working a five-day week. Despite earlier desired policy changes, some 70% of the cars made were still leaving the factory in kit form for customer build and, as always, the most popular engine was the 1622cc MGA unit. Coventry Climax engines had to this point been fitted to about 25% of all TVRs, while the Ford 109E unit had not been popular and had been phased out with the Mk1. Unfortunately, whatever engine was under the bonnet, the cars all suffered from a distinct lack of finesse due to poor quality control and non-existent road testing, two areas with which David Hives was to become increasingly involved.

The result of recent magazine publicity, along with late 1961's energetic input from Bryan Hopton, was that fortunes were temporarily revived. Increased orders immediately came from America and Canada. An appearance by a slightly revised Grantura Mk2A, with tuned 1622cc MGA engine, wire wheels and improved interior and exterior finishing, on the TVR stand at the January 1962 Racing Car Show at

London's Royal Horticultural Halls also provided more orders, all supplied in kit form. Further exposure at the show came thanks to TVR East Anglia distributor WJ Last Ltd running another stand displaying a Grantura alongside an Elva Courier. One of the TVR show cars was painted in British Racing Green and had its interior trimmed in white leather throughout – not to be forgotten in a hurry!

Prices at this time were quite stable at £1188 including purchase tax for a fully built car or £888 for a kit-form car. Such affordability, along with the show exposure, meant the company was clearly doing something right – whereas the Hoo Hill premises had been chock-full in September 1961 with no less than fifty-five kits and finished cars unsold and in stock, and only ten orders on the books, by February 1962 orders had been doubled and stock reduced by three-quarters. On the great roller-coaster ride that encapsulated all things TVR, the horizon was looking clearer; the TVR wheel of fortune seemed to have turned yet again.

Even so, there was now a school of thought that the Grantura was beginning to look dated, despite its styling being only four years old. Bryan Hopton had been right about the need for a new model. The other directors mostly agreed, feeling the Grantura might suffer badly when compared with its soon-to-be-introduced competitor, the pretty Lotus Elan, which enjoyed smooth, well proportioned, modern lines. The short, squat TVR certainly had an individual shape, one that people either loved or hated, but was it stylish enough for a growingly fashion-conscious market?

▲ While the Grantura Mk2A was being produced, most customers chose the 1622cc MGA engine, which produced around 90bhp. Many performance tuning parts could be specified. An HRG cylinder head, for instance, raised power to over 105bhp. (Peter Filby)

◀ Built during 1961 and much of 1962, the Mk2A was TVR's most successful early model. Early in1962 it cost £888 in kit form or £1188 fully built. (Brigit van Steijn)

THE AITCHISON - HOPTON ERA

The eighty or so members of the TVR Car Club certainly tended towards the former opinion, but the motoring public at large perhaps needed more convincing.

Cars on the road in the UK and USA now numbered several hundreds, which had been enough to encourage the formation of the TVR Car Club in 1961. Anthony Oakes-Richards of TVR distributor, Research Garage of Nuneaton, was made President and Bunty Scott-Moncrieff was actively involved. In his first newsletter, Bunty had addressed the early total of fifty-one fully enrolled members, number thirty-eight being Trevor Wilkinson. The list had grown steadily since then: Trevor would have been absolutely startled if he could have looked into a crystal ball and seen that many, many years later club membership numbers would be in their thousands.

Developments continued at a hectic pace. Bryan Hopton wasn't sitting about, not even in the relative luxury of his newly and expensively appointed office, its deep-pile carpets and wood-panelled walls shaming any previous 'executive' accommodation at Hoo Hill. Exports were going well, now plans needed making for an international works competition programme to start creating a racing pedigree – and also to support the forthcoming Mk3 version of the Grantura.

To have any hope of success, an experienced competition manager would be needed, and in January 1962 Ken Richardson, famed for his work with Standard-Triumph and BRM, got the job – he'd led Triumph's competition department to many successes over seven years, including forays to Le Mans. He'd also previously been involved in the development of the notoriously unreliable V16-engined BRM racer of the early 1950s. Its massive power unit too powerful for the gearboxes and clutches of the day to cope with, that car broke down during most of its races and became something of a white elephant. Whatever, some ten years later Bryan Hopton

▼ Like wire wheels, a smart wood rim steering wheel was a necessary optional extra for any Grantura Mk2 or 2A. (Hugh James)

Regardless of its faults, there was something quite special about the Mk2A. It was the mainstay of TVR production in the early sixties. More than 200 were built, which made it the best selling of all the Granturas.

was fully confident that the existing Mk2A chassis would be up to the challenge, and so three factory cars were entered for the famous Sebring 12-hour race in Florida in March 1962. The world's greatest motor race, the Le Mans 24-hours, would come later.

Highly experienced in international racing and rallying with sports cars, Ken Richardson immediately used his contacts and gained an impressive £5000 sponsorship from Shell, more than paying for himself. But would the balance be adequate for TVR to offset the prohibitive cost of big-time racing? Also expected to be expensive was the decision which saw Tony Clarke now departing for New York. Taking up residence there, he would assist Dick Monnich with the still small American import business and encourage sales both in the USA and Canada, all at TVR's growing expense. Bryan Hopton was spending lavishly. The other directors wondered where all this money was coming from – international racing was an expensive business and the company was not ready to shoulder such a substantial programme of events with so little sponsorship.

Yet, having expressed their concern, none of them felt like sticking their necks out and being flattened under Hopton's headlong charge towards glory or doom. Company policy had already dictated that sales on the UK market might be better off taking a back seat, partly owing to the certain amount of notoriety achieved by the TVR to date. It was felt that precedence should be handed to the US market despite the fact that the few early Jomars and rather more Granturas already exported had created much the same reputation amongst customers there, though spread over a much wider area.

More recently, the new management at Blackpool had not yet learned enough lessons, despite warnings, and had neglected to tighten-up strongly enough on quality control. Grantura Mk2As were still going out with repeated snags – bad detail finish, poor steering, carburettors fouling the chassis tubes, noisy gearboxes and whining differentials, badly fitting doors, handbrakes fouling gearbox mountings, etc. Such faults were a matter for serious concern, but they were largely ignored: everyone was confident that these were inherent design deficiencies that would be eliminated

THE AITCHISON - HOPTON ERA

▲ At Liverpool docks *en route* to America for the Sebring 12-hour race in March 1962 are the three factory Mk2A racers, all with the new Mk3 bonnets.

▼ Only one of the above trio managed to finish the Sebring race – in 25th place. The driver was a then little known Mark Donohue, who would go on to become very famous.

with the much needed introduction of the planned new Mk3 model using John Thurner's all-new chassis. And there were other new TVRs on the cards...

The proposal for an exotic Italian-styled TVR had not been forgotten though was already badly delayed. Trevor Wilkinson's earlier design for a convertible TVR roadster was still thought to be viable, and around this time there was also talk of a strange new blob-like machine of advanced concept and aerodynamic design, to be known as the P5 (*covered fully in the next chapter*). Resigned to possible extinction amidst all the schemes and rumours flying about, the long-suffering, stumpy little Grantura would for the moment be lucky to stay alive, even when underpinned by the Thurner-designed chassis and graced with a modified Mk2A body.

As for the Sebring 12-hour race, competition mechanic Bob Hallett (now Ken Richardson's number two) and David Hives, now chief mechanic, played a major part in the construction and preparation of the three lightweight Grantura Mk2A works racers to contest the event in March 1962. They were all fitted with heavily tuned 1588cc MGA engines, complete with HRG light-alloy crossflow heads, twin 40DCOE Weber carbs, special camshafts and close-ratio MG gearboxes. Oddly, they weren't equipped with the front disc brakes specified for the Mk2A but, for optimum stopping, had a big Alfin finned aluminium drum on each wheel. Each car also sported an early example of the new Mk3 bonnet with its raised air intake.

In February the smartly turned-out racers, finished in TVR's new race colours of white with twin green stripes, went by boat to New York and were then driven on the road down to Florida for the race. The plan was to gently run them in during the trip and then service them at Sebring before the race. But it was a fairly madcap idea, especially in view of the huge distance involved and the strong chance of some speeding. Sure enough, Tony Clarke, who was driving one of the cars, soon got stopped by the police and was roughly spreadeagled over the TVR's bonnet by a mountain of a cop wearing dark glasses and sporting cowboy-style guns. In a brief but terrifying incident, the traffic lawman apparently frightened the pants off TVR's Sales Director!

American importer Dick Monnich hoped for decent results at Sebring, knowing how much good they could do for TVR's reputation. Unfortunately they weren't of the calibre expected. After two hours the first car, driven by Peter Bolton and Mike Rothschild, succumbed to axle failure. The second car, with Ray Cuomo at the wheel (his co-driver was Tom Payne), suffered engine failure after four hours. Happily, the Grantura of a then unknown but fast emerging Mark Donohue (Jay Signore was his partner) did manage to finish. In fact, with only just over an hour to go it was well placed, quite close behind and keenly attacking the leading Porsches. Then an unfortunate shunt resulted in the car limping back to the pits, its steering operative on one wheel only. After much time spent in the pits having a new steering arm fitted, and losing many laps, it regained the track to complete the race in 25th place, but all to no avail. The verdict was that it was an expensive and inauspicious start to TVR's big-time international racing career.

Bryan Hopton witnessed the unfortunate debut. According to a newspaper report, 'he had worked himself cruelly into a thoroughly bad state of health in putting the business back on its feet'. In fact, *en route* to the Sebring race he had travelled to the United States in elegant luxury on Cunard's fabulous ocean liner Queen Elizabeth, saying that he needed a rest cure. Not all his colleagues found the affair wholly credible. More raised eyebrows were to follow…

In various ways, not the least being Hopton's often seemingly lavish expenditure, the seeds of doubt regarding TVR's current management had been sown. The factory no longer enjoyed its previously happy atmosphere. Had the takeover by Aitchison-Hopton

◀ Despite its canal-side premises being rather grotty, the Aitchison-Hopton dealership was very enthusiastic and positive about TVR and consequently sold a lot of cars.

◀ With no opening rear window, luggage had to heaved through the tiny door, over the seat and onto the rear deck. The spare wheel was right at the back. (Hugh James)

THE AITCHISON - HOPTON ERA

▲ In 1962, when this Mk2A first hit the road in Britain, there was much talk at the factory about a new model. Lack of money was the reason it never happened. (Brigit van Steijn)

(Engineers) Ltd all been one huge mistake? A lot of money had been spent and wasted on the Sebring effort. Likewise, development of the new but premature Grantura Mk3 was proving expensive. Though he found Hopton an interesting fellow, Bernard Williams was concerned that he imagined he was Enzo Ferrari. Also that his ideas and ambitions were much too big for a company the size of TVR Cars Ltd. Arnold Burton was even more concerned: "After the January 1962 Racing Car Show we had received an exorbitant bill for rather a short stay in a London hotel. It seemed that some excessive entertainment had taken place."

Certainly, there were now worrying indications that the new Managing Director's business acumen, and possibly his intentions, were not all that the longer standing directors had been led to expect. As ever at TVR, there were certainly some unorthodox financial moves afoot. Whereas the original idea had been to utilise common finances between TVR and Aitchison-Hopton (Engineers) Ltd, the cash flow seemed to be moving mainly in the wrong direction from TVR's point of view. The situation did not warrant the risky over-expansion that was taking place.

The imminent appearance of the important new Grantura Mk3 very sadly coincided with the departure of the company's oldest and closest link with its origins.

▶ Quite possibly the only early '60s TVR to be used as a wedding car! Newlyweds Sidney and Janet Adams pose on a snowy day with their Grantura Mk2A early in 1963. (David Adams)

109

▲ While working for TVR and designing the new Grantura Mk3 chassis, engineer John Thurner often raced his own Mk2. He's seen here at Silverstone in August 1961. (National Motor Museum)

The split had been on the cards for months, even years. A quiet, unassuming character, Trevor Wilkinson had always got on extremely well with Jack Pickard, John Ward and most of his other early colleagues. But, proving to be the most dominant character in the team, the persuasive Bernard Williams had pushed company developments along since mid-1955 and sown the first seeds of Trevor's loss of control. The sudden appearance of a host of new directors late in 1958 had begun the rot. As life had become more complicated amidst the constant turmoil, his TVR dream drifting further and further out of reach, the modest Trevor had taken the easy option and slipped gradually into the background – he'd never relished the limelight anyway. He had continually spoken out against the alarmingly rapid growth that was being forced on to the company, but it had been a voice in the wilderness.

The most awful mistakes had been made and people had been enticed into the project purely because they were prepared to hand over some cash – rarely because they were experts in the engineering and production of specialist motor cars. Trevor had often been over-ruled by these people and had become increasingly unhappy. Most recently, with the company fast outgrowing him, he hadn't even had much of a say in developments. The arrival of Ken Richardson had been the last straw. It was 'with great regret' that the board accepted Trevor's resignation as a working director on 5th April 1962.

Shop foreman and old friend Jack Pickard and some of the longer standing directors were very upset that it should end this way. So was Trevor: "TVR was well known in the motoring world by then and I felt really miserable about it. I had nothing left, having lost all my machinery and tools, which now belonged to the company. I remained a 'sleeping' partner for some months and attended some board meetings

THE AITCHISON - HOPTON ERA

in that capacity but, of course, things were soon looking ominous again. It was like being shipwrecked on a desert island – in a way you're happy to be off the wreck but you're still in trouble stranded on the island."

Now married to girlfriend Jean and aware of his responsibilities, Trevor wasn't going to allow himself to be totally beaten but now had to face up to starting a new business all over again. "Before I left TVR I bought two cars from the company, a Mk1 lightweight with Electron wheels, rack and pinion steering and Alfin drums but with no motor, and a Mk2 that had been driven under the back of a truck. I rented some small premises off Central Drive, Blackpool, to start work as a custom moulder. I now had two cars, an empty workshop, four weeks rent and a set of drawing instruments presented to me by TVR's directors. Luckily I was able to sell the Mk1 and the proceeds kept me going until contracts could be found. The Mk2 was eventually repaired and I used it as personal transport for a number of years. My firm was called Trevini Auto Marine Plastics and about six months later, when TVR was again in liquidation, Jack Pickard came to work for me."

For the meantime Jack battled on at Hoo Hill always sad at the way the original dream had broken apart. Possibly Trevor's careful, more down-to-earth approach to business might have seen his original company still stable and operating happily in 1962 under his full control. It might not have built so many cars – by April 1962 a total of over 500 TVRs had been supplied since the early days – but it almost certainly would have been operating on a more solid footing than the latest company, TVR Cars Ltd, as so frantically propelled along by Bryan Hopton.

▼ The works Grantura Mk2A pictured in 1961 during the RAC Tourist Trophy at Goodwood with Colin Escott leading a GSM Delta. Co-driver Keith Aitchison also raced this TVR on several occasions. (Ferret Fotographics)

TVR's founder, the man who started it all, had departed. If Trevor had been unassuming, methodical, conservative, unprogressive and at times difficult for some of the workforce to get on with, current boss Hopton was projecting himself as truly dynamic. His ideas certainly looked good on paper and some of them were well judged. For instance, the concentration on export sales was proving wise enough for the moment. His ambitious plans for tearing apart the world of international motor sport sounded exciting too...

After the Sebring debacle, the ambitious 1962 international works competition programme was to continue with three cars competing in the International Tulip Rally in May, three cars attending the hugely demanding Le Mans 24-hours race in June (only one was to race in the event proper) and three cars in the international RAC Tourist Trophy race at Goodwood in August. At the factory there was the question of organising regular production for the Mk3 and planning for the TVR stand at the British motor show in October. All these events were to prove a huge drain on the company's cash. With sufficient funds failing to appear in the bank account, nothing made any commercial sense. And so the TVR dreadnought lurched on.

Competition in 1961

RACING EXPLOITS FOR TVR had until now concerned mainly private entries in club events, although a few semi-works entries had appeared too. Sensibly, the company had not given serious thought to entering big-time international events because of the prohibitive cost involved. In club racing the 1961 season's efforts showed good promise and justified the winter's construction at Hoo Hill of three lightweight Mk2A body/chassis units. They were completed with MG engines and John Thurner enjoyed several works outings in one of the cars, as did Keith Aitchison and, on a couple of occasions, Colin Escott. Indeed, Aitchison again did an excellent job of upholding TVR honour on race tracks during the year. Escott, on the other hand, was winding down his racing activities due to a medical condition.

There weren't many memorable competition successes for the marque during 1961 but there was plenty of activity and the cars were becoming more and more competitive. Ex-World War Two fighter pilot Tommy Entwistle campaigned his 1500cc Climax powered Grantura Mk2 over many weekends through the season, but although he quickly became well known, his engine wasn't reliable enough for Tommy to score any notable wins this year. His time would come.

Also notable for his WW2 efforts flying in the RAF, TVR man James Boothby was more likely to be seen this year at the wheel of his Jaguar D-type, often at his favourite venue, Firle hillclimb. After only one season racing a TVR, his good friend Mary Wheeler was already a popular driver, blasting her green 1216cc Climax powered Grantura Mk1 up the

▼ The TVR team managed 12th position in the 1961 Birkett Six-hour Relay race at Silverstone in August 1961. This is John Wadsworth in the ex-Keith Aitchison Grantura Mk1.

Competition in 1961 cont'd.

hills and around tracks such as Goodwood and Brands Hatch at every opportunity. At Goodwood for the Whit Monday meeting in May, she did particularly well in the Grand Touring Car race, taking second place in the 1300cc class behind Gordon Jones' similarly powered Marcos.

John Wadsworth (in the ex-Keith Aitchison Mk1), Peter Bolton, John Woolfe (who married Arnold Burton's niece) and Dave Baldock were other well-known TVR pilots during 1961. Finished in blue, Woolfe's MG powered Mk2A lightweight (one of the factory built cars) was regularly on the grids, and in August he was part of the TVR team that competed in the 750MC's Birkett Six-hour Relay event at Silverstone, the other drivers being Tommy Entwistle, John Thurner, John Brown, Anthony Oakes-Richards and John Wadsworth. Despite inevitable problems with the cars – overheating, fuel starvation, oil pipe fracture, low oil pressure and a cracked exhaust manifold amongst them – the team finished in twelfth position after completing 287 laps.

On the international rallying scene, wealthy motor trader Peter Bolton waved the TVR flag in 1961's RAC Rally, while the intrepid Arnold Burton, an accomplished driver who also enjoyed hillclimbing, was another rally competitor. Indeed, he clocked-up something of an achievement in his 1588cc MG powered Grantura Mk2 by just about reaching the finishing line in May's Tulip Rally (his co-driver was Paul Rutland-Barsby), albeit in last place. Wending his way through Europe from the start in Holland, he didn't enjoy the experience: "The car was a nightmare! It had so many faults that in all the two years I drove it we never got the thing right. During the rally we had suspension problems and were constantly stopping all the way round to have bits welded up. Oh, it was a real struggle!"

◀ Suffering many problems with his 1588cc MGA powered Grantura Mk2, Arnold Burton had a terrible struggle just to finish May 1961's Tulip Rally. He came last!

CHAPTER SIX

Collapse in 1962

Propelled dynamically forwards during 1962 by MD Bryan Hopton, TVR Cars Ltd's new model agenda included an advanced aerodynamic coupé of bizarre appearance, a sharp looking Grantura fastback coupé and a proposed exotic GT car with superb styling – not forgetting the hugely improved Grantura Mk3 with its all-new, all-independent chassis. Also scheduled were further ambitious entries in international races at Le Mans and Goodwood. But the result of much extravagant expenditure was disaster: the company's collapse in October.

Since the Aitchison-Hopton takeover in autumn 1961, the TVR marque's existence in the hands of the enigmatic Bryan Hopton had at least displayed sporadic signs of inspiration and progress. But a lot of money had been spent and there were many serious doubts about his style of management. Unimpressive results in March 1962's Sebring 12-hour race hadn't exactly enhanced

▼ With its rear bodywork identical to the Grantura Mk2A, this model was actually called a Mk2B. The third page of this chapter will reveal why. (Michael Osborne)

THE EARLY YEARS

the company's already fluctuating fortunes. But still Hopton's energy was unstoppable, particularly on the new model front.

Despite the forthcoming launch of the important Grantura Mk3, proposals for further new TVRs were legion. Trevor Wilkinson had departed at a point where there'd been discussions about a possible four-seater TVR. That hadn't been feasible, but Trevor's earlier design for a convertible TVR had since been revived and given deeper consideration. Indeed, further development had been done on what would have become a Grantura Mk3 roadster. Despite the ever-tightening grip of inadequate finance, Hopton had already told Dick Monnich that such a car was in the course of development and Monnich had given him three orders! A TVR shaped roadster would undoubtedly have been welcomed with open arms in the United States but, like the four-seater, it was another project that never got off the ground. Indeed, there were several other projects complicating the issue, the most startling of which was known as the P5...

P5 stood for Project 5 – Costin Auto Project 5 in full. Brilliant aerodynamicist Frank Costin had earlier approached the Aitchison-Hopton car sales business in Chester with what he called a 'truly exciting project'. He lived and worked near Llanberis, North Wales, only about an hour's drive from Chester, and duly turned up early in 1961 for a meeting armed with a scale model of his proposed car of the future. Recalled Keith Aitchison: "Costin was a respected and highly experienced individual in both the aircraft world and the fields of stress engineering and aerodynamics for competition cars – with companies like Vanwall, Lister and Lotus. We immediately formed a friendship. Looking at his scale model, the concept was obviously light years ahead of its time and had great potential, so funds for the prototype's construction were provided by Aitchison-Hopton (Engineers) Ltd, myself personally and Arnold Burton. The TVR people in Blackpool had no knowledge of it to start with."

Frank Costin built the P5 prototype in his remote Welsh workshop over the second half of 1961 and early 1962. It was an advanced aerodynamic, lightweight coupé with its engine mounted at the back and three-abreast seating in its cabin. Slightly bewildered by the whole concept and not greatly enthusiastic about it, Bryan Hopton merely called it 'an entirely new type of motor car' and he wasn't far off the truth! Power was supplied by a 1000cc three-cylinder, two-stroke DKW engine built by Keith Shorrock using one of his own superchargers. Of monocoque construction, the car was built using a combination of glassfibre and plywood sections and glassfibre body panels. One reason for its ground-breaking existence was the hope of participating in the Thermal Efficiency Challenge at Le Mans – that at least went some way towards explaining its bizarre appearance and reflected its remarkable power-to-weight ratio.

Following on from his involvement with the

▼ Frank Costin's remarkable styling for the 1000cc three-cylinder DKW powered P5 prototype was dictated purely by aerodynamics. It never made production. Perhaps thankfully!

▲ As confirmed by the amazingly knowledgeable TVR parts expert, Stan Kilcoyne, it was the special bonnet with an additional air intake for radiator cooling that identified the rare Grantura Mk2B. With 1622cc MGA power, this car was registered in April 1962. (Michael Osborne)

ungainly looking Marcos 'Ugly Duckling' Gullwing GTs of 1960 and '61, Costin's lack of interest in attractive styling was patently obvious. Naturally, his shape was dictated by aerodynamic efficiency, but the car looked extraordinary to say the least. One wonders what effect it must have had on other road users as Costin eventually drove the finished prototype from North Wales to Blackpool to show it to the management there. TVR's directors had long been agreed about the severe limitations of the Grantura's unusual styling, but they certainly hadn't been prepared for Costin's remarkably free-thinking approach to sculpting the P5. Quite frankly, the amazing gullwing-doored machine would probably have stopped the traffic anywhere and everywhere, although Arnold Burton was one of the few who appreciated its futuristic appearance and potential for TVR: "I thought it was quite splendid if rather impractical."

"The P5 was an incredibly advanced package," reckoned Keith Aitchison. "Frank's choice of engine wasn't right but it had been selected for its light weight, fuel economy and compactness, not primarily for its performance characteristics. It was really the only suitable unit that was readily available at the time and did its job perfectly. The car performed magnificently in terms of power-to-weight and economy. We kept it secret for some time but once it had been revealed at Hoo Hill, the plan was for TVR to put it into production."

Before going to the 1962 New York motor show to launch the Grantura Mk3, Bryan Hopton took the precaution of slipping pictures and specifications of the P5 into his briefcase to conduct an early survey of the potential US market. Having indicated that the car should be production-ready in time for the British International Motor Show in October that year, upon his return from America Hopton outrageously claimed that thanks to the immediate reaction of American dealers, he'd taken provisional orders for no less than 1000 P5s for 1963 delivery – subject to satisfactory testing and demonstration. His public relations mentality was obviously

THE EARLY YEARS

moving into overdrive – he even suggested that the American dealers planned to charter a special aircraft in order to visit Earls Court and place firm orders. "We should have no difficulty in accepting orders for some 2000 units," he said. "We have in the P5 a car which, properly handled and sufficiently financed, could have an impact as great as that of the Jaguar E-type."

Despite Hopton's vivid imagination and obvious intention to take the P5 into production, the extraordinary vehicle never had much chance of even limited commercial success, let alone such vast sales. In fact its existence was shrouded in secrecy so far as the British motoring press and public were concerned. David Hives was responsible for the testing that did get carried out and found it highly entertaining. "It wasn't really feasible as a practical road car because, thanks to its low windscreen and thick A-posts, you couldn't properly see out of the bloody thing! I took it out on the road several times over the weeks, and with the supercharger on the DKW engine it proved very quick. I got well over 100mph from it and it was very stable at that speed.

"At Hoo Hill," continued David, "we often had various cars of other types coming in for work (generally they belonged to friends of Bernard), one of them being a fabulous Zagato bodied Aston Martin. Well, the little lightweight P5 would leave that Aston standing! But there were lots of snags that we never sorted out ready for manufacture. After a while it was left under a dust sheet for a long time while we discussed what to do with it. We never did decide!"

Arnold Burton conceived the name Trident for the Costin 'blob', and eventually ended up with what was left of it. "Yes, I was eventually left with the remains of the P5. We did talk seriously about putting it into production but we would have needed a lot of capital to do so and it transpired that we couldn't get supplies of DKW engines, so we ordered an Imp engine, which never arrived! Having created this highly sophisticated automobile for about £7000 in nine months, Costin had run out of money by the time the snags appeared, and there was then a dispute. He refused to go on developing it without any more money and we refused to give it. He hadn't proved so clever. The whole thing proved ultimately impossible!"

The world was spared of having to confront the clever but rather barmy P5, and the prototype languished for at least a year in dusty retirement in the first-floor glassfibre workshop of what was then Grantura Plastics. A third new prototype project under way in 1962 was being given rather less time in the Hoo Hill development shop – which was located in a partitioned-off area of the first floor body moulding shop above the brick kilns. Bernard Williams had prompted the project and Frank Nelson, a brilliant designer who worked on development alongside David Hives, John Ward and John Thurner, had created it along with input from Thurner.

Although the proposed design's front end was little changed from the Grantura,

▼ At a time when new designs were abundant, 1962's attractive restyled rear end proposal for the Grantura was the work of Frank Nelson and John Thurner. The front end bodywork and tiny doors would have remained unchanged. Lack of funds caused the project's demise. (John Bailie)

118

▲ With its new bonnet and redesigned chassis, the Grantura Mk3 made its debut at the New York motor show in April 1962. An exaggerated 1.5 million dollars' worth of orders were claimed to have been placed on the stand! (LAT)

▼ Side profile of the rare Mk2B was identical to that of the Mk2, Mk2A and Mk3. (Michael Osborne)

the fastback rear end was dramatic and modern: a stylish new TVR body to fit the new Mk3 chassis perhaps? Like the others, however, it never reached production. Intended as a sort of poor man's Ferrari, the project was dispensed with later, having reached the stage where the near-completed shape was in full window-less 'plug' form ready for making body moulds. As ever, the lack of sufficient funds and available time could well have had something to do with it.

Last but not least in this creative period of 1962 came Bryan Hopton's ambitious plan for a truly beautiful, Italian-designed drophead bodyshell, also to fit the MG powered Mk3 chassis. The hopelessly over-optimistic Chairman had suggested spring 1963 as the release date for this proposal, hopefully in time for the Geneva Motor Show. American importer Dick Monnich was firmly behind the scheme. In the USA, Italian styling was now definitely in vogue. The saga had begun earlier in 1962. Two motoring enthusiast friends of Bernard Williams were going to Italy on business, so Bernard asked them to have a look at the various coachwork specialists out there and get some idea of what a styling commission would cost. "A company called Carrozzeria Fissore could be your answer," came the reply. "It's not too big or too expensive and is looking for this type of work."

The advice was noted, but for the time being even the dynamic Hopton failed to find time (and money) for the project. Such was the continuing pressure of work – and the continued struggle to keep his company afloat. So much had been going on that he must have been having trouble determining exactly what his real policy was. Ideas for new models, the search for capital and the plans for a new factory were all buzzing through his mind. Above all, there was the big headache of how to get Grantura Mk3 production rolling.

Announced to the press somewhat prematurely in April 1962 and publicly revealed later that month at the New York International Motor Show to try and take advantage of the growingly healthy US export market, the new Grantura Mk3 was clearly TVR's best effort to date. But its debut at the New York show almost didn't happen. At the time of the show car's despatch from the Blackpool

THE EARLY YEARS

factory, the parts department was short of hub adaptors. Instead of having two left-hand and two right-hand adaptors, the car was hurriedly put together with the only available stocks – four left-handed items. There was no petrol tank, either, but the new prototype did look essentially complete for display and so was OK'd for delivery to Liverpool docks.

Despite factory warnings not to drive the car, when he collected it from New York docks Dick Monnich's US Sales Director Tony Clarke apparently fixed a temporary petrol tank in the boot and decided to go straight to the New York Coliseum – his first try in a Mk3. Unfortunately, the drive wasn't that impressive. Cruising through, of all places, a very busy Times Square in central New York, Tony Clarke and the immaculate new show car were suddenly hugely embarrassed when a wheel fell off and rolled into the gutter – not an easy situation to deal with in the midst of heavy traffic. And it didn't help when Clarke asked a passer-by, a rather strong looking black gentleman, for a push and was promptly told to fuck off! Other onlookers had broad grins on their faces but eventually Clarke received help, got a jack under the stricken Mk3 and fitted the spare wheel before continuing his journey to the Coliseum.

For the honour of TVR, that little incident was kept very quiet. Once on the show stand, the Mk3 was extremely well received and, indeed, many sales were booked. But the stand's out-of-the-way position and, due to the ongoing acute money shortage, the general lack of an adequate press and publicity campaign to back-up the announcement, did somehow discredit Bryan Hopton's claims on returning from New York (later reported in an English newspaper) that he had received a massive 1.5 million dollars' worth or orders. This represented almost four hundred TVRs – enough to keep the Hoo Hill staff, which now numbered over eighty, working flat out for well over a year! Indeed, to cope with the apparent explosion of orders Hopton stated that new, much more spacious factory premises were imperative to provide the company with the professional facilities it needed for such increased production numbers. Not surprisingly, he also decreed that TVR's working capital would have to be substantially increased to pay for all this proposed expansion.

Describing how Hopton lived in a Blackpool hotel for some time and relaxed out of office hours by sitting in his darkened room thinking through the next day's business problems, the same English newspaper report continued in an equally humorous vein. Hopton was reported as saying: "I am dedicated to making a million pounds and no power on earth will stop me," and claiming, "My good name and the confidence and trust of my shareholders are the only things in life that I hold sacred."

Henry Moulds already had the measure of the Chairman's rather arrogant and almost bitter personality. "Hopton himself wrote that newspaper article! He did an awful lot of devious manoeuvring while he was in charge. The problem was that he wanted to run the whole thing himself, but of course it was really a team job that needed running by team work."

Conceptually, the Mk3 chassis was a big step

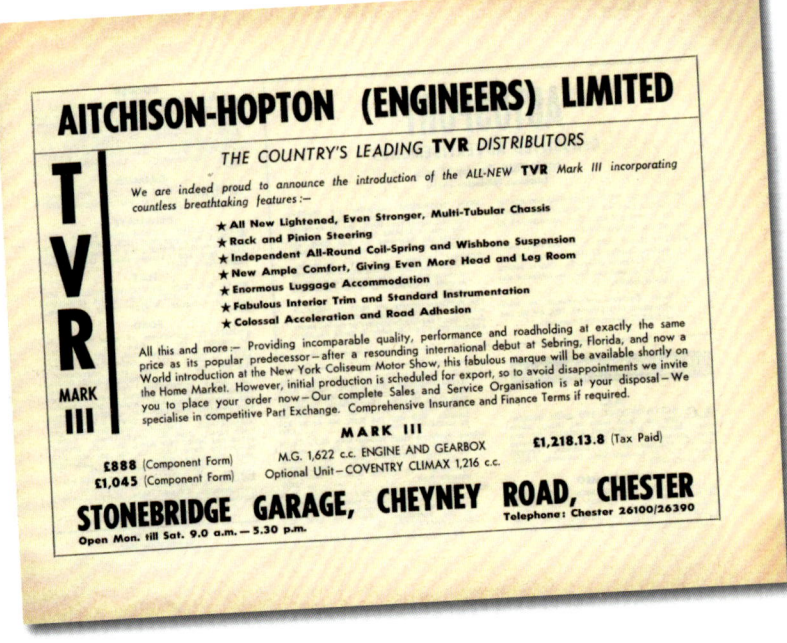

▼ Dated April 27th 1962, this *Autosport* advert for the new Mk3 was in reality rather premature in terms of the British market. Production at the time was running at snail's pace and didn't really get into gear until the coming of the Griffith V8 early in 1964.

COLLAPSE IN 1962

▲ Designed by John Thurner, the all-new Mk3 chassis of 1962 featured double-wishbones and coilspring dampers at each corner along with rack and pinion steering.

▼ This superb cutaway drawing of the radically changed Grantura Mk3 was originally published in *The Motor* in August 1962. (LAT)

forward for TVR. Intended to eliminate all the basic faults of the existing chassis designed by Trevor Wilkinson, the all-new assembly brought about the TVR's biggest design change so far. As it transpired, the Thurner chassis was to remain in production for almost ten years and would prove suitable for a wide range of power units from the mild 1300cc Triumph Spitfire up to the big grunt of the 271bhp 4.7-litre Ford V8s.

John Thurner had been working on his new chassis design since early 1961, generally being assisted by David Hives and John Ward during the construction of the prototype assembly. A brilliant engineer, Thurner had concluded that he'd stick to a similar basic layout to the 'old' chassis – a multi-tubular design with integral backbone – but needed to add greater rigidity and strength via better triangulation. The new assembly was also a more efficient design, which meant it would be easier and more economical to manufacture – at least, by the standards of the day! Its wheelbase was 1.5in longer and particularly important was that it should receive a more supple ride. If there was a problem with the earlier cars' suspension, it was principally the general lack of such a thing!

The harsh and generally uncomfortable ride given by Trevor Wilkinson's torsion bar and trailing arm suspension of VW origin had been further complicated by its tendency to allow a modicum of rear wheel steering – due to the rubber bushed mounting of the kingposts to the trailing arms both front and rear. Drastic damping to harden the ride still further might have cured this disconcerting tendency but would not have been customer-friendly. And so TVR now became one of the first

manufacturers to use all-independent wishbone suspension in a production car, and the results proved to be very good indeed.

Trevor's chassis had not been particularly rigid in torsion across the cockpit, leaving the bonded-on fibreglass bodywork with a tendency to crack. Although Thurner's new multi-tubular semi-spaceframe was some 20lb heavier, the increased weight was devoted mainly to the additional bracing tubes, which increased torsional rigidity. Unlike Trevor, Thurner was a fully qualified engineer and his design, built in 1.5in diameter 16-gauge steel tubing, showed it. Four main longerons formed the backbone and were spaced wider horizontally and closer vertically than Trevor's effort, producing a somewhat wider and taller transmission tunnel, which intruded further on the TVR's already confined interior. Outriggers extended to the sides while the tube network extended at the rear to carry the spring mountings and larger petrol tank (up to ten gallons capacity). The engine could now project higher above the top main chassis tubes, improving its already excellent accessibility.

Moving on to suspension, the new chassis replaced the earlier design's VW Beetle transverse torsion bar and trailing arm system with more advanced twin wishbone and coilspring assemblies front and rear. In other words, it now had suspension that worked properly! At the front end the lower wishbones and uprights were of Triumph Herald origin, while the upper wishbones were fabricated by TVR. The company also made its own wide-based upper and lower wishbones for the rear suspension along with the special light-alloy hub carriers. Special coilspring damper units were used all round and Triumph rack-and-pinion steering replaced the old Ford worm-and-peg system. A front anti-roll bar completed the specification, while braking was capably handled by 10.75in Girling discs at the front and 9in drums at the rear.

MG engines had long been the most popular in TVRs and the introduction of the enlarged 1622cc MGA unit had only served to back this up. The time of offering a large choice of engines had now passed, and the 90bhp MGA four-banger was now specified as the standard engine. In case anyone insisted, the 1216cc Climax FWE and 1340cc Ford Classic 109E units were still available, though only while stocks lasted. Styling-wise, the stumpy Grantura bodyshell remained little changed to the casual onlooker and was still bonded to the chassis. While the rear bodywork continued as per the Mk2 and 2A, at its front end the Mk3's bonnet received a restyled nose with its air intake raised and made more upright to get more air into a larger radiator (in fact, this revised bonnet was already being used for the last run

▲ This immaculate Grantura Mk3 is believed to be only the twelfth example made. It started life with a 1622cc MGA engine and was first registered in July 1962. (Peter Filby)

COLLAPSE IN 1962

▲ There were no changes to the Mk2-style dashboard for early Mk3s. (Peter Filby)

▼ The only external distinguishing feature for the early Mk3 was its raised and enlarged nose aperture. (Peter Filby)

of Mk2As). The indicators were now placed either side of the intake area.

Overheating problems had always been a threat with Granturas and, apart from the new radiator, the opportunity was now taken to improve the general coolant flow arrangement. Most customers to date had specified the optional electric cooling fan which now became standard equipment. Another small but important improvement was the addition of integral inner wheel arches (they were moulded-in as part of the front wings) to stop under-bonnet damage from stones thrown up by the front tyres.

Although the new chassis's wheelbase was 1.5in longer than before (the front wheels were now that much further forward and had slightly more bodywork behind them), the Mk3's overall length remained unchanged at 11ft 6in. Unfortunately, the narrow doors were unchanged too, but the TVR had always been difficult to get into and always would be! At least general revisions to the interior layout now gave 1in more headroom and 3in more legroom (thanks to the seats being mounted further back), and the car was now much quieter in the cabin thanks to extra sound-deadening felt applied over the complete lower half of the interior – and a cloth roof lining over the upper half. There were small improvements for the dashboard, its simple layout remaining unchanged from that of the Mk2 and 2A, but there was no increase in the minimal luggage space behind the seats and the spare wheel still sat

THE EARLY YEARS

awkwardly in a well at the very back of the cabin. The transmission tunnel running through the cockpit was now more bulky than before – this had been a feature of TVR cockpits since the Mk1 and was going to remain so for the next ten years.

On the road the 14cwt Mk3 was more refined, had a much more comfortable ride and enjoyed improved handling. The 0-60mph dash took just over nine seconds, while maximum speed with standard 90bhp MG power driving through the four-speed MG gearbox remained at around the 100mph mark. Bryan Hopton was proved right – the Grantura Mk3 was refreshingly better than the Mk2A, or so the prototype indicated. If the car's many improvements over its predecessor were to be reflected in proportionately improved sales, the company might at last look like a viable proposition.

It was a pity, therefore, that having announced the Mk3 rather loudly in April 1962, the factory couldn't gear itself up to start manufacturing the car until around June that year, especially as the New York show display had supposedly generated orders for 1.5 million dollars' worth of cars. In those early days of the Mk3's existence, the last 2As were still in production while the new model was being made at only a snail's pace. Confusion over the US orders situation and a shortage of readily available cash at the factory were the predictable answers to the problem. Getting the Mk3 into full production was a major financial commitment and the biggest departure technically that TVR had yet become involved with.

After some test experience, Keith Aitchison was delighted with the development team's efforts. "The Mk3 was 1000% better," he enthused. "It now had proper suspension travel and was correctly sprung and damped. Technically speaking, it was now an up-to-date product, and in action the roadholding and refinement were considerably better than the market competitors. After the first batch of Mk3s had left the factory clothed with Mk2/2A main bodies and the new bonnets, we soon realised the production moulds were in need of replacement and so commissioned new ones to give the Mk3 a much better overall finish. The styling might not have looked as good as it should have done but we really didn't have the money to do a restyled body. That was also the reason why the new moulds were delayed."

◀ The Grantura Mk3 was a hugely improved car but sales in 1962 were slow, mainly because production was even slower! Also, the huge effort required to get to Le Mans that year was a major distraction.
(Peter Filby)

COLLAPSE IN 1962

▲ Anne Hall and Val Domleo's works Mk2A (with Mk3 bonnet) in action on the Tulip Rally in May 1962.

▼ A break in France during the Tulip Rally. Support team members were Stan Pateman (left) and David Hives (behind the white Mk2A). Car number 38 was Stan Pateman's Mk2A.

In view of the struggle taking place while an out-of-date design was being phased-out and an entirely new one taking its place, any further international competition effort for the already ailing company would clearly involve considerable risk. Yet despite the Sebring 12-hour race failure in March, TVR's ambitious sorties into international racing were to continue unabated through 1962. What little success there was occurred largely in the USA. The Sebring racers were sold, one to TVR's Canadian distributor, Sports Car Accessories of Toronto, and the other two in the 'States, one of them staying with Dick Monnich. Amongst American club racers there was an impressive spell of racing results during 1962: over a four-month period various TVRs gained twelve first places and one second in thirteen outings. Amazingly, one of the cars was entered in five races during a one-day meeting at Lime Rock Park, Connecticut, and proceeded to take five first places!

Following Sebring, the next important works-sponsored event was the May 1962 Tulip Rally, which started and finished at Noordwijk-aan-Zee on the Dutch coast and thrashed down to Monte Carlo for an overnight halt. In a big push for publicity, the TVR team consisted of two private entries – Arnold Burton and partner in the Burton Mk2 and Stan Pateman and partner in a Mk2A – and one full works entry: Anne Hall and Val Domleo in the 1622cc MG engined, factory-prepared Mk2A sporting a Mk3 bonnet. Fitted with all available performance extras, including an HRG crossflow head and twin Weber 40DCOE carburettors, which raised power output to 108bhp at 6000rpm, the ladies' car was prepared by David Hives, now in charge of all racing preparation under

THE EARLY YEARS

Ken Richardson, and Richardson's assistant Bob Hallett.

It was a job that David didn't always find rewarding: "He was a great personality but we had a right nightmare with Ken. He made us screw everything on and off about ten times. If it wasn't absolutely 100 per cent right, it came off and had to be done again. Eventually the car was ready and then, twenty-four hours before it was due to leave, this all-synchromesh ZF gearbox arrived at the factory. So we had to take the whole thing apart again! That gearbox had the first diaphragm clutch we'd ever seen and it didn't seem to match up or work properly. In the end the girls just had to set off for Holland with it and hope for the best."

▲ Anne Hall pauses in Holland during the 1962 Tulip Rally to receive flowers from a well-wisher. Val Domleo is in the passenger seat.

Despite an eventful southbound trip to Monte Carlo, things were looking good for the TVR team on the return trip back though France, the cars at one stage holding the first three places in class. Then it was sudden disaster for the ladies' car when Anne Hall fell asleep at the wheel and her TVR ploughed off the road and was unable to continue. Much better fortune befell the Grantura Mk2 of Arnold Burton which finished a highly creditable third in class (behind a pair of Porsche 356s) and twentieth overall. It was the first international trophy ever won by a TVR.

With the Tulip Rally over, Ken Richardson, David Hives and Bob Hallett now

◀ Night time stop during the Tulip Rally. To the left of car number 38 are Bob Hallett, David Hives (in overalls) and Stan Pateman (leaning on the car). On the right are Pateman's co-driver John Brown and Arnold Burton with his Mk2, car number 30.

looked forward to TVR's first outing to the Le Mans 24-hour race in June. It was the world's most famous motor race and great commitment was required to prepare for it. The three men might later have wished they hadn't bothered. At quite some expense, the assembly of three brand new, factory-prepared, lightweight Grantura Mk3s was started – even though the model wasn't yet readily available to the public. Apart from one prototype that designer John Thurner had been running around in and evaluating for some time, they were the first three production Mk3s built and were all painted in the factory team colours of white with twin nose-to-tail stripes in British Racing Green. Two of the cars were all-out, no-frills racers while the third was a spare to be taken to Le Mans and cannibalised for parts if necessary.

The team had been accepted for one firm entry in the race along with one reserve place, so the best possible scenario was that only two of the trio had any hope of starting the race. It didn't help that the cars weren't ready for the practice sessions held some time before race week proper. This meant that they missed out on the vital testing that might, just might, have eradicated the overheating problems that were to cause such disappointment on the day of the race – and on future race occasions too.

Power for each car was courtesy of a competition tuned 1622cc MGA engine producing about 125bhp and driving through a close-ratio MG gearbox. Special parts included a light-alloy HRG crossflow cylinder head, twin Weber carburettors, special pistons and a special camshaft, and stopping power came from the standard Mk3 set-up of front discs and rear drums. In the case of the first Le Mans racer to be completed, this braking system was soon to prove a little down on muscle – in an incident that happened during testing...

David Hives recalled a devastating early blow for the TVR team: "Bob Hallett took one of the race cars out on test from the factory and we naturally assumed he'd taken our regular five-minute route. When twenty minutes had passed and Bob hadn't returned, I went out to try to find him. He wasn't anywhere on our normal route so I went further afield and soon found this awful mess. Bob had failed to brake hard enough for a tractor coming out of a field towing a trailer loaded with straw bales. He'd hit the trailer broadside-on and wiped the top clean off the car!"

Badly injured, Hallett was rushed to hospital, where he was kept for several days. With the car needing a total rebuild, the pressure was on and, in classic TVR style, the whole Le Mans project turned into a mad rush. Indeed, things became so fraught that David Hives was fired several times by Ken Richardson. "In fact, he fired me about six times

▼ The pits area at Le Mans in 1962 before practice. On the weighing scales is the TVR that never turned a wheel in the race. (Judd Wheldon)

every day," laughed David. "He was a strong and very amusing character. He also fired me most days while we were at Le Mans!"

There was, however, one personality who could get the better of Ken Richardson. For some time there'd been a large dog that was something of a fixture on the Hoo Hill estate – a rather dominant and aggressive Alsatian called Rinty, which belonged to a joiner and cabinet-maker who rented one of the old brick kilns. If you caught Rinty in the wrong mood, there could be trouble, as David Hives had witnessed: "At around tea-time one day Ken was going off to the dreadful toilet we had on the estate and, as you do, he was shouting at the lads: 'Get some bloody work done, you lot'. Unfortunately, he also shook a leg at Rinty and alarmed him. I'll never forget it because the dog jumped up, ripped into Ken's trousers and pants and nearly bit his arse off! Ken threatened to sue Rinty's owner over the incident but he eventually calmed down."

'Calm' was not a word that adequately described the whole nature of TVR's preparations for Le Mans. 'Frantic' and 'ill-judged' were much closer to the truth. As the team had been nowhere near ready for the first series of practice sessions at the French circuit, a compromise was decided upon and Aintree circuit hired for a day's testing of the racers. Even then, things started with an upset. Ex-MG driver Ted Lund was one of the testers who attended. He'd previously won his class at Le Mans with a works-prepared MGA twin-cam coupé but, initially at least, he didn't get on so well with the TVR. Within three laps he had skidded off the track, careered into a ploughed field and ended up with the car stricken on its side!

With Le Mans race day little more than a week away, TVR's financial constraints meant that the two racers and one spare car would have to be driven on the road all the way down through England and France to the track. A predictable last-minute panic to complete the final assembly of the third team car led to it setting off from Blackpool with its green racing stripes still wet – and soon collecting flies in their hundreds. But eventually the cruise southbound was in full flow, including the race team, a sizeable back-up crew and many others. Indeed, the great TVR convoy included, in the inimitable words of David Hives, "everybody and their bloody uncle!"

The two racers and one spare car were driven by David, Ken Richardson and Bob Hallett. Arnold Burton was in his Mk2 and Bunty Scott-Moncrieff and wife Averil were trusting 'The Coffee Bean' to make the journey without incident. Henry Moulds was there with his Jaguar, as were Bernard Williams, John Thurner, Frank Nelson and racing driver John Woolfe, who was hoping to participate in the big event itself. As for the back-

▲ Mk3 at speed through the Esses during practice, with John Woolfe behind the wheel. (Judd Wheldon)

▼ Discussion in the TVR pit area. From left to right are David Hives, Ted Lund, Robbie Slotemaker and, in the helmet, Ninian Sanderson. (Judd Wheldon)

COLLAPSE IN 1962

up people, their transport included the TVR Morris Minivan, two hired vans carrying tyres and spares, a hired Volkswagen caravan and various other vehicles carrying supporters and would-be race marshals. This was to be the big one, and a suitably comprehensive level of support was obviously needed.

But there were several frustrating problems during the journey south. One was due to a recurring blockage in one of the race cars' fuel systems, while another involved Ken Richardson's chariot failing to brake quickly enough at the London end of the M1 motorway. Hardly used during the journey, the brakes' racing linings were still cold and simply didn't work as Richardson tried to slow for the roundabout – with the result that driver and car ploughed straight across!

The TVR entourage's hotel in France was in a small village a short drive from Le Mans, and not surprisingly they virtually filled the place. As luck would have it, just across the square from the hotel was the local garage. "We more or less commandeered the place," recalled David Hives, "and it was just as well the proprietor was enthusiastic about helping us. The first job I did there was sort out the fuel system that had caused so many stops for that car during the trip."

There was much worse to come. Official practice for the race took place late in the afternoon and during the following evening, and though the temperature had dropped, there were alarming overheating problems for both the TVR racers. Boiling point for each car came at the end of the flat-out charge down the long Mulsanne straight when the engines were suddenly deprived of cooling air as the cars slowed

▼ On the ramp during scrutineering at Le Mans is the Mk3 that never made the race. (Judd Wheldon)

right down for the following bends. It was a major blow to the team's hopes, and the situation wasn't helped when a mechanic in the pits poured cold water into one of the engines and promptly cracked its HRG aluminium cylinder head!

And so to race day. Weary after another late session in the little French garage near their hotel, the TVR crew were well aware that they'd run out of time to fully rectify their cars' overheating problems. It didn't help that the temperature that day had risen significantly as the race start drew closer. With no place on the grid for the reserve racer (it had been due to be driven by Ted Lund and co-pilot Rob Slotemaker), it was all down to Peter Bolton and Ninian Sanderson to uphold TVR's fragile honour. They were both experienced racing drivers: Bolton had driven a works TR4S at Le Mans in 1961 for the Triumph team managed by Ken Richardson, while Sanderson had been a Le Mans winner in 1956 with a team Jaguar D-type run by Ecurie Ecosse.

▼ The start of the Le Mans 24-hours endurance race in 1962. Peter Bolton rushes to get away, little knowing that disaster wasn't far down the track. (Judd Wheldon)

COLLAPSE IN 1962

▲ Storming away from the start, Peter Bolton's Mk3 turns a wheel in anger at Le Mans. But not for long – during only its third lap the engine boiled and lost all its water. It was the end of the race for the TVR. (Judd Wheldon)

Unfortunately, all that experience counted for nothing. At 4pm, amidst all the frenzied excitement and expectation of one of the world's most famous motor races, Peter Bolton ran across to his Grantura Mk3 racer (for the road it was registered YFR 751) and blasted off down the straight desperately hoping his engine wouldn't overheat. Sadly, there was no such luck. On only its third lap, braking hard at the end of the Mulsanne straight, Bolton's engine boiled again and lost all its water. Disaster! End of TVR's race.

Ken Richardson and his team were shattered. TVR's reputation in serious competition had again been severely dented – and at huge cost, reputedly upwards of £10,000. David Hives' view of the situation was characteristically forthright: "With all those people attending the race, including the four drivers and their girlfriends, it cost TVR a small fortune. With their water cooling systems not working efficiently and their construction not remotely robust enough to last twenty-four hours, the racers were never fit to go to Le Mans in the first place. It was all a bloody fiasco!"

TVR Cars MD Bryan Hopton had to shoulder much of the blame for the Le Mans debacle. He'd been pushing relentlessly for a strong international competition image – and expecting success – of which the brand was just not capable. Not surprisingly, it was bad news again from the International Tourist Trophy race at Goodwood in

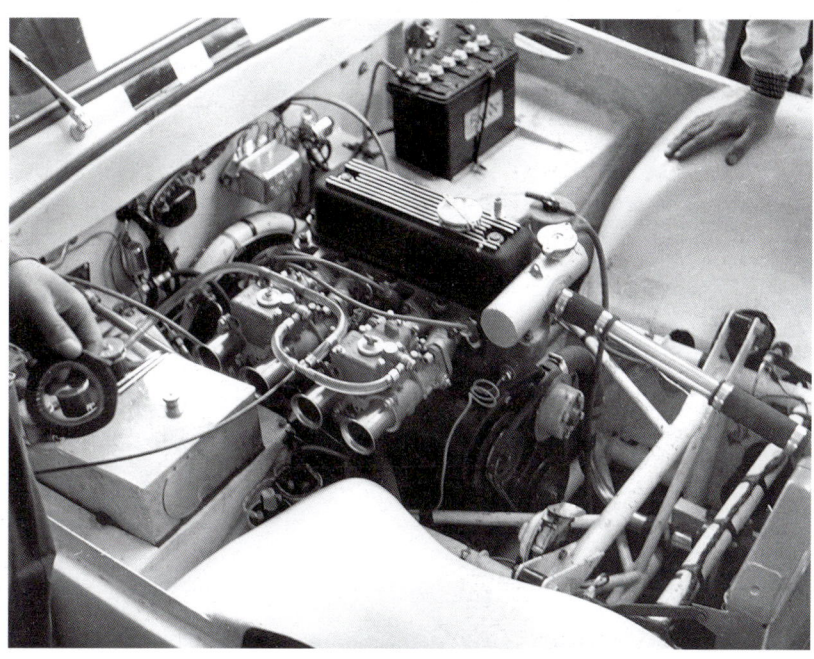

▶ Each of the Le Mans cars were fitted with a highly tuned 1622cc MGA engine with a light-alloy HRG crossflow head, twin Weber carburettors and a special camshaft. The modifications brought power output up to around 125bhp. (Judd Wheldon)

THE EARLY YEARS

The Race That Never Was

AS LONG AS cars and drivers were available, a team of TVRs would compete each year in the 750 Motor Club's Birkett Six-hour Relay race at Silverstone. That was certainly the plan for August 1962's edition of the famous club event, at least until a combination of situations conspired to spoil everything. The end result was that, thanks to withdrawals and a certain amount of confusion, only one TVR turned up for practice, which it did on its own. So, not surprisingly, the decision was taken to withdraw the team's entry.

Ah, but don't let's forget the power of the press. Amazingly, in its report on the race *The Motor* mentioned that the whole TVR team had blown up in practice! Even more intriguing, but certainly kinder, was the *Motoring News* report, which said that the team finished in a decent eighth place after completing 291 laps!

mid-August, with only one of the three TVRs entered managing to finish. They were the same cars that had been to Le Mans and, in two cases, still their overheating problems hadn't been sorted out. There was a much brighter note, however, on the TVR club racing scene. Familiar names like Chris Summers, Peter Bolton, John Thurner, Keith Aitchison, Nick Downie and Mary Wheeler had been joined by a host of newcomers, so much so that the Blackpool bombers were now a regular sight on circuits throughout Britain.

Some of the most outstanding race exploits during 1962 came courtesy of Tommy Entwistle. Ex-RAF pilot Tommy had campaigned an MGA in the late 1950s and had enjoyed reasonable success with it. But he felt the car was too heavy and so for 1961 swapped it for an early Grantura Mk2 lightweight with 1500cc Coventry Climax power, which he raced regularly without any great success.

◀ Ex-World War Two flying ace Tommy Entwistle was the best known TVR racing driver of the 1960s. He's seen here rushing to start his lightweight Mk2A for the 1962 Birkett Six-hour relay race at Silverstone.

COLLAPSE IN 1962

Frustrated with what he felt was an under-powered engine, Tommy replaced the Climax unit in his new lightweight Mk2A with a tuned 1622cc MGA engine – and in 1962 he immediately started to get results. Indeed, he finished the season with the runner-up slot in the Freddie Dixon Challenge Trophy series. Ultimately, Tommy was to become the most famous TVR racer of the day.

While Bryan Hopton's grand works competition plans for 1962 had been disastrously shattered, certain other company plans had been severely dented as well. In the heat of summer that year, life at Hoo Hill was not only hot but was becoming rather bothered and exceedingly sticky. The management's weaknesses, in particular Hopton's ridiculously over-ambitious pretensions, presented an alarmingly shaky picture that was cracking at every corner. Hopton seemed oblivious to this – he was now talking about making at least ten cars per week and finding the money to put both the stylistically challenged P5 and the unfinished Mk3 roadster into production.

Sadly, the US export order for large numbers of Mk3 coupés supposedly obtained by Hopton at the New York motor show in April (and claimed to be worth 1.5 million dollars) was looking more and more transparent by the day. Shop foreman Jack Pickard soon realised what was happening: "When they came back from the New York show, I thought 'beautiful, great'. But needing to be informed of production plans, to be able to order enough materials accordingly and supervise what would obviously be much busier production, I wasn't getting much information. It was always 'Oh well, leave it, we'll let you know later'. I think I knew right then that there was a big question mark hanging over the deal."

With early Mk3s being completed and the last Mk2As still lingering on in production, over late summer 1962 much time was wasted looking at new

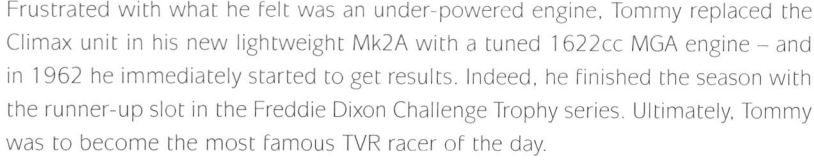

▼ Early Grantura Mk3s had unchanged rear bodywork. The position of the number plate was later raised onto a special plinth and the flat back panel filled in and rounded off. (Peter Filby)

premises to carry production for the fictional order. Factories on the industrial estate at Blackpool's Squires Gate Airport were viewed and negotiations were opened on the most suitable building, but there was to be no return to the site of Trevor Wilkinson's jubilant early morning test drive of the very first TVR in 1949. Next there was the question of the urgently needed additional finance. The ever-loyal (and hopeful) Arnold Burton had helped out again, but the ambitious promise of a large sum from Aitchison-Hopton (Engineers) Ltd had not materialised. Explained Keith Aitchison: "If I had not taken a realistic stand on this issue at that time, the Chester business would also have been brought to its knees."

▲ This early Grantura Mk3 was first registered in Britain in September 1962 with an MGA engine. Much later it was shipped to Australia – hence the special number plate. (Richard Warne)

At a board meeting one day in September there was a strong protest about Aitchison-Hopton's failure to provide more funds and also about Bryan Hopton's excessive expenses and hotel accommodation charges (he was living at Blackpool's Imperial Hotel), all debited to the company. Tony Clarke's hotel residence in Long Island, New York, had also cost the company a healthy packet. There had been an awful lot of money going out, thousands being spent on unrewarding competition outings, and relatively little coming in from sales of the much delayed Mk3.

Then there was the question of actually making the cars, which just happened to be the company's principal function! Amidst all the hustle and bustle thrown up by race car preparation and new model development, one stark fact stood out: the Mk3's New York release in April had been embarrassingly premature. Some genuine orders had come from the show, but due to the delay in making new body moulds, it had been at least two months before the factory had started making any production cars – and then only slowly. Although the first batch of Mk3s had been built in June, full series production was some way off. Alarmingly, the brave new TVR wasn't yet generating enough income to offset the dangerous financial shortages that had delayed its production in the first place.

To compound matters, some irate component suppliers had been refusing to budge until their long-overdue accounts were paid. This meant a shortage of components, which in turn ruined the development and production programme. As soon as a factory Mk3 was allocated for further development, it tended to find itself being sold to provide cash or cannibalised to provide components to help finish off a production car. An old TVR ailment, this consequent lack of thorough development had led to various snags, including certain rear suspension faults, on the early Mk3s that did escape the factory, and rectifying them took time and money.

If the TVR manufacturing process had soldiered on more steadily, it might at least have helped the situation. But now, in September 1962, there were some mystifying developments on the sales front. The concentration on US sales through the year had taken a damaging toll on home market sales, which were coming in at a rate of only one or two per week. Worse, some English distributors and agents were starting to lose confidence – WJ Last Ltd had ceased placing orders, various potential agents had gone quiet and two others, David Buxton Ltd of Derby and Research Garage of Nuneaton, had gone bust.

This alarming trend was ignored by the management. Perhaps to compensate, there were reputed to be existing orders, on which hopes (or dreams?) were pinned, from an extraordinary range of countries: South Africa, Switzerland, Chile and Germany, while negotiations were said to be under way in Jamaica, Ceylon, Greece, Japan, Hong Kong, Southern Rhodesia and Uruguay! It rather sounded as though Bryan Hopton's sales patter had gone ballistic again.

And so to the next set of alarm bells: nobody at TVR had been prepared for the sudden break-up with the company's prime US promoter, Dick Monnich, over his non-payment for cars (maybe he'd got wind of the problems at the factory) or for the sudden halt in deliveries to Canada when the Government there imposed a 10% duty on imported British cars. Indeed, financial problems and cash shortages once again seemed to lurk in every corner of Hoo Hill. Some Mk3s had been manufactured in June and July, but by the end of August the sales situation once again looked poor – just as expectations were rising for the new car's impact on the market.

The final Mk2A Granturas weren't completed until September 1962, some five months after their replacement model had been announced, raced and lined-up for the factory production system. Between them, the Mk2 and 2A were made for well over two years, during which time about 400 examples left the factory – at least 150 of those were exported, mainly to the USA, while most of the UK-

▼ Bill Last's garage in Woodbridge, Suffolk, originally delivered this Mk3 to its British owner. 660 NBJ was its UK registration before it reached Australia. (Richard Warne)

delivered cars were sold as kits for building at home. Faults or not, these cars were by far the best-selling TVRs to date. Even the hugely improved Mk3 wasn't to reach anywhere near such dizzy heights.

Ideas for the long-proposed Italian-styled prototype were still being discussed but the delays were to carry on for at least another eighteen months. Before Dick Monnich had fallen out with TVR he had suggested that, in the event of a complete lack of new models, the company should make renewed efforts to modernise the Grantura's rear bodywork (such a development was finally to happen with the restyled Mk3 1800S of 1964). Accordingly, Bryan Hopton had indicated that a modified car could be ready for the British International Motor Show at Earls Court in October, but then he'd said lots of things would be ready by showtime…

The truth was that TVR Cars Ltd was now in desperate financial trouble, its collapse seemingly unavoidable. It was shocking timing, because new body moulding tools had been made, the Mk3 was at last in production and sufficient orders were on the books. But cars couldn't be made without money for parts, materials and wages, and re-financing the company would take time. At least £40,000 was apparently needed for TVR to continue, but something more like £100,000 could have been closer to reality. Inevitably, all movements at the company's Hoo Hill base finally ground to a halt around the time of October's British motor show, the factory doors closing with a gloomy and, for many, shattering clunk.

Sadly, the workforce received only a few minutes' notice of their fate and were all sent home immediately with no redundancy pay. The situation was terminal, although an unlikely glimmer of hope had been authorised by the company's bank manager. Explained Bernard Williams: "We'd already booked the motor show stand and paid a deposit. The bank manager's view was that we should go through with

▼ Beautiful Australian scenery and a pristine wire-wheeled Grantura Mk3. Bliss! Only a small number of TVRs ever went down under. This one was imported over 45 years after it was built. (Richard Warne)

COLLAPSE IN 1962

▶ Built at Hoo Hill in September 1962, this Mk3 was later modified with Manx-tail rear bodywork before a full restoration returned it to its original, and correct, specification. (Rob Wells)

▼ The much improved new Mk3 made its UK public debut at the British motor show at London's Earls Court in October 1962. Tragically, TVR Cars Ltd crashed out of business during the show!

it as he felt we might even find a bidder for the company there. Also, despite his feelings about the dire situation, Bill Last kindly paid in advance for two cars, which helped us out."

Two lovely Grantura Mk3s graced the TVR stand at Earls Court 1962 and made quite an impact. An impressed motoring public was keen to place orders, and a German MG importer, based in Cologne, even made an extraordinary offer to sign-up for 200 cars. But of course there was no hope of fulfilling such demand. No bidders for the company materialised and, behind the glamorous show facade, it was all over for TVR Cars Ltd. Ironically, it was at that very same show that the brilliant Lotus Elan S1, the new MGB 1800 and the first AC Cobra, the 260 version with 4.2-litre V8 power, all made their public debuts.

TVR's undignified final death warrant came with the directors calling in the receivers: the extraordinary Aitchison-Hopton era had ended suddenly and dramatically in poverty with debts to the tune of £77,000. No-one was surprised that Bryan Hopton had already resigned from his position as MD. "There was little else I could do," he said in a newspaper article. "I am out of the firm because we were too successful. We had hundreds of orders suddenly and needed more capital to expand production. Naturally the directors looked to me, but I wasn't rich enough. I feel bitter because of all the work I did trying to get the firm off the ground. Now I'm out of a job. I expect an offer for my shares (51 per cent) any day." Somehow, his comments failed to sound sincere...

As the Earls Court show ended, the only men left on the TVR stand were Bernard Williams and Ken Richardson. When they returned to Blackpool next day they called at Stan Kilcoyne's house to discuss the sorry situation. It transpired that Bryan Hopton and Keith Aitchison were both unavailable. Convinced that the TVR had ended its days once and for all, Jack Pickard went off to rejoin its founder, Trevor Wilkinson, who had set up another business, Trevini Plastics, in Blackpool making industrial fibreglass products. Jack was extremely sad about the situation but the sheer enormity of the problems he and Trevor's creations had faced over the years seemed now to make the TVR's cause a hopeless one. It was time for a more stable and settled existence, even if it wouldn't be anywhere near so much fun.

The TVR Cars Ltd creditors' meeting was held one morning early in December in the first-floor workshop at Hoo Hill and was attended by some very irate people – about thirty of them. Henry Moulds and Bernard Williams had to face their wrath. One of the biggest creditors was the Board of Trade, which had much earlier loaned TVR £15,000 and hadn't seen it back. Claiming later that he had misunderstood the meeting's timing, Bryan Hopton was at home in bed at the time! He'd believed the meeting was to be in the afternoon. And needing to recharge his batteries, Keith Aitchison had flown off to the Canary Islands for a holiday. The great irony of the situation was that a pleasantly complimentary report on the Mk3 had just appeared in the motoring press...

▲ With September 1962 as its build date, this was one of the last Grantura Mk3s to leave the factory before TVR Cars Ltd went bust that October. The car was much later used for classic sports car racing. (Rob Wells)

Printed in *Autosport* on November 23rd 1962 was a well-balanced road test of the 1622cc MGA powered Grantura Mk3 written by John Bolster. The car in question was one that had been very speedily assembled by Bernard Williams and helpers from a painted body/chassis unit and components held in stock by Grantura Engineering, which of course operated independently from TVR Cars Ltd and had escaped the crash. These were some of Bolster's opinions: 'The body is extremely well made and beautifully finished. The scuttle is unusually high and the seating very low, making forward visibility a problem for a short driver. As the car is quite light, the MGA engine gives it a lively performance... a 0-100mph acceleration time of 28 seconds. The steering response is substantially neutral, the rear end steering of the first TVRs having been completely eliminated by the new wishbone suspension. The cornering power is also very much higher than that of the earlier TVR model'.

'The whole structure is commendably rigid, no scuttle shake being experienced. The suspension feels quite taut and deals with poor road surfaces remarkably well, while there is marked absence of roll. Entry to the low seats is much easier than would be expected and the general impression inside the car is of a small luxury vehicle rather than a stark sports model. There is no built-in ventilation and the quarter lights at the front of the doors do not swivel. The machine is entirely practical as everyday transport and the attention it attracts is quite flattering. The Grantura is a pleasant little sports car and it has many endearing characteristics'.

So, here was press confirmation that TVR had finally produced a genuinely desirable sports car good enough for spirited driving on both road and track (a lightweight version was available). An increased top speed of 110mph was possible with the right gearing and the car was generally very well mannered. In full kit form the Mk3 cost from £862, while the price for the complete car with wire wheels (as

COLLAPSE IN 1962

▲ This is the rebuilt 1800cc MG engine in the red Mk3 pictured on previous pages. (Rob Wells)

▼ Restored and lovingly cared for, YFR 751, the only Mk3 to race at Le Mans in 1962, is still active in classic car racing. (John Lowey)

tested) was £1218 13s 8d including purchase tax. What a shame such an apparently big step forward in the Grantura's reputation and ability came at a point when TVR Cars Ltd had just gone out of business! Competition exploits finished on a rock-bottom note, too. News of insurance man George Humble crashing out of the 1962 RAC Rally in November signed-off the list of failures that year. One side of his TVR's rear suspension had broken, lowering the car so much that when it went over a great hump in the road the bottom was knocked pretty much clean out of the car!

At the end of 1962 about twenty Grantura Mk3s in various stages of completion stood forlornly on the silent production line in the main building at Hoo Hill. It was a sad sight. The only rays of light in the whole depressing situation were that TVR Cars' associate company and parts supplier, Grantura Engineering, was still alive and in business – just about! Several more body/chassis units also sat in the company's large workshop above the brick kilns, and in the vain hope of being able to build these up into complete cars, Managing Director Bernard Williams was already making desperate efforts to obtain more funding – just for a change! Some members of the TVR workforce (numbering about ten) were even volunteering to carry on assembling the cars, giving their services free. Amazingly, great spirit, loyalty and resolve were still present amongst these men. Though it seemed extremely unlikely, there was still the faintest shred of hope…

Competition in 1962

TVR'S ATTEMPTS AT competing in prestige international racing in 1962 with works-backed cars were extraordinarily ambitious and largely disastrous. After the failures of the three Grantura Mk2As in March's Sebring 12-hour race (*described in chapter 5*) came a half-decent result in the Tulip Rally in May, with Arnold Burton's car finishing third in class. Things then took another turn for the worse with the Le Mans debacle of June and continued with more upset in mid-August's RAC Tourist Trophy at Goodwood, Britain's most important international Grand Touring car race.

The same two works Grantura Mk3s that had disgraced themselves at Le Mans were entered at Goodwood along with the spare car, but once more during practice there were engine overheating problems. The unfortunate outcome of this was that Rob Slotemaker's car didn't get beyond the marshalling area, Peter Bolton's car boiled and blew its cylinder head gasket after only ten

◀ Competing in the Tulip Rally for the second time, Arnold Burton's Mk2 finished a creditable third in class and twentieth overall in 1962.

▼ Great action for Tommy Entwistle's lightweight Grantura Mk2A in 1962 as he battles with an early AC Ace.

Competition in 1962 cont'd

laps, and Keith Ballisat's car actually finished – in eleventh place overall and fifth in the 2-litre class. In fact, Ballisat's drive was a fine effort, his Grantura completing eighty-seven laps of the 100-lap race and finishing ahead of several Lotus Elites.

Only Tommy Entwistle's efforts in club racing brought any true honour to the TVR marque this year. The dashing World War Two fighter pilot had raced a 1500cc Climax powered Grantura lightweight in 1961 but it wasn't until 1962 that his name came to prominence. The secret was more power from a better engine, a tuned MGA 1622 unit. For the '62 season Tommy raced most weekends and competed in the Freddie Dixon Challenge Trophy series, straightaway winning on a regular basis.

At one point he was well placed to grab the title outright – until disaster struck. During practice at Oulton Park in August, Tommy's flying Grantura ran out of road at Druids corner, shot into the banking at high speed and rolled over before sliding back on to the track. Unlike the Spitfire fighter aircraft he'd piloted during WW2, he immediately discovered that the TVR wasn't quite so capable when travelling upside-down. In fact, it would only keep going in this position for some fifty yards at the most!

On a more serious note, Tommy was incredibly lucky to escape largely uninjured, because the car had no roll-over cage and simply disintegrated as it scraped along the track's surface. He wasn't wearing seatbelts, either, and only by pulling himself up inside the car (towards the floor) and hanging on to the steering wheel for dear life did he survive – with little more than ruined driving gloves and grazed knuckles!

Using all the undamaged mechanical parts, the car was rebuilt at the Blackpool factory with a new extra-lightweight Mk3 shell and was back in action in double-quick time. At the season's end, Tommy was up there in the series' runner-up slot, receiving all the encouragement he needed to have another go at the Dixon Trophy in 1963. But he'd never forget his disappointment at not being named as one of the TVR Le Mans drivers, regardless of the fiasco it had turned out to be.

Another bright spark on the 1962 TVR club racing scene was ex-Lotus Elite driver and 1960 *Autosport*

▼ Brian Barr's Mk2 holds off a Morgan in a BRSCC event at Silverstone in 1962. (Ferret Fotographics)

THE EARLY YEARS

Competition in 1962 cont'd

Championship winner Chris Summers in his extremely quick, Arden-tuned, MG powered Grantura lightweight (it belonged to Research Garage Ltd). Driving in the Autosport Championship and often dicing with the very rapid Mr Entwistle, Summers was competitive all season, a typical result being a fine third place at Silverstone in June behind the E-type Jaguar of Ron Sturgess and the Aston Martin DB4 GT of Nick Cussons. Other Granturas in the same championship were those of Nick Downie, Peter Simpson, Ninian Sanderson, Dennis Morgan, Keith Aitchison, B. Coombes, Peter Bolton, John Thurner, Brian Barr and John Baker in the ex-John Woolfe car.

The ever-enthusiastic Mrs Wheeler's Climax powered Grantura Mk1 was often in action this year at tracks like Goodwood and Brands Hatch, and Mary naturally attended her annual favourite, September's Brighton Speed Trials – in which she achieved a fine third in class. And if there was a hillclimb event taking place at Firle, East Sussex, she was unlikely to miss it. Dedicated to motorsport despite never having enough money to make her car truly competitive, Mary was a lady of many talents and interests, amongst them painting, fishing and caring for her horses and various other pets. Her most notable achievement in 1962 was founding the British Women Racing Drivers' Club, an organisation aiming to develop the interests of women in motorsport.

Church Lawford aerodrome, near Coventry, was the venue in August for the first competition effort by Solihull man Roger Stanger, who had bought his red Grantura Mk1 the previous April – it was a 1588cc MGA powered, standard road-going machine, which Roger had seen in the showroom of TVR dealer Kieft Sports Car Company of Withall, Birmingham. The event was a sprint meeting and Roger propelled the car rapidly enough around the track to achieve third in class and fourth FTD. Over the next few months he would compete regularly in sprints before expanding his TVR activities to the race circuits.

Back in action in mid-September '62 was YFR 751, the one Le Mans racer that had actually turned a wheel in anger on the track. The car had been bought by haulage contractor Tommy Wood from Bradford, and that month he gave it its first competition outing under private ownership. Harewood hillclimb, located at a farm owned by Arnold Burton, was the venue – indeed, this was the inaugural meeting there – and Tommy was third in class. Over the next ten months he used YFR 751 in several sprints and hillclimbs, mostly doing well with the car.

▼ R.Wilkinson's Grantura leads an early AC Ace in a club race at Mallory Park in June 1962. (Ferret Fotographics)

CHAPTER SEVEN
Survival Time

From the dying embers of TVR Cars Ltd late in 1962 a faint flicker of hope was rekindled by TVR parts supplier and associate company Grantura Engineering Ltd. By early 1963 the revival had gathered pace, the Grantura Mk3 was back in production and ex-TVR Cars Ltd director Keith Aitchison was back at the factory working with Bernard Williams and David Hives. Amazingly, the dogged TVR had survived disaster once again. Better still, 1963 was the year of Tommy Entwistle's first victory in the Freddie Dixon Challenge Trophy.

I t was November 1962 and, nearly four years after Trevor Wilkinson's TVR Engineering Ltd had collapsed, Bryan Hopton's TVR Cars Ltd had also succumbed to catastrophic commercial failure. Not unnaturally, those who had followed the marque's eventful life assumed that now the long expected crash had arrived, the individual, stubby TVR shape was quite likely gone forever. Though a vastly improved and now more desirable sports car, the Grantura Mk3 hadn't

▼ Previously a keen rally driver, John Akers began autocrossing in 1963 with his Grantura Mk3 1600. Driver and car went on to become extremely successful at the sport.

been exactly state-of-the-art at the time of its demise. Many eager competitors were ready to plug the gap: well known specialist sports car makers like Ginetta, Marcos, Elva, Turner, Tornado and Rochdale. Strongest of all was Lotus with its brand new Elan, a sure winner which some industry cynics felt made the 'new' TVR look rather middle aged.

After some fifteen years in existence, it seemed that this could be the end of the road for the TVR name. But down in the depths of the old Hoo Hill factory something stirred. Not just the rats in the brick kilns or the ghost of Bryan Hopton. A small group of stalwarts – Bernard Williams, David Hives, John Ward, John Thurner and Stan Kilcoyne amongst them – huddled round the dying embers of the marque, hoping to create a spark of life, maybe a flickering flame. The Grantura had always enjoyed an enthusiastic following, and not just from the members of the TVR Car Club (Bunty Scott-Moncrieff was now President) who had numbered over 150 by mid-1962. Despite the car's various inadequacies and long-drawn-out development, there had always been a loyal band of devotees ready, generally eager, to own a very special, characterful sports car. The question was, how could they be tempted back again at this desperate time?

While the previous directors and shareholders departed to write-off their losses, the small band of devoted and still optimistic diehards stayed together and held on to faint hopes. In fact, only TVR Cars Ltd had gone bust. One of its largest creditors was of course its sister company, Grantura Engineering Ltd. This company had been little more than a legally necessary background name supplying parts (like engines, gearboxes, suspension components, electrical parts, trim sets etc) while TVR Cars had taken most of the up-front responsibility for body moulding, finishing off rolling body/chassis units and handling kit sales, publicity, reputation and image. But Grantura Engineering had always owned a certain amount of machinery` and facilities of its own, enough now to provoke its ever-durable Managing Director, Bernard Williams, into action.

Grantura owed more money to suppliers than it had in the bank at this stage but, with an inevitable struggle and some borrowing here and there, Bernard felt sure those stalwarts left in the team would help get the business rolling again. He still had huge enthusiasm for everything TVR, and those around him found that enthusiasm extremely contagious. The still potentially large US market would be the one to concentrate on; orders from Dick Monnich were outstanding from the October '62 crash and little more than the surface of American TVR interest had been scratched so far. The big problem was that some of the essential components with which to build cars and complete kit packages now belonged to the receiver and had been moved to a secure area. The situation would require more than one negotiating session with the receiver, who was also in control of all the vital body moulds.

Not surprisingly, there was a huge task ahead and there were several highly charged meetings between the leading men aiming to start a new chapter in the story of

▼ One of Bernard Williams's many roles at TVR was flying the flag, and he would always attend the big race meetings. Here he is at Goodwood with David Hives (right) and friends. (Judd Wheldon)

SURVIVAL TIME

▲ Roger Stanger's Mk1 about to leave the line in an August 1962 sprint event at Church Lawford airfield near Coventry.

▼ Two of TVR's key men during the early 1960s. John Ward (left) and David Hives are pictured in 1975 with John's own personalised Grantura Mk3. (John Bailie)

one of the country's best known specialist car makers. Stage one came in November 1962 when Grantura Engineering began its battle to survive in the Hoo Hill brick drying sheds. In total about ten men remained, undoubtedly spurred on more by their hope, loyalty and love for the TVR than by the belief that they might very soon get decently paid jobs again. Recalled David Hives: "The spirit of TVR was still alive but it was a grim period, with no regular parts supplies, no wages, no nowt. Yet we still felt we could do it."

Though his forceful character had been submerged somewhat by the last management, the resourceful and dedicated Bernard emerged once again as the natural leader. Forever calm and positive, he was an amazing man, an engaging personality who was always pleasant, had no temper and certainly never swore! Using his effusive charm, he now managed to buy time and even organised his company's continued use of the entire Hoo Hill premises previously occupied by TVR Cars Ltd. No question, Bernard was the driving force, the main reason why the marque had already survived for so long in its incessantly precarious position. And still he was holding everything together!

Without completely dismissing existing proposals for the Grantura's revised rear end styling and the much vaunted Italian design concept, Bernard knew that for the moment it would be a test of everyone's resolve just to continue making the standard Grantura Mk3. The first priority was to be able to actually produce some cars and, shrewd and persuasive as ever, he somehow managed to acquire from the receiver the various body moulds that were available. Exactly how he did this no-one could explain but it was certainly a master stroke.

Just as cleverly, the completed and part-built body units that lay discarded in the body shop also came into Bernard's hands. The target was to finish off the cars, sell them and regenerate the cash flow. This wasn't easy without a fully stocked stores department, but some of the creditors were helpful and TVR's new leader was able to persuade them to supply him with small quantities of vital parts. "We really had to scratch around for everything," recalled Bernard. "From the time TVR ground to a halt in October 1962 through to early in 1963 we just managed to complete about five cars, most of them going to the USA."

Stan Kilcoyne knew one fellow worker who found a much simpler answer to the parts problem. His way didn't involve all the awful crawling, it just meant a little climbing, that's all. "There were all these vital components upstairs belonging to the liquidator. So what this chap did was nip up there every morning and grab enough stuff to keep us going for the day! You know, enough to finish a car or two. Well, one day some kid started doing an audit of what was there. Each day he'd come back to continue the job and would find these boxes getting emptier and emptier. And he was getting more and more confused, angrier and angrier. One day he just threw his papers up in the air and said 'fuck it, that's my lot!' And he never came back. We'd got rid of him OK. Eventually, we bought the whole lot for about £2000 and the cheque bounced! We did square it in the end."

As if the daily existence at Hoo Hill wasn't already harsh enough, the whole country was hit just after Christmas 1962 by dreadful blizzards that resulted in plummeting temperatures and snow drifts in some areas more than 18ft deep. Power lines were brought down plunging whole areas into darkness, the railway system was thrown into chaos and roads were impassable across the country. Lasting nearly three months, it was the coldest winter for over two-hundred years – not the ideal conditions in which to be attempting the revival of a sports car company.

Regardless of the discomfort, disarray and instability surrounding the grinding rebirth of TVR production, several loyal UK dealers and distributors were still supporting the marque and trying to generate orders. Early in 1963 demonstrations of the Grantura Mk3 were being offered by East Anglia distributor WJ Last Ltd of Woodbridge, Suffolk. Bill Last was also a Lotus, Elva and MG dealer, and at London's Racing Car Show held at Olympia in the second half of January his stand displayed a Mk3 and an Elva Courier. Other companies involved in marketing TVRs were London and Home Counties distributor Tony Brooks Ltd of Weybridge, Surrey, Woodbourne Garage of Brighton, The Chequered Flag of West London and Nottingham, Anthony Oakes-Richards, his Research Garage now trading as GT Cars in Atherstone, Warwickshire, and Fisher's Garage (Edinburgh) Ltd, the sole TVR distributor for Scotland.

The most surprising name on the list was that of Aitchison-Hopton (Engineers Ltd). Yes, despite all the awful blunders made by Bryan Hopton's management of TVR during 1962, his Chester sports car garage, now in more modern premises and being managed by Keith Aitchison and Tony Clarke, was still advertising itself as a 'leading distributor for the all-new Mk3 Grantura' and offering early delivery. Prior to TVR's collapse, the Chester operation had bought, and taken delivery of, a large number of Mk3 kits (between fifteen and twenty) complete with all parts, and these would at

▼ This brochure is from the late 1962/early '63 period. Both the factory and its distributors were trying desperately hard at the time to revive interest in the struggling marque.

▲ In this picture the Grantura Mk2A looks well proportioned and almost elegant! (Sidney Adams)

▼ First registered in May 1963, this Mk3 was built to special order earlier in the year with a 1798cc MGB engine. It was possibly the first TVR to be so fitted. (Jim Lowry)

least keep the supply chain going for some time. But the relationship between TVR and its thriving dealership would, however, last only a few more months, as Aitchison-Hopton was undergoing a long-term change to become a VW main dealer – ultimately a highly successful one, too.

While all TVR's agents were doing their level best to keep the marque alive, slowly at first, maybe two or three times a month over early 1963, a 1622cc MGA engined Grantura Mk3 would be ticked off as complete and dispatched from the factory. As had happened before, the atmosphere at Hoo Hill soon became a pleasant one for those present – even if temperatures outside were still rock bottom! Free of earlier pressures, everyone could relax and the relentless struggle no longer seemed so exhausting. True, it wasn't exactly ideal that there were no wages to pocket, but the lads weren't keen to give up on the TVR dream. They'd lived TVR for a long time and were determined to keep those cars rolling out, however slowly.

Any available cash was generally shared, the majority going to those most needy. Some of them were on the dole, so every week they would pop out and collect a few meagre pounds from the gloomy dole office. The regularity of those absences quickly caught John Thurner's attention, so he attempted to join the queue, only to be forced to reveal his qualifications and promptly have to move early in 1963 all the way back to his original starting point at Rolls-Royce, which he re-joined in a senior engineering capacity.

The fact that Grantura Engineering was surviving at all in this desperate stage of the TVR

THE EARLY YEARS

marque's career was quite astonishing. Considering the enormity and complexity of reviving and rebuilding a specialist sports car manufacturing operation that had crashed so heavily, it was a tribute to the determination and courage of the small team that they were holding everything together. Unflappable and controlled as ever, Bernard Williams was in charge but was well aware that there was a steep mountain to climb before any form of real stability could return. If they were going to create something out of nothing, the TVR diehards would have to continue showing great commitment and carry on working hard for little money, lots of satisfaction and maybe, just maybe, the remarkable resurrection of a now well known marque.

▲ Aitchison-Hopton magazine ads were relentlessly bright and persuasive. And gushing! This ad was from the period when Bryan Hopton and Keith Aitchison owned most of the shares in TVR.

Further lifelines would be needed, though. Another injection of support came from Dick Monnich's company, RM Imports, with confirmation that it would once again take delivery in the USA of more Granturas. Despite earlier disagreements with TVR, Monnich even bravely agreed to put up some payment in advance. No such luck was enjoyed by Bernard when he cautiously asked Bunty Scott-Moncrieff if he might care to re-invest in TVR, because Bunty had decided to stick to rather more distinguished motor cars than the Blackpool bombers. "Sorry chaps, I haven't got any more money," came the response. "It's all tied up in Rolls-Royces now." But more help was about to materialise...

Spring 1963 saw the unexpected reappearance at Hoo Hill of former TVR man Keith Aitchison, who'd driven to Blackpool one day to meet Bernard and see how the revival was progressing. Keith hadn't chosen the best day because Bernard was for once moaning about all his problems and let it slip that the bailiffs were due at the factory later that day. "They were apparently coming to take away a pipe bender, which was a vital machine for production operations," recalled Keith. "Bernard said that the whole place would come to a halt if he was to lose that machine – it was as serious as that. So I paid the bailiff and effectively put £250 into the company.

"But Bernard wasn't finished. In conversation he revealed that Grantura Engineering was actually in dire straits and could I help in any further way. I'd already been a sleeping director of TVR Cars Ltd in 1962, so I took a deep breath and said I'd come to Blackpool for a while and do my best to help out. Once installed in a small family hotel at nearby Poulton le Fylde, I immediately started to do a five-day week trying hard to get TVR back on the road again. Initially, I did anything and everything hands-on except work with fibreglass in the body shop, and I got to know the product in real depth. My main role became Marketing and Sales Director, and I stayed there for more than two years!"

Not long after Keith's arrival, another new name to appear on the scene and invest a few hundred pounds in the company to acquire shares was Richard Barnaby. A wealthy young man who'd raced Lotus Sevens and wanted a new interest in life, Barnaby had then bought a blue Grantura Mk3 and decided to become involved at Hoo Hill, if only on a part-

SURVIVAL TIME

▲ Paddy Gaston was a notable TVR racer during 1963. This is his Mk3 at Brands Hatch.

▼ Inside the factory in 1963. On the left is mechanic Ken Ronson, on the right is shareholder Keith Aitchison.

time basis. His and Keith Aitchison's investments meant, technically, that the two men now owned Grantura Engineering between them – Bernard Williams only having a tiny number of shares.

Concentrating on technical development, Barnaby's main objective was to improve the TVR, and one of his first projects was to assess a possible V8 powered, four-wheel-drive car, which would have been an incredibly innovative attempt for the time. A meeting was held with Major Tony Rolt, boss of Ferguson Developments, and the project discussed, but the idea of a technically advanced TVR was really a non-runner, as Keith Aitchison explained. "The transfer box mechanism and differential that Ferguson was using would not have fitted into our chassis. For them to have built their system into a new chassis and engineer all the special parts required meant we'd have to design a completely new car, and there was no way we had the money for such a scheme. We later heard that Major Rolt had also been in talks with Jensen."

Returning to reality, as 1963 progressed, so did the laboured re-birth of TVR. Thanks to Keith's excellent racing results and hard-earned improvements on the sales and marketing fronts, life was gradually returning and Grantura's depleted but dedicated band of survivors could attempt to speed up car construction, generate

THE EARLY YEARS

income and slowly begin to pay-off creditors. A rather preposterous PR claim was made, no doubt by Bernard, that the factory was again building up to four cars per week, most of them heading across the Atlantic ocean to RM Imports. It was a wishful exaggeration but the fire had certainly been rekindled and progress was being made. Following the October 1962 collapse, bad press coverage of TVR's misfortunes had led people to believe that it was all over. Even the better informed onlookers from the motoring world were quite amazed at the unexpected revival happening in Blackpool.

A small but important element in the company's improving image at this time was the design of a new TVR logo and badge. Bob Hallett, still operating in the dual roles of competition mechanic and customer service manager, had additional skills in graphic design, and he was asked to come up with something more stylish. Although it wasn't pressed into immediate use on the car's bonnets, the new design soon appeared on some of TVR's promotional material and was the direct forerunner of the logo/badge that would still be in use more than forty years later.

Still charging around the racetracks in his very quick Grantura Mk2A, Keith Aitchison felt it was again time for TVR to become involved in certain competition exploits and maybe take advantage of the consequent development of wider markets. Several excellent drivers – Tommy Entwistle, John Woollon, Nick Downie, Paddy Gaston, Mary Wheeler and Peter Simpson amongst them – were successfully piloting their TVRs in club events, but a return to the international arena wasn't to be a happy one for the marque, at least not until the long-standing race engine overheating problems had been completely cured.

While the TVR works team had burnt its fingers at the Sebring 12-hour race in 1962, an American team of three 1622cc MG powered Granturas was entered for March 1963's event by Dick Monnich's company RM Imports. Unfortunately, the results were worse than in 1962, none of the cars managing to finish. The Ben

▼ This immaculate Mk3 is from the mid-1963 period when Grantura Engineering was struggling to stay afloat. Like so many Mk2As and Mk3s, it began life with a 1622cc MGA engine. (Peter Filby)

▲ Lew Shulz checks the 1622cc MG engine in one of the 1963 Sebring 12-hour racers. (Gerry Sagerman)

▼ The Donohue/Sagerman racer before the Le Mans-style start at Sebring. Donohue is in the red overalls with Sagerman just behind in white. (Gerry Sagerman)

Warren/Jere Mosiman car was scratched even before the Le Mans-style line-up, while the George McClure/Dick Semko car failed early on with a cracked cylinder head. The up-and coming Mark Donohue, who was sharing his drive with Elva Courier racer and TVR enthusiast Gerry Sagerman (Donohue had at least finished the 1962 event), had to retire his Grantura Mk3 early in the race with a damaged oil cooler.

Both drivers were very disappointed but Sagerman was sufficiently impressed by the car to buy a new, 1622cc MG powered Mk3 with HRG crossflow head and twin Webers and start racing it soon after. It was the birth of a transatlantic relationship which would become long and loyal: early in 1966 Sagerman was to become the USA's sole TVR importer, a role he would play for well over ten years. As for Donohue, he was set for international fame as the winner of many American championship races, including the Daytona 24-hours in 1969 and the Indianapolis 500 in 1972, the latter at an average speed of 162.962 mph – a record that stood until 1986. He would also be a winner in Can-Am and Trans-Am events and would drive at Le Mans and in Formula One.

After the international disasters of 1962, 1963's TVR competition activities in Britain were mostly restricted to national and club events. The leading exponent, after his 1962 near-miss in the Freddie Dixon Challenge Trophy, was once again the frantic flier, Tommy Entwistle. His car this year was a new, ultra-lightweight, 1622cc MGA powered Mk3 built at Hoo Hill by David Hives and John Ward. Weight was removed from virtually every possible component on the car and three cooling vents were cut out along the bonnet's leading edge. As part of the big works effort, David Hives devoted much of his spare time to acting as Tommy's chief travelling mechanic. Said David: "I prepared the car, regularly rebuilt the engine, drove it to many of the circuits for Tommy and lived, ate and breathed the whole exercise. It was supposed to be a part-time hobby but it seemed like a full-time job to me!"

The works support certainly produced the desired results. In TVR's most outstanding British competition achievement to date, Tommy battled against the Morgan brigade, mostly beat them and won the bulk of his races through the season to grab victory in the

THE EARLY YEARS

Dixon Trophy series for 1963. "I suppose the MG engine was the winning part of it," he reflected later. "It wasn't always the easiest of cars to drive but its light weight and the terrific power that David Hives coaxed from the engine made up for this."

On a number of occasions during the 1963/64 period Tommy also partnered Keith Aitchison in both men's TVR racers at various events, including the prestigious RAC Tourist Trophy at Goodwood, with some success. Now he had the bit between his teeth, Tommy was really motoring, and he would go on to win the Freddie Dixon Trophy twice more, in 1965 and 1966. Despite all the severe storms it had weathered, the TVR sports car's performance and handling abilities were now better than ever. The Grantura had always provided great entertainment whether it was on track, on the road or even at the factory…

1963 represented a very tough time for the company, but Hoo Hill's traditional practical jokes were still happening. One day it was discovered that the factory's welding torch magneto could be used to excellent effect on the steel mesh partition between the machine shop and the production line. When somebody called through the partition for some component or other, they would often hang onto the mesh, giving a fair impression of a monkey in a zoo… until some practical joker connected the magneto to the wire and switched on, providing a sharp electric shock. And then the magneto disappeared. Amongst his various tasks, Stan Kilcoyne, a mine of information on TVRs almost from day one, was now again looking after the replenished parts department, and so he became the prime suspect in the case. The lads were simply further amused by Stan's failure to appreciate their childish antics.

David Hives was probably the ringleader. "We felt sure that bloody Kilcoyne had taken the magneto. One day I went into the parts stores and Stan made the mistake of telling me to go and look for the part I wanted. Well, what should I find in a cupboard but this magneto. So I got it out and we formed this plan. While Kilcoyne was out at lunch, we bolted a pulley on to the magneto and fixed a long length of string on to the pulley to make it all work like you'd start an outboard motor. We coupled this up to the Yale lock on the back of the parts department door. One lad hid the

▲ Pictured at Vineland track, New Jersey, in early summer 1963, Gerry Sagerman's MG powered Mk3 had not yet been modified for racing. (Gerry Sagerman)

▼ Tommy Entwistle crowned a superb 1963 season by winning the Freddie Dixon Challenge Trophy in his lightweight Grantura Mk3. It was the first of three such wins.

◤ Gorgeous and pristine Mk3 with a rather more monstrous machine that's a little less concerned about appearance and more focused on function. It's a Vulcan bomber. (Steve Reid)

string in his hand and we're all sat round the fire. In comes Kilcoyne shouting the usual 'come on you blokes, let's have you, you little rats, get back to work'. And with that he sticks his key in the lock, the signal was given and the string pulled. Poor Stanley was transfixed by the shock, yelling for all he was worth! He collapsed in a heap on the floor, still stuck to this lock!"

Stan wasn't the sort of guy who would take this lying down and he soon rose to the occasion. He had lunch one day with the ever-increasing number of apprentices. Despite his spotty face, one of the young lads had a healthy interest in the opposite sex and regularly took them out in the borrowed TVR van. "You've got a dose, that's what's wrong with you, all those spots on your face," said Stan. "Any moment now you'll be peeing blue and then there won't be much that any hospital can do for you."

Stan knew exactly how to pee blue – he'd had kidney trouble and the prescribed pills

THE EARLY YEARS

did the trick. So next day the smallest, meekest apprentice was scared out of his wits and threatened with all manner of awful endings unless he agreed to mix one of these pills into some sweets to give the spotty lad. David found it all extremely funny. "They offered the lad a load of Smarties knowing he ate like a cannibal, and the greedy bugger took the lot and stuffed them down. That night he went out drinking with a couple of the lads, and next thing he's gone for a pee and come back frightened as hell, yelling 'I'm peeing blue, I've got a dose, I've got a dose!' He went flying off to the nearest hospital and went crazy when he found out what we'd done."

Amidst all the tomfoolery, some form of order had now returned at Hoo Hill. 'Prosperity' wasn't really the word for it, but money was coming in and wages were becoming a viable proposition once more, so the premises were readied for better efficiency. Machining, assembling and trimming were still being carried out in the main workshop, and sales of the Grantura Mk3 were now steady enough for Bernard Williams to return the first floor body moulding shop above the brick kilns to full-scale operations. Early in 1963 a new company had been formed to handle all the fibreglass moulding work and sales thereof – it was called Grantura Plastics Ltd, a move Bernard made to comply with HM Customs and Excise's tax laws affecting the sales of kit cars. As Managing Director of the new company, perhaps more than ever since his association with TVR had begun in 1955,

T.V.R.
WOODBOURNE GARAGE.
The T.V.R. Distributors for Sussex, Kent and Hampshire.
1960 Mk. I T.V.R.-Climax, in dark B.R.G., full Stage III engine, just rebuilt. This is the well known Mary Wheeler car of noted reliability in racing £575
1961-62 Mk IIA T.V.R.-Climax in red, close ratio gears, Marchal lamps and every possible long-distance touring extra. Very low mileage £699

Woodbourne Avenue, Brighton, 6, Sussex.
Tel.: Brighton 55694.

▲ The sales manager of Brighton's Woodbourne Garage in 1963 was ex-Squadron Leader James Boothby, one of the great TVR characters.

◀ Just inside the first floor entrance shown here were the offices of Bernard Williams's fibreglass moulding company, Grantura Plastics. At the other end of the building were the large doors through which TVR bodies and cars were moved in and out. (John Bailie)

SURVIVAL TIME

▶ Early in 1963 the Grantura Mk3 received this new dashboard design. The standard steering wheel was still the huge 17inch diameter plastic rimmed item shown here. (Peter Filby)

▼ Beauty and the beast? Well, nearly but not quite. No-one ever claimed the Mk3 was beautiful but it had a certain '*je ne sais quoi*' about it! (Steve Reid)

Bernard was now the key person in the whole operation.

Chassis manufacture had always taken place in two of the brick kilns underneath what was now the Grantura Plastics moulding workshop. One kiln was used for tube storage and cutting, the other for the welding together of the tubes. Neither kiln was particularly pleasant but the latter one was thoroughly filthy thanks to the general dirt and dust created by the grinding and welding. Because there were no extraction fans, both its specialist inhabitants were generally covered in grime: Wilf, the experienced and highly skilled old-timer, and Ronald 'Benny' Bentham, his younger assistant. It was always fairly dark in this kiln (there were lights but no windows) but despite his failing eyesight, Wilf could do absolutely anything with a welding torch.

'Benny' hadn't yet reached that lofty level and was more notorious for being the dirtiest, most scruffy bloke imaginable – and for a little extra part-time job he maintained. It was with the local lifeboat club and came about thanks to his in-depth knowledge of the area's tides and dangerous seas. When called upon, he would use

155

that knowledge to locate drowned swimmers or people who'd committed suicide, fish their bodies out of the sea and, using his motorcycle with large box sidecar, deliver them to the Blackpool mortuary!

Not surprisingly, the natives in the chassis kilns were regularly in line as the subjects of some wicked mickey-taking. David Hives laughed as he recalled one particular incident: "It was early evening at the beginning of November and getting dark. Some kids had come to the factory wanting pennies for their Guy (Fawkes). So we borrowed it, stuck a coat and hat on it, balanced it on a bicycle and positioned it outside Wilf's kiln. One of us then called out, 'Wilf, there's somebody outside on a bike who wants to talk to you', and Wilf, in the gloom and with his poor eyesight, went up to the guy and asked him what he wanted! He then went back into the kiln and innocently said 'the bloke didn't answer me'! We had such a good laugh over that."

Throughout 1963 the mainstay of TVR's limited production effort was the excellent Grantura Mk3, easily the best of the breed produced to date. Output was shared between the American and the UK markets and no more than small detail changes had been made since the model's introduction in mid-1962. At some point the ride had been further improved and acceleration wind-up reduced when a second telescopic damper was fitted in front of each hub on the rear suspension. Early in 1963 another development involved an all-new dashboard, its shape at the top gently curving from A-post to A-post, making it equally suitable for both right-hand and left-hand drive cars. It was finished in coarse-grained leathercloth and featured a revised layout for the instruments and switches. At the same time there was some mild restyling of the rear bodywork, namely the filling-out and rounding-off of the tail area beneath the rear window and the provision of a moulded-in mounting panel for the rear number plate (this was done, it is believed, after Mk3 chassis numbers had moved into the fifties).

▲ 1963's new dashboard was a simple curved design that was usually trimmed in leathercloth. (Peter Filby)

◀ A Mk3 rolling chassis shown with the slightly more powerful and more torquey 1798cc MGB engine that was introduced as TVR's standard fitment in August 1963. The company claimed a rather optimistic 120mph maximum speed for the Mk3 1800.

SURVIVAL TIME

▲ With twin SU carbs, the 1798cc MGB engine produced 95bhp at 5500rpm and 110lb ft of torque.

More significantly, by August 1963 an engine change had been announced, the 90bhp 1622cc MGA unit giving way to the more recently introduced 1798cc MGB unit, which produced a maximum of 95bhp at 5500rpm. Now the standard fitment, the new unit also gave an improvement in torque – up from the MGA's mediocre 97lb ft to a stronger 110lb ft. The standard MG four-speed gearbox was retained and there was the option of overdrive.

With its greater capacity MGB engine, the latest TVR now became known as the Grantura Mk3 1800 (it was also sometimes referred to as the Mk3A, which indicated improved suspension and increased ground clearance). At £872 for a 'standard' kit or £1054 for a fully completed car, its price had marginally increased, as had its top speed of 110mph – 10mph higher than the earlier Mk3 with standard gearing. The chassis itself was unchanged but other detail changes upon the advent of the 'B' engine included improved steering, the addition of a more efficient Kenlowe electric radiator fan as standard, and the revision of the spring rates and damper settings in yet another attempt to improve the ride. The cabin now gained distinctive quilted leathercloth padding on the transmission tunnel, while optional extras included wire wheels, performance tuning parts and a heater.

In September 1963 *Autocar* provided some initial test impressions of the new 1800cc powered Grantura: 'A short run over rough local streets proved that the suspension modifications have smoothed-out the low-speed ride successfully, while

THE EARLY YEARS

the same surfaces provoked very little kick-back at the steering wheel. Particularly pleasing was the general feeling of tautness, the low noise level and the improved tractability with the MGB engine. General finish of this demonstration model was excellent'.

After 600 miles on the road, The Motor's verdict on the Mk3 1800 was equally positive: 'The car impressed us mainly with its built-in safety. There was obviously some performance in hand at 110mph. The road holding is exceptional. This latest TVR should be very welcome to anyone seeking individual high performance with a fair degree of refinement'.

David Hives, Richard Barnaby, Bernard Williams and Keith Aitchison had 'sorted' the car rather efficiently. John Bolster supported this in his road test of the Mk3 1800 in Autosport of December 1963. 'In general, the TVR Grantura is particularly well-made, delightful to drive and has a personality that is all its own. The driving position is very comfortable; it is a particularly fast little car, its light weight being reflected in sparkling acceleration; it is stable at high speeds and rides well on reasonable surfaces, the suspension only giving a hard ride on bad roads at low speeds; the car is well balanced, being fast on corners and feeling particularly safe on wet roads; the brakes are powerful; there is a praiseworthy absence of road noise inside the body'.

The only criticisms made by Bolster involved 'the annoying kick-back on the steering (on bad roads), the hard ride on bad roads at low speed' and the fact that there was 'little provision for adequate ventilation'. Summarising, he said: 'The Grantura is an attractive small closed sports car. This machine has all the attributes of a fierce little car while possessing the advantages of a closed body. It appeals particularly because it is more refined than most of its kind'. What Bolster failed to mention was the car's irritating tendency to

▲ This ad appeared in Autosport in August 1963 prior to James Boothby finding his Reece Mews, South Kensington, premises for his London TVR centre.

▼ Although it has a later registration, this 1963 Mk3 is believed to be the first regular production example to have 1798cc MGB power. (Jim Lowry)

leak when it rained and fry its occupants when the sun was hot!

Benefiting from the magazine publicity, efforts to market the Mk3 1800 were in full swing between autumn 1963 and mid-1964. Indeed, although it was still only made in limited numbers, the car was doing an important job bringing bread-and-butter income to Hoo Hill. After all the problems of late 1962, East Anglia dealer Bill Last's loyalty to TVR was once again shining through. As already mentioned, his company also handled MG, Elva, Lotus and Wolseley cars but he always retained a particular fondness for the Blackpool sports car. Most of his customers were American servicemen from the many USAF bases in Suffolk and Norfolk, and his operation had its own dedicated transporter for TVR collections – and the return of faulty cars! At one stage the Blackpool factory even set up a special production area for left-hand-drive Mk3 Granturas ordered by Last for the UK based Americans.

A significant new name on the distributor list in September 1963 was The TVR Centre based in Reece Mews, South Kensington, London SW7, handling sales in London and the south. In charge was a splendid, tall and imposing character, Squadron Leader James Boothby (retired), an ex-RAF flying officer who'd flown Hurricane fighters in the Battle of Britain. According to legend, his greatest sortie was the shooting down early one morning of three German aircraft before returning to base ready for breakfast! Apart from his booming voice, Boothby was notable for his big personality, his generosity and his preposterously large handlebar moustache, which was fully waxed and measured nearly 12in from tip to tip. Matching his appearance, his character was imposing and entertaining – not too dissimilar to that of his friend and accomplice, one Gerry Marshall, who in fact worked for Boothby at the TVR Centre for a short period of time.

Never short of fascinating and entertaining stories, many of which naturally tended

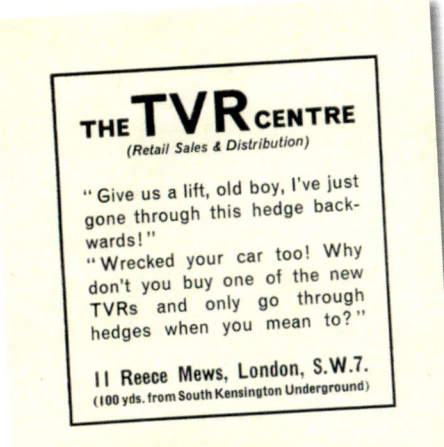

▲ Probably the work of James Boothby, this ad was from November 1963.

▶ Ex-Squadron Leader James Boothby set up The TVR Centre in Reece Mews, South Kensington, London SW7, during autumn 1963. The premises were too small to take any more than one car! Here is Boothby on the right with wife Sylvia and Bunty Scott-Moncrieff.

THE EARLY YEARS

▲ It's a 1963 car but this Mk3 was still going strong in classic car racing over 45 years later. (Jim Lowry)

to get exaggerated, James Boothby had, to his friends and associates, long been one of British motorsport's great characters. One wicked tale did the rounds years later: it recounted how he'd been hit by a bullet going straight through his head during World War Two, causing the fitment of a permanent steel plate to protect his skull – but apparently it wasn't true! Boothby's racing career began in 1937 with a 1½-litre Bugatti, and he went on to construct his own car, the Mercury V8 powered JBM, soon after the end of World War Two. In 1958 he became general sales manager for St James Motors in Brighton, handling such marques as Goggomobil, Berkeley, DKW and the occasional TVR.

Having enjoyed much success racing his yellow 692cc engined Berkeley in 1959, the ever-competitive Boothby next acquired a mildly lightened Grantura Mk1 in 1960 and, in his first outing with the car, grabbed a fine second place in class at Goodwood. His dark blue TVR was a regular on southern tracks that year, but it was a white ex-works D-type Jaguar that further enhanced the Boothby reputation between 1961 and 1964, particularly when it came to hillclimbing. Then, having set up a car sales business at the Reece Mews premises earlier in 1963, several months later he secured a deal with the TVR factory and began to spread the word. Indeed, being a big V8 enthusiast, he even produced a basic design for a V8 engined example of the marque (whether this related in any way to the Griffith V8 project born in the USA later that year seems very unlikely).

The first TVR to reside in Boothby's tiny Reece Mews showroom (there was only room inside for one car) was a lightweight Grantura Mk3

▼ Pictured many years later, the 1962 Le Mans Mk3 racer's highly tuned 1622cc MGA engine was still remarkably tidy. (John Lowey)

160

1800 delivered from the factory by David Hives. The ex-Squadron Leader made an immediate impression on David: "He was a typical Battle of Britain type, an amazing, over-the-top character – a loud, entertaining bloke who was physically big and made a big impact everywhere he went. In fact, he had a voice as loud as an elephant blowing off! Having got the Mk3 to him, I had to stay overnight in a pub across the other side of London. Boothby knew the bloke who owned it, but it was a right scruffy hole, one of the worst. Gerry Marshall, who had just started racing Minis at the time, took me there in his full-race lightweight Mini-Cooper. I'd never known a bloody Mini go as fast in my life. When we reached the pub, I was shaking and as deaf as a bloody dodo!"

The outrageous James Boothby and the miniscule London TVR Centre were to figure regularly in TVR life and times over the next year. The lightweight Mk3 1800 delivered to Reece Mews by David Hives was employed both as a demonstrator and a race car, although when Boothby competed with it he didn't necessarily wear his usual racing overalls. The story has it that because he believed so ardently that the TVR was a true grand tourer, he preferred to race in a rather smart business suit!

A great TVR enthusiast and highly skilled social drinker, Boothby never managed to sell many cars, mainly because he spent so much time in the local pub – The Hereford Arms in nearby Gloucester Road, Kensington. Just around the corner and a short distance along the road from Reece Mews, this was a popular hang-out for the area's car enthusiasts and racing types, most of whom used to retire there after work for a few pints and a good natter. Boothby's other fascination was thrashing his Mk3 during his daily

▼ Although it only lasted three laps before overheating, YFR 751 is notable for being the 1962 Le Mans racer. (John Lowey)

▲ The Le Mans racer was one of the first MK3s made – in 1962. After three years in production, the model was replaced by the new Manx-tailed 1800S. (John Lowey)

commute to South Kensington from his home in Hassocks, Sussex, often dicing with other fast road cars. Given his love of V8 engines, it was hardly surprising that during 1964 he was to nurture a particular fascination for TVR's forthcoming big banger, the wild and wonderful Griffith V8.

Supplied in the UK almost always in kit form, the Grantura Mk3 1800 was displayed at the Racing Car Show held at London's Olympia over the last week of January 1964. Once again it was Bill Last who organised the stand, an impressive presentation that included the latest Elva Courier and a striking Mini conversion, the Viking Hornet Convertible. Also shown was a range of MG tuning equipment marketed by Last's other company Viking Performance.

The MGB powered Mk3 was to continue in production at Hoo Hill until early 1965, by which time its successor, the restyled 1800S, was also being made. In total, only about ninety of the first two Grantura Mk3 models, the 1600 and 1800, were built, a figure that didn't represent a particularly notable success for what was really a very good TVR. But the car had suffered a bad start to its life, its impact on the market being severely damaged by TVR Cars' collapse in 1962, and the quantity made probably would have been much greater had the monstrous Griffith not dominated events at the Blackpool factory from early 1964 onwards. Indeed, the Ford 4.7-litre V8 powered projectile was to have a drastic effect on TVR's very existence.

Advance news of the strange happenings across the ocean in New York first filtered through to Grantura Engineering late in 1963. The full enormity of the project became apparent when Dick Monnich visited Blackpool at the end of the year to meet Keith Aitchison and Bernard Williams. The American reported that he was involved with Long Island Ford dealer Jack Griffith, one of the most successful and progressive Ford agents in the New York area, who had been playing around with the installation of a powerful

Ford 4.7-litre V8 engine in an unsuspecting Grantura Mk3 engine bay. The result, he said, was a seriously muscular TVR capable of amazing acceleration. According to Keith, Monnich's words were: "Look, I know you're struggling and need to sell lots more cars. The machine we've built will eat a Cobra. What we have in mind is a deal whereby you build the cars complete but less engine and gearbox and then ship them to New York, where we will fit the V8s and finish them off."

For the men who'd been battling so hard to re-establish the TVR marque it was an enticing proposal, and they were to waste little time in evaluating it. The number of TVRs sold through 1963 was extremely disappointing and it was felt that the V8-powered Cobra crusher had come onto the scene just in the nick of time. Keith Aitchison's view was that the company had no option but to go ahead with the American project. Hence the next phase of Grantura Engineering's existence was to involve a quite sensational Anglo-American hybrid that, it would soon be claimed, was 'the fastest road car in the world'. To the motoring world at large, it seemed as though TVR was magically emerging intact from what had started as a desperate year. Rather more incredibly, the company now had quite sensational possibilities in store...

Competition in 1963

ALREADY DESCRIBED IN this chapter are the disappointment of TVR's entries in the 1963 Sebring 12-hour race in the USA and the brilliant effort of Tommy Entwistle in winning the Freddie Dixon Challenge Trophy for the first time. Aside of Tommy, the army of British TVR club racing drivers had grown significantly larger for 1963. Notable racers who competed throughout the season and gained plenty of class wins included Peter Simpson, Keith Aitchison, Paddy Gaston, John Edmonds, John Woollon, John Forrest and Nick Downie with his unmissable yellow, MG powered Grantura Mk2A lightweight.

Alistair McHardy added his name to the TVR racing clan during 1963. Aberdeen-born Alistair placed his order for a lightweight Grantura Mk3 kit with James Boothby on the TVR stand at the January 1963 Racing Car Show in London. At the time Boothby was sales manager of Hove, Sussex, based TVR dealer Woodbourne Garage, and Alistair lived only a short distance away. As luck would have it, the Scot was offered a job as a salesman at Woodbourne Garage, and he quickly became good friends with both Boothby and TVR racer Mary Wheeler, who ran the garage's parts department.

Assembly of the McHardy Mk3 lightweight wasn't finished until late summer 1963. With 1622cc MG power, the car was built as a dual-purpose road and race machine. One of its first outings (if not *the* first) was in a marque scratch event at Aintree late in September, where Alistair drove superbly to finish second behind Tommy Entwistle – the very race in which Tommy secured the Freddie Dixon Trophy. Like many other drivers of the day, Alistair always

▼ Entertaining action in the Eight Clubs meeting at Silverstone in June 1963, the leading Grantura Mk2 of John Woollon being chased by Roger Stanger's modified Mk1.

Competition in 1963 cont'd

drove his TVR to events, regardless of it having a very loud racing exhaust system, full race suspension and very little in the way of cockpit trim! But he was immediately addicted to the thrills of battling with other cars at breakneck speeds and quickly established himself as one of TVR's most impressive racers.

Again campaigning her trusty Climax powered Grantura Mk1, the relentlessly energetic Mary Wheeler charged through another enjoyable season without gaining any notable results. Unfortunately, 1963's works entry for the international RAC Tourist Trophy race at Goodwood in August was entirely forgettable, the TVR team of Tommy Entwistle and co-driver Keith Aitchison finishing in next to last place.

Previously concentrating on sprints, Grantura Mk1 driver Roger Stanger first ventured on to a race circuit in June 1963, when his MG engined car competed in the Eight Clubs meeting at Silverstone and achieved a respectable result. It was the first of many race events for Roger, whose regular haunts over the next three years were to be Silverstone, Mallory Park and Castle Combe.

A new motorsport activity for TVR in 1963 was the rough and tumble arena of autocross racing. However unlikely the car seemed as an off-road

▲ Nick Downie's Mk2 was seen regularly on track during 1963. (Ferret Fotographics)
▼ Tommy Entwistle's lightweight Mk3 chases Adrian Dence's Morgan Plus Four during their battle for 2nd place in a GT car race at Goodwood in June 1963. Tommy failed to pass the Morgan and finished 3rd.

THE EARLY YEARS

Competition in 1963 cont'd

challenger, a Chorley, Lancs, based painting and decorating contractor called John Akers specialised in autocross and was soon regularly achieving FTDs with his battle-scarred Grantura 1600. John had become involved with motorsport during the 1950s, when he started rallying a Sunbeam Rapier. This was followed by a Riley 1.5 and a Triumph Herald, both of which were rallied, before an MG powered Mk3 Grantura was bought in kit form, assembled by the factory and prepared for the rigours of autocross.

Success came quickly and John was soon a well known name in his chosen field. His TVR became quite notorious too. The car was also campaigned in the occasional rally, but John now found he much preferred autocross – and sand racing – and he would continue to be a winner in the sport for several years hence.

Other competition TVRs during 1963 included the sprint cars of A. Lambe and N.H. Barnes and the hillclimb machines of John Forrest, T.J. Henderson and E.Preston. As for the most famous motor race in the world, despite the Le Mans disaster of 1962 a TVR was surprisingly amongst the eighty-nine applications made for a place to compete in the hugely challenging 24-hour event in 1963. Perhaps thankfully, the entry didn't figure amongst the fifty-five cars accepted.

▼ Tommy Entwhistle was not only a skilled racing driver but was also one of the great TVR characters. This is his lightweight Mk3 cornering hard during 1963.

CHAPTER EIGHT

The Monster from America

The explosive performance of the 4.7-litre Ford V8 powered Griffith Series 200 of early 1964 made it arguably the fastest production car in the world. Built to out-perform the AC Shelby Cobra, and priced to undercut it, the American TVR special was an affordable supercar that had huge and instant appeal. But due to rushed production and a lack of proper development, the sensational Griffith quickly gained a notorious reputation as a monstrously fast but unreliable hell-raiser. Predictably enough, the project eventually ran into trouble.

▼ Jack Griffith appears rather happy with his AC Cobra racer in the pits at Lime Rock circuit in Connecticut. It was his success with this car that inspired him to create his own Anglo-American monster. (Jack Griffith)

Without its enthusiastic American following, TVR might never have outgrown the confines of Trevor Wilkinson's original Beverley Grove workshop. From the point in mid-1956 when Ray Saidel imported his first TVR chassis to the USA, the seeds were sown for what was to become an extremely healthy – and at one point life saving – export market for the Blackpool sports car. With their UK sales graphs forever fluctuating wildly, the various companies responsible for making TVRs often came to rely on sales from the USA for at least a healthy percentage of their income. But the most extraordinary American connection was yet to be made...

It all came about almost by chance. Dick Monnich, importer of TVRs to the North American region since 1961, was a keen racing enthusiast and, indeed, regularly competed in his own TVR. After he'd been involved in some racing projects funded by

THE EARLY YEARS

TVR Legend...

OVER THE YEARS there have been several stories telling how, in autumn 1963, the little Grantura came to have its engine bay filled with a bulky 4.7-litre Ford Fairlane 289cu in V8. Here's how David Hives remembered the transplant story: "Dick Monnich had been having trouble with the MG engine in his racing Grantura and had left it at Jack Griffith's Long Island premises for some rectification work to be done. The engine had already been removed but the mechanics were spending most of their time working on Griffith team racer Mark Donohue's Shelby Cobra, the engine of which had also been extracted. When Monnich came to the workshop one day, he was angry that not enough work had been done on his car and so he gave the men some stick about it.

"Irritated by Monnich's attitude, the men decided to play a prank on him before he returned. In the next bay was the Cobra's 4.7-litre Ford V8, and the dirty deed they came up with was to lower its V8 into the Grantura's empty engine bay to really give Monnich something to think about. With no ancillaries on it, the V8 just about went in and was left resting on the Grantura's chassis. The bonnet was then put back in place.

"When Monnich next called into the workshop, he noticed his car's front end sitting lower, then sat in the driver's seat and, assuming his MG engine had been fixed, tried to start it. When there was no sign of life, he got out, opened the bonnet and dropped his jaw. Waving his arms around excitedly, he yelled: 'What the hell have you guys done with my car?' It gave the lads a lot of laughs."

Andrew Jackson Griffith Jnr, president of the White-Griffith Ford dealership at Hicksville on Long Island, New York, Monnich was offered full-time employment maintaining and developing one of the dynamic Griffith's other projects, his AC Shelby Cobra race team. While watching TVRs race in the Sebring 12-hour event in March 1962, Griffith had met Carroll Shelby at the track and the two men had got on well. The outcome for Griffith was two-fold: he became the first US east coast dealer to handle the Cobra and he also acquired his own full-race Cobra, an early example which was campaigned by Griffith and his friends Bobby Brown, Bob Johnson and Mark Donohue for the 1963 season (very successfully, too).

While working for Jack Griffith, Dick Monnich remained a part-time TVR importer, and it was he who sold to Griffith the unsuspecting Grantura Mk3 that was to carry in its engine bay an outrageous transplant. There have been, over the years, several fanciful stories telling how, during autumn 1963, the little TVR came to be loaded with a powerful 4.7-litre Ford Fairlane 289cu in V8, but according to Gerry Sagerman, who often drove his TVR to visit Monnich at the White-Griffith Ford premises, it was just the logical outcome of typical car enthusiast chat. Yet there *was* a specific day when Gerry parked his TVR right next to the Griffith Cobra racer, prompting discussions between Jack Griffith, his mechanic George Clark (who maintained Griffith's Cobra race car) and Dick Monnich about the possibilities of an engine swap. Perhaps at the root of it all was Griffith's somewhat ambitious belief that he could beat Carroll Shelby at his own game – creating a sports car legend.

The concept of a small, lightweight sports car with serious V8 grunt clearly had

THE MONSTER FROM AMERICA

▲ The Griffith's birthplace was at the premises of the White-Griffith Ford dealership in Hicksville on Long Island. (Keith Aitchison)

▼ The engine that caused all the fuss – Ford's 289 small-block V8, as used in the AC Cobra.

immense potential. The Ford V8 was a robust, powerful and extremely torquey unit, and it wasn't too heavy; fitting it into a compact and slim TVR would create all the makings of a machine that could out-run the notoriously brutal Cobra. Griffith's immediate enthusiasm for the project would see the birth of an awesome beast of a car with massive performance; he could visualise a hell-raising thunder chariot that would maybe enhance both his and TVR's reputation – in more ways than either may have wanted! Using the same 4.7-litre V8 engine, Shelby's Cobra was already selling like hot cakes in the USA, about ten cars per week being shipped from AC's Thames Ditton factory to Shelby American Inc in California. Thanks to the TVR's light weight, Griffith envisaged that 'his' car would be quicker than the Cobra and could have a cheaper price tag than the Cobra's $5995, and he naturally wanted some of the action.

But first a prototype had to be built, and George Clark was asked to perform the operation on a standard Grantura Mk3 supplied by Dick Monnich. The job was done in a workshop at the White-Griffith Ford dealership. Dropping the fully kitted-out Ford V8 – it was a small-block unit but physically quite bulky – into the TVR's engine bay wasn't straightforward and called for serious modifications to widen the front of the tubular backbone-style chassis assembly. By all accounts, the work didn't display the best craftsmanship, a state of affairs that apparently permeated throughout the prototype's build.

For instance, despite the serious nature of the engine swap and the safety implications behind the performance potential, the entire suspension and braking systems were left untouched – exactly as they were in the MG engined base car. Although one would have thought the MG differential and driveshafts needed beefing up, they remained untouched too. Visually, the car was immediately distinguished by a modified bonnet and chunky looking 72-spoke, knock-off wire wheels, while at the rear were twin pipes for the exhaust system. The clear downsides to the prototype were that the transplant was a complicated job in terms of the effect the big V8 engine would have on the rest of the little TVR's mechanical components and, secondly, the whole scheme of things was rushed along somewhat recklessly right from the start – thus the car suffered from serious under-development.

THE EARLY YEARS

The re-engined TVR 'special' was completed in October 1963. Griffith, Clark and Monnich were quite prepared for bonkers performance when it came to the machine's first test outing but even they were amazed. With 271bhp from its high-performance version of the 4.7-litre Ford 289 V8, the prototype could storm to 60mph in under five seconds and, if the driver was brave enough, could thunder on to a maximum of over 150mph. Its straight-line performance was quite outrageous by any standards. To further evaluate the monster and discuss the availability of factory-fresh engines, Monnich now took it to the Ford Motor Company's Dearborn proving grounds – Ford's performance people also fancied the chance to stir up its four-speed manual gearbox and experience the resulting thrills.

The results of the Dearborn testing were mixed. Although the Ford V8 engine was heavier than the MG four-banger it replaced, the TVR prototype's handling was thought perfectly competent and only became tricky when it was driven hard or thrown into corners. Clearly there had been a change in weight distribution and this *did* affect the car's balance. No-one was under any illusions about the obvious need for more thorough development, but the acceleration was ferocious enough to impress the men from Ford and they promised to take seriously Griffith's request for engines.

Other tests conducted on the prototype car brought equally varied results. Involved in these sessions was racing driver Mark Donohue, the same up-and-coming maestro who'd partnered Gerry Sagerman in the TVR team at Sebring in March 1963. Donohue had since progressed to racing one of Griffith's Shelby Cobras – in which he was exceedingly quick – and he joined Sagerman in trying out the TVR Griffith prototype at the small Marlborough racing circuit on Long Island. Again it was noted that the car was indecently quick in a straight line but suffered from worryingly flawed handling. Braking power wasn't great either, the standard 10.75in Grantura front discs and 9in rear drums (sourced from the Triumph TR4) not being up to the job. Yet during this testing Donohue improved on his own best lap at Marlborough achieved in his well-sorted Cobra.

Though crudely built, the prototype was performing beyond expectations and certainly had the makings of a genuine contender for the Cobra's high-performance

◀ Dick Monnich poses with the prototype Griffith 200 early in 1964. Little could he have guessed that such an incredible sports car manufacturing saga was about to unfold. (Keith Aitchison)

▲ George Humble at the wheel of the works Grantura Mk3 in wintry conditions during the 1964 Monte-Carlo Rally. The co-driver was Bobby Parkes.

crown. Excited by his creation's vast potential, Jack Griffith now began discussing plans for the project. They were extremely ambitious plans, too, involving large numbers of TVRs being shipped to the USA for engine and gearbox installation there. But first the whole situation needed to be thrashed-out and a deal formulated with Grantura Engineering, so late in 1963 Dick Monnich was despatched to Blackpool to discuss production arrangements with Bernard Williams and Keith Aitchison.

Monnich, of course, was already aware of the Trident project and while at Hoo Hill he learned more details of what was an entirely different animal from the rough, raucous Griffith prototype. Sleeker, longer, more luxurious and much more desirable, the beautiful Trident had instant appeal, and though it only existed as a set of styling drawings, clearly it would propel the Griffith organisation into a new, more sophisticated world. Progress was made on arrangements for making the existing Griffith but Monnich was convinced the Trident represented the future. Once he'd seen the first styling proposals, Jack Griffith was in agreement.

If the Trident project had been much more advanced, it's fascinating to think that the Griffith V8, destined to become one of the most outrageous road rockets the world has ever seen, might never have happened. But no Tridents had even been built, let alone developed and given price tags, so for the moment the Griffith had a clear road ahead. When Keith Aitchison flew to New York in February 1964 to visit the Griffith premises and finalise business arrangements between the British and American companies, he suggested that Griffith should get things under way with the existing project, adding the Trident to the line later on when it finally came on stream. And so the little British sports car with the thundering great American engine rumbled ominously forwards.

THE EARLY YEARS

Keith's trip was also to see the Griffith prototype, drive it, discuss development, weigh-up the whole project and thrash out a deal. "That first car was an amazing experience," he recalled. "It was hugely fast, under-geared thanks to its MG differential, and no way were the brakes good enough. In truth, the car was really a shocker. I actually said to them: 'This car is rubbish and you can't even think about marketing it as it stands'. But at the time we were hardly selling any MG powered TVRs in the UK and desperately needed this deal and the work it would provide, so I agreed to take on the project as long as they would supply an engine and gearbox for us to build another prototype in Blackpool. I also warned them not to under-estimate the large amount of development work still needed. But I was delighted to be given an order for several hundred cars in fully finished form but less engines and gearboxes. Exactly how we were going to make so many was another matter."

▲ Hard to believe sometimes that the little Grantura Mk3 could accommodate muscular Ford V8 power and gain world-beating acceleration. (Peter Filby)

Jack Griffith's intended transition from Ford and Shelby Cobra dealer to fully fledged sports car manufacturer was beginning to roll. Believing 'his' car to be capable of becoming 'the world's fastest production car', he envisaged great sales numbers – the incredible suggestion was that he would want the Blackpool factory's entire production (and more) of engine-less Grantura Mk3s: at least 500 cars a year. The astonishingly daring project's success would clearly revolve around whether Grantura Engineering was capable of supplying the goods at a far greater rate than it had previously managed. In the Hoo Hill factory's antiquated and inadequate facilities, turning out five or more cars per month wasn't easy, let alone five or more cars *per week*!

▼ Ford's 289 V8 came in two stages of tune. The 'cooking' version gave 195bhp, but this is the high-performance version with 271bhp. (Bob Goldschmidt)

To have any chance of coping, a huge amount of preparation would have to take place at Hoo Hill. The proposed production quantities, parts buying and necessary working arrangements (workforce, factory layout, systems etc) would need careful detail planning in advance. Quite prepared for something very special having a major impact on his factory, Bernard Williams realised that Grantura Engineering needed a serious injection of funds to deal with the situation and develop the commercial opportunities for the company. So he approached someone who had a special affection for TVRs and was wealthy enough to have brushed aside his loss of quite a pile of money when TVR Cars went bust in October 1962. It was Arnold Burton.

THE MONSTER FROM AMERICA

While Arnold was carefully considering another investment in TVR, Jack Griffith's enthusiasm was growing by the day. He now received Ford's approval for regular engine supplies and had already booked a stand to launch his new projectile at the prestigious New York auto show in April 1964. The pressure was increasing, especially at Hoo Hill, as the American seemed to be in no hurry to send the vital Ford V8 engine and gearbox needed for installation in the first Griffith prototype to be built on British soil.

It was at around this stage in proceedings that arrangements were made for Dick Monnich to make a second visit to Blackpool, this time accompanied by the hastily built American prototype. The plan was to show off the car to all concerned and do a short promotional tour of British TVR dealers. According to the rumours flying across the Atlantic, the men at the factory were quite prepared for an exceedingly rapid projectile, but not for one that performed as though it was possessed by the devil. In a straight line, the monster from America had absolutely blistering acceleration. Weighing about 17cwt, it certainly matched up to those early reports of its fantastic performance. But there was great concern about its various inadequacies and the heavy-handed surgery that had been performed under its bonnet. The whole concept needed a serious re-think.

David Hives, now chief design and development engineer at Hoo Hill, was distinctly unimpressed by Griffith number one. "It was a lash-up, a cut-and-shut job with a minimum of proper engineering modifications done to the chassis. To get the engine in, they'd hammered and squashed chassis tubes and made a right crude mess of it. Glassfibre had been cut away in the footwells and the holes then covered with bent aluminium panels, and there was an inadequate, standard exhaust system and no air filter. The back end still used standard MG driveshafts, differential and stub axles – unchanged from the Grantura. A second prototype urgently needed to be built, starting from scratch, with a proper job done on it."

Against his better judgement, David sat in the passenger seat while Monnich demonstrated the Griffith's power. David was shocked by the experience: "Its performance was devastating. It was a bloody flying machine, but he nearly frightened me to death in it! There were no bloody brakes on it – those Triumph discs and drums were nowhere near good enough."

By all accounts, Dick Monnich was a wild driver who only knew two speeds – being at a standstill or thrashing the car flat out. An outrageous stunt he performed one day during his visit to Hoo Hill was a drag race-style start in the Griffith prototype. Backing the car up against the wall of the brick kiln building, which ran parallel to the main assembly building, he aimed it at the workshop door opposite (yes, it *was* open!), revved

▼ Some late Grantura Mk3 1800s featured an improved dashboard with polished wood panels. It used a layout not unlike that of the Griffith. This car also has a remote gearchange linkage for its MGB gearbox. (Peter Filby)

the big V8, dropped the clutch and, with smoking rear tyres and front wheels off the ground, did a crazy 'wheelie' lasting about 30ft! Somehow, after clearing the door and entering the workshop, the car *did* stop.

There was one other notable event concerning Monnich and Griffith number one, and ultimately it was to have a great bearing on the very future of the TVR marque. Taking the car for the planned short promotional tour of TVR dealers – with David Hives again bravely passengering – Monnich demonstrated it to Peter Simpson, Bill Last and Paddy Gaston, all of whom were amazed by its sheer ferocity and keen to see more. Last on the list was James Boothby, who ran the London TVR Centre in Reece Mews, Kensington. The arrangement was to meet Boothby at a hotel close to London Airport the evening before Monnich was due to fly back to the 'States.

◀ The Griffith badge. In the long run Jack's dream of building his own car was to cost him an awful lot of money.

Monnich and Hives were dining together at the hotel when they were joined by Boothby, his wife and another fast car devotee, Martin Lilley. David's meal was suddenly under attack. "That completely over-the-top bloke Boothby from the TVR Centre in London walked in talking loudly enough to disturb everyone, then sat down at our table and immediately started pinching my chips! The other guy, Martin Lilley, was rather more reserved and didn't say much. Dick took both of them out in the prototype for short blasts up the A4, and that was the last I saw of Martin for about eighteen months."

Martin, who'd been encouraged to attend the meeting by James Boothby, found that brief encounter with the car was to leave the initials TVR firmly imprinted on his brain. Already an interested follower of the company's fortunes, he was immediately hooked by the American hot rod's shattering turn of speed. Despite the prototype's obvious shortcomings, he made a mental note to place his order as soon as right-hand-drive Griffiths were available. Perhaps he didn't realise it at this point, but his name would soon enough become synonymous with that of the Blackpool sports car maker.

▼ The cover of Jack Griffith's first sales brochure. That's a very strange look on the bloke's face!

After making its point and indicating its intentions in no uncertain terms, the beast from America was shipped from Liverpool docks back to the lair from whence it came. Opinion was divided as to whether that was the best thing for it, but the next job in the development shop at Hoo Hill was to build a second, *properly* engineered prototype – a 'mule' test bed that would enable TVR's workforce to learn more about the whole concept and turn it into something more manageable.

David Hives, Keith Aitchison and Richard Barnaby were the men charged with the task of building the new

THE MONSTER FROM AMERICA

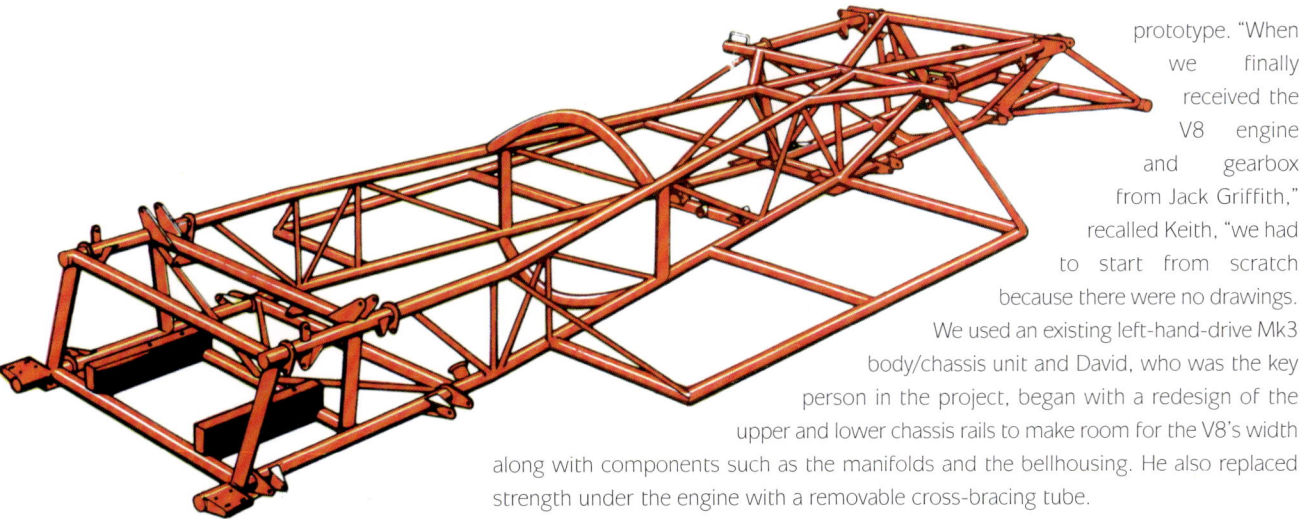

▲ As it appeared in the Griffith brochure, an artist's rendering of the Series 200 chassis.

▼ Front end of the TVR chassis, as modified by David Hives to take the Ford V8 engine and gearbox and become a Griffith. (David Hives)

prototype. "When we finally received the V8 engine and gearbox from Jack Griffith," recalled Keith, "we had to start from scratch because there were no drawings. We used an existing left-hand-drive Mk3 body/chassis unit and David, who was the key person in the project, began with a redesign of the upper and lower chassis rails to make room for the V8's width along with components such as the manifolds and the bellhousing. He also replaced strength under the engine with a removable cross-bracing tube.

"The car required a lot of reworking – strengthened suspension pick-up points, a second coilspring/damper unit mounted *ahead* of the hub on each side of the rear suspension (replacing the sole damper unit previously fitted to the chassis), this being to provide added acceleration wind-up resistance and greater rear end stability. To compensate for the V8 engine's extra weight, we also revised all spring and damper settings. The steering was redesigned, there were new exhaust manifolds, better cooling etc, and we developed as much as we could within the ludicrously short time available. Everything considered, it was absolutely crazy that we were being pressured into building and developing an extremely high performance sports car in such a short space of time. There was an extraordinary lack of appreciation from Griffith for the enormity of what was being asked."

The creation of this first British-built Griffith prototype was a trial run to hurriedly prove the changes made, but there simply wasn't time to incorporate them into another rush job: the building of three more fully finished but engine-less cars wanted by Jack Griffith in time for the planned launch in April – including the New York show debut. The British 'mule', as it was known, was finished in burgundy red, retained an MG differential and received a good quality Kenlowe radiator with a single electric fan. Its bodywork was basically standard Mk3 fare but was distinguished by the large bonnet bulge needed to cover the Ford V8's air filter.

"A bit rough" was how Keith Aitchison described the 'mule', but it was certainly a huge improvement over the first American prototype. While the car was getting as many test miles under its belt as time allowed (not many!), the next three Griffiths – wanted urgently in New York – were rushed through the Hoo Hill factory in as little as three weeks, all of them having to make do with completely standard MG-type TVR chassis. David Hives was in the thick of the action: "It was a ridiculously short space of time and far harder than any normal challenge. Twice we worked round the clock, staying at the factory for the full twenty-four hours, and I had to sleep on the trimmer's bench! Thanks to my lack of decent sleep, it sometimes became difficult to concentrate and one time an engine fell on my hand and badly injured it. Some sinews were cut and the hand became permanently bent."

With the three 'production' Griffiths reaching Jack Griffith's workshop on schedule, there was simply no stopping the extraordinary project. Recognising the big profit potential, Arnold Burton had agreed to finance the British side of the tie-up. Recalled Keith Aitchison: "Arnold came to the factory to drive our prototype and generally have a look around. He thought the car was fantastic and committed his support with a large amount of money. For this gamble with TVR, he faced the situation with a much more businesslike approach than before. One of his conditions was that both myself and Richard Barnaby should relinquish our shares, and Arnold then became the main shareholder, took over control of Grantura Engineering and made himself Chairman. He also warned us of impending reorganisation – with plans to appoint a new Managing Director, overhaul the dealer network and sort out more efficient production systems."

With the British side of the project now amply capitalised to do the job, Jack Griffith was wasting no time. A human dynamo who at times found it difficult to stand still, he was already in the process of selling his Ford dealership to provide substantial capital for his new business, and had signed the lease for the modern 10,000sq ft factory in Syosset, Long Island, where the cars were to be completed in decent surroundings. All seemed to be set for the realisation of Griffith's almost preposterous dream to put the Shelby Cobra in the shade by building the fastest production car in the world. It would be known as the Series 200 model, and it would *not* be branded a TVR.

The Griffith Series 200's public debut had been made at a regional motor show in Boston, Massachusetts, some weeks before the much bigger New York event. It was at the International Automobile Show at the New York Coliseum in April 1964 that the V8 projectile's full launch took place, and it was a great success. Finished in silver blue metallic paint, its cabin trimmed largely in white and sitting on relatively narrow 5K x 15in wire wheels shod with 185-section tyres, the show car looked little different from the two innocent 'little' MG powered

▲ This dramatic looking machine was number eleven off the Griffith 200 production line. (Mike Mooney)

▼ From early 1964 onwards Griffith production took place at this modern factory in Syosset, Long Island. (Mike Mooney)

THE MONSTER FROM AMERICA

▶ Finished in silver blue with white interior trim, the Griffith 200 made its full public debut at the New York motor show in April 1964.
(Randy Hartigan)

▼ Early Griffiths such as this could be distinguished by their large side vents and simple horizontal flares over their rear wheel arches. (Mike Mooney)

TVRs with which it shared the Griffith stand – despite the whopping 271bhp of muscular grunt waiting to be unleashed from under its bonnet.

Predictably enough, reaction to the Anglo-American hot-rod's wild performance potential was phenomenal, with plenty of orders being placed there and then. Word at the show was that the V8 powered TVR would be savage enough to embarrass not only the Cobra but more exotic machines such as Ferraris, Maseratis and the E-type Jaguar, at least in straight-line performance. It seemed as though it could be the ultimate road-going missile of the day, and at $3995 its price tag was way less expensive than the $5995 being asked for the Cobra.

Of the first three 'production' Griffith 200s built so hurriedly at Hoo Hill and shipped to New York, one was the show display car, one was probably kept at the Griffith factory as a demonstrator, and the third had hit early problems when it was badly damaged by a packing case that was dropped on it at the docks! The old TVR hoodoo was clearly still hovering around, something that Arnold Burton sensed soon after he'd invested in the project. Grim faced, he recalled the scenario: "The Griffith was a fantastic idea but it soon turned into the old, old story. Virtually all we needed was a few thousand down to get the thing off the ground, so I agreed to put it in.

177

THE EARLY YEARS

Things then started moving and before long they were moving in the most terrible direction!

"When I saw the first Griffith-built prototype I thought it was a frightful bodge-up! Quite incredibly, the early 'production' cars built at Hoo Hill were delivered on time, but they also turned out to be completely, utterly and absolutely useless! Once completed by Griffith's workforce, each one broke down almost immediately. Of course, our first British prototype had never been given enough proper testing in Blackpool. It was ludicrous the way we'd pushed the cars into production, because squeezing a big engine into a tiny bay was an obvious recipe for overheating, so naturally they all tended to boil over after short distances on the road. They wouldn't steer properly, either. The mistake was that Jack just said 'copy the prototype' and in all the panic to get production going, we followed his directive. He'd even said 'don't worry about the problems, we'll sort out the cars'. So when given the green light, we'd begun to churn them out."

By May 1964 the Griffith Motors factory at Syosset, Long Island, was completing cars as fast as the American workforce could push things along. Already some five or six Griffiths per week were going through the system, the UK side of things struggling to cope. Indeed, the rather grim Hoo Hill factory had never seen such action, and staff numbers had already been increased substantially to uprate production. Keeping the momentum going required an extraordinary effort by the entire workforce, the remarkably capable Bernard Williams being the driving force, especially when it came to co-ordinating the vital supplies of parts. Credit for the successful working of the scenario also went to the various large companies that made and supplied all the necessary components. Despite remembering the big TVR collapse of October 1962, they maintained a helpfully positive attitude to the extraordinary revival at Blackpool.

▲ The cosy looking interior of the superb silver car below, another early Griffith 200. (Bob Goldschmidt)

▼ The upright panel behind the front wheel opened to allow fresh air into the footwell. It was an optional extra. (Bob Goldschmidt)

Griffith Grief

THE NON-STANDARD, RATHER bulbous appearance of this early Griffith's rear bodywork (below) is easily explained. Carrying chassis no.11, the car was built in April 1964 and used as a factory research and development 'hack'. As such, it was often evaluated at high speed by the factory's test driver Mike Mooney. One tendency Mike noticed was some lift owing to the wing-like profile of the roof line. "We were having some trouble keeping the car on the ground above130mph, then shop foreman Dick Triano got the brilliant idea of putting a 'whale tail' on the rear for added stability."

Given the go-ahead to prove the modification worked, Mike headed out for another test drive in mid-1964. All went well until he reached about 125mph. "At this point the Griffith got squirrelly and suddenly, with a loud bang, I was completely air-conditioned! The entire rear of the car had torn loose from the top of the rear window down to the license plate frame and deposited itself all over the highway."

On investigation it was found that the added aerodynamic aid had only been bolted on to fibreglass bodywork. In their haste the Griffith shop fabricators had forgotten to attach the new fixture to anything structural. So the car's entire rear body had to be reconstructed by hand without the use of a body mould, hence its rather strange profile.

Responsibility for keeping a grip on the whole Griffith saga and its effect on the TVR factory rested largely on the efforts of Bernard, Keith Aitchison and David Hives, but welcomed back on the scene at around this time – to help keep things moving – was Henry Moulds, who had been a TVR director and stalwart between late 1958 and late 1962. Henry had always been rather smitten with the TVR business and was once again keen to get involved. Particularly interested in time and motion efficiency, he was immediately made production manager and was soon back on the board of directors.

While the Griffith project was fizzing away and threatening to erupt at any time,

THE EARLY YEARS

Dick Monnich was still operating independently as the sole official importer of TVR Mk3 1800s into the USA. Between 1962 and 1964 his only dealer had been Lew Schulz, whose company S & R Motors was a sports car specialist with premises in Hanover, New Jersey. In 1963 Shulz had managed the unsuccessful Sebring 12-hour race effort for the American TVR team. Bullish as ever, Griffith insisted on marketing his cars independently, so an agreement was thrashed-out and, while retaining his TVR import business, Monnich also became a director of the Griffith Motorcar Company. After selling his own company, Shulz was now employed as Griffith's sales manager. Another Griffith demand was that the TVR badge should be dropped and the V8 powered car be called simply the Griffith. His latest brochure went one stage further, calling it 'the Grrrrreat Griffith Series 200, the world's fastest, most dramatic production automobile'.

Two engines were available: standard fitment was the 4.7-litre Touring version of the famous Ford 289 cubic inch V8, which produced a hefty 195bhp (this was the figure that prompted the Series 200 name tag) at 4400rpm, while for the braver driver there was the optional High Performance version of the same unit producing a storming 271bhp at 6500rpm. Both versions used the Ford all-synchromesh 4-speed gearbox. While approximate maximum speeds were at least 140mph and 160mph respectively, the first 60mph could be reached in less than five highly entertaining seconds. But it didn't help the Griffith's reputation when cynics said that after 160mph the front wheels lifted off the ground, while after the five-second dash the back of the car usually overtook the front! In reality, to get the best from the car a careful approach and an educated right foot were needed. The handling was, for the average driver, all about nose-heavy understeer.

Regardless of the Griffith's savage performance, many components were carried over directly from the considerably more docile Grantura Mk3. Surprisingly, for most of the Griffith Series 200 cars the standard MG differential and driveshafts were retained, although beefed-up stub axles made from heat-treated metal were fitted to help cope with the hugely increased performance. Later, when the restyled Series 400 cars appeared towards the end of 1964, the stronger Salisbury differential (as used for the E-type Jaguar) was introduced as a standard fitment to deal more robustly with the Ford V8's power and torque and provide higher gearing. The men at Blackpool were still in touch with John Thurner and he was asked to produce a set of design drawings for a tubular carrier to accommodate the much larger Salisbury unit. The carrier was then fabricated at the factory and fitted to all subsequent cars.

▼ Jack Griffith was an excellent and imaginative sales promoter. This brochure cover revealed his Scottish ancestry and described what was clearly not a bad car!

THE MONSTER FROM AMERICA

▲ If engine bays can possibly be described as beautiful, this Griffith one certainly is. (Sonny Poarch)

▼ Looks typical TVR, doesn't it? But this one's really a ferocious beast.

The various suspension modifications developed for the first British Griffith prototype – the left-hand-drive car finished in burgundy red – were applied to production cars as soon as possible, but in the meantime nothing changed for the Triumph TR4-sourced brakes. Servo-assisted front discs (10.75in) and rear drums (9in) were fitted to both the 'slower' car and its more brutal sister despite intentions of giving the latter disc brakes all round. Both models had 72-spoke, 5K x 15 knock-on wire wheels with 185-section tyres that were fatter than those on standard TVRs. To provide enough cool air, two thermostatically controlled electric fans worked in tandem with a large Kenlowe radiator, which was deep in section and held a lot of water. But cooling issues were to remain a niggling problem with the Griffith for some time ahead. Few changes were made to the standard TVR interior apart from a little more luxury, a slightly revised dashboard and improved bucket seats.

Body-wise, a small but noticeable change was introduced by the Hoo Hill fibreglass workshop early in the Griffith 200 production run. This involved the horizontal flair strip over each rear wheel arch being altered so that it ran around and down to the bottom of the wheel aperture (at its rear) to create a more complete look. Another

181

THE EARLY YEARS

▲ Subtle it ain't but this Griffith 200 looks seriously aggressive with its outrageous colour scheme and big after-market alloy wheels, for which the arches have been neatly widened. As one motoring writer put it: 'The difference in acceleration between the Griffith and being hit in the back by a runaway train is small'. (Marshall Moore)

development, this one made at the Griffith factory, involved much larger, grille-style bodyside vents to improve the release of heat from the engine bay. They were fitted to many (but not all) of the first thirty-odd cars but were dropped after being found relatively ineffective. The large bonnet bulge was of course present on all cars, while the vertical, flip-open air vents in the body panels behind the front wheels (they drew fresh air into the footwells) were optional along with a luggage rack and various competition-related performance extras. Most cars' bonnets were also fitted with a set of louvres placed each side of the central bulge.

So far, so good. The Griffith 200's successful launch at the New York motor show and the reorganisation at TVR's Blackpool factory had already led, despite problems, to around twenty cars per month being shipped across the Atlantic and completed at Griffith's factory during summer 1964. To keep the momentum going, the relentlessly energetic American had established a national dealer network: some fifteen outlets covering most areas of the USA. The project seemed to have a good chance of success, but already tensions were rising at Syosset. As fast as orders were coming in, faults with the cars were emerging, customers were complaining and the assembly line was beginning to resemble a repair workshop.

Because of the manner in which the project had been rushed along, quality had been compromised and testing and development had so far been minimal, a woeful situation for such a high performance missile. The result was an alarming series of problems: some early engines were gutless beyond 4000rpm and turned out to be of marine spec; the fuel tanks were found to be porous; there were electrical glitches; some of the MG differentials were chewed-up when cars were hammered; and of course there were the inefficient brakes and the overheating tendencies. The temperature was rising relentlessly at the Griffith plant, while the workforce in Blackpool were not finding it easy to churn out more and more cars whilst maintaining the standard of finish required.

One area where quality control wasn't in question was paint finish, the man responsible for this being David Hives' father Tommy. Like his son, Tommy was an

▶ The place to be for electrifying acceleration, a stirring exhaust note and highly illegal top speeds. This is the cabin of the car below. (Sonny Poarch)

▼ The dramatic colour scheme of this restored Griffith 200 aims to show what a Griffith factory racer might have looked like had there actually been one.
(Sonny Poarch)

extremely skilled engineer, but since the Hives family garage had foundered several years before, he'd done a variety of jobs including training at Rolls-Royce as a gentleman's chauffer. Now, in 1964, he was a general dogsbody at Hoo Hill though was highly respected for his skills at paint spraying. With Griffiths being churned out at a healthy rate, the cramped production line at the factory was always incredibly busy. This would often lead to minor paintwork damage and Tommy was the maestro who always sorted it to perfection. Later, after TVR's next collapse, he would wind up restoring and rebuilding classic cars in Bunty Scott-Moncrieff's workshop at Basford Hall.

Another man who'd been part of the Blackpool team for some time was local motorsport enthusiast Graham Wallwark, who often turned up to support Tommy Entwistle in his Freddie Dixon Trophy races. Graham confirmed that the office staff at Hoo Hill were struggling too. "I joined as the parts buyer. At the time both Stan Kilcoyne and Alf Thomas were trying to order parts whilst doing various other jobs too, and they weren't coping. I was surprised that there were no parts lists, no drawings and no proper ordering system. Money seemed to be in very short supply

THE EARLY YEARS

and it all appeared to be pretty disorganised. Everyone at the factory was trying very hard, but perhaps the whole set-up was a bit over-ambitious. It seemed like no-one could say no to Jack Griffith."

Despite all the warning signs, an interesting variation on the Griffith theme appeared during the first half of 1964. This was a one-off, topless roadster, the concept cooked-up by Jack Griffith and Dick Monnich as a potential Cobra killer on the racetracks. Based on the standard body/chassis unit and retaining road-spec suspension, it was built in Blackpool as a rolling assembly, its bodywork styled as a stripped-down, lightweight racer with twin aero screens ahead of the cockpit and an aerofoil and boot spoiler at the rear.

▲ Shown in unfinished form before it left the Hoo Hill factory, this Griffith roadster was designed to race. It remained a one-off but surely would have sold well had it been produced. (John Bailie)

With its Ford V8 and gearbox fitted at Syosset, the roadster was due to be driven by Mark Donohue and was intended to bring the Griffith marque to international notice in competition (which it surely would have done). But despite Dick Monnich's great enthusiasm for the project, there were serious concerns at the TVR factory that the Americans lacked the skills to complete the roadster to full race specification and thus do justice to its potential. The men of Hoo Hill were right – apparently it sat around incomplete for some time and was eventually sold, after which the new owner later raced it successfully in the USA's mid-west area. Its ultimate fate was to become a pile of scrap parts following a bad crash during a race several years later..

Back in Blackpool David Hives and Keith Aitchison were building another Griffith 'mule', this time a right-hand-drive prototype (the first as such) that would be used for intensive testing in preparation for the ultimate production of cars for the UK market. The V8 engine and gearbox were lifted out of the earlier left-hand-drive 'mule' – which was by now so chopped, changed and chewed-up that it was scrapped – and bolted into the front end of the new car. Completed by June 1964 and painted pale blue, this 200-series Griffith was registered BFR 400B and used as a daily 'hack' by

◀ Completed by Gene Balmes, an official Griffith dealer, during 1965, the unique Griffith roadster was raced that year by Balmes himself. Finished in black with yellow ribbon stripes, the car is in action here at Meadowdale Raceway in October '65. (Randy Hartigan)

THE MONSTER FROM AMERICA

Aitchison. Furthermore, it was subjected over the next few months to the thorough kind of development testing which the first 'mule' should have received. Areas given close attention were the handling, braking, pedal box and position of the steering system. By all accounts this car capably demonstrated the Griffith's full supercar potential, but unfortunately it came to a very nasty end in January 1965 – as we shall see later, in chapter nine.

If Keith Aitchison had got his way, together with David Hives and perhaps two or three more skilled men from Grantura Engineering, he would have flown to Syosset, Long Island, and sorted out once and for all what was really a very straightforward process – the fitting of an engine and gearbox into an otherwise already complete car. But it wasn't to be. The Griffith factory was intent on churning out cars regardless of glaring faults and, as if these weren't warnings enough, the Anglo-American hot rod's reputation was suffering badly as word got around about its idiosyncrasies.

With a kerb weight of about 1450lb, the Series 200 was some 500lb lighter than a Shelby Cobra, so with the same engine it was significantly quicker – and genuinely one of the fastest accelerating cars in the world. But people like American journalist Rich Taylor didn't help the car's future prospects when they wrote such things as: 'There has never been a more dangerous production vehicle'. Another magazine report said: 'A Griffith parked in the garage is more dangerous than a motorcycle at full chat at Daytona Speedway!'

Despite such startlingly bad publicity, orders continued to rain in and the Griffith factory thrashed on. Ever since the launch of his marque, Jack Griffith had planned an ambitious range of different models, a dream that had no doubt been spurred on when Dick Monnich, during his visit to Blackpool in December 1963, had learnt about Grantura Engineering's plans for the beautiful TVR Trident. Griffith had immediately wanted a slice of the action, so in mid-1964 the American blew the lid on what he called the Griffith Series 400 convertible and the Series 600 coupé, both cars with aluminium and steel bodywork and power from the 271bhp Ford V8. In fact, these two Trident designs still only existed as drawings at this stage. It was yet another extraordinarily premature and misleading announcement, especially as Griffith was saying prototypes were already under construction and was talking figures of at least 500 of *each* model to be produced at Syosett during the second half of 1964!

Back to reality: with Series 200s leaving the hectic Hoo Hill production line at a startling rate – now up to around ten units a week – Arnold Burton had contacted a firm of management consultants and employed someone with first-class qualifications to run Grantura Engineering in an

▲▼ Mid-way through 1964 Jack Griffith released these drawings of 'his' new models and confidently called them the Series 400 roadster and Series 600 coupé. In fact, they were the TVR Trident designs and their release was extremely premature.

185

Aussie Export

THE VERY FIRST TVR to be exported to Australia reached Sydney during the summer of 1964 and was soon distinguishing itself on the racetrack.

The name Peter Owen was well known on the Australian motor racing scene during the early 1960s. He made a good living from his sizeable tyre and wheel sales business in Brookvale, a suberb of Sydney, but his real love was racing. Early in 1964 he arranged with the TVR factory to become the car's sole distributor down under, and soon after a full Grantura Mk3 kit was shipped from Blackpool together with a standard 1798cc MGB engine. It was the very first TVR to reach those far away shores.

▲ Soon after it reached Australia, Peter Owen's Mk3 was in race action. From its first four outings in 1964, the car scored two wins, a 2nd and a 3rd.

Assembled by Les Merrick, who worked part-time for Owen, the car was finished in grey and featured red leather trim and wire wheels. With its engine tuned to give over 100bhp, It was almost immediately pressed into action as Owen's road car and also became the publicity vehicle for his fledgling TVR import business. In August 1964 it was on display at the Sydney motor show before being tested by motoring journalists for reports in several Aussie magazines. And pretty complimentary the reports were too.

While building the Mk3 Les Merrick had also helped prepare it for racing, and the car was in track action under the Peter Owen Racing banner several times during the second half of 1964. The drivers were Owen himself and Kevin Bartlett, a notable Aussie racer who would go on to win the Macau Grand Prix in 1969 and the great Bathurst 1000 event in 1973. Both men enjoyed success with the little TVR, the car being gradually developed so that by 1965 its engine was pushing out 145bhp and its rather badly widened wheel arches were covering ugly steel wheels with fat tyres. At around this time the bodywork was treated to some fresh white paint with blue stripes.

▼ The above car a year later in its new livery and displaying flared arches over its wide steel wheels.

In its dramatic new livery, the Owen Mk3 was still racing in 1967, performing impressively in the Rothmans 12-hour sports car race at Surfers Paradise on the Gold Coast south of Brisbane. Co-driven by Graham Wood, David Haldane and Brian Lear, the TVR finished 6th in class and 14th overall from twenty-seven starters. After that, the car was eventually sold and would pass through several owners before finally

THE MONSTER FROM AMERICA

Aussie Export cont'd

returning 'home' and being restored in the UK some thirty-five years later.

As for Peter Owen's TVR import efforts – his business was called Motor Imports Pty Ltd – the trail runs dry after 1966. But while a few more Granturas and Mk3 1800S models are believed to have been sold in Australia, one Griffith V8 Series 400 certainly did reach Sydney during the second half of 1965. It had a cooking 195bhp engine, but a writer for *Modern Motor* magazine was amazed at the car's ferocious turn of speed, exclaiming: 'The performance was shattering'.

▼ The first TVR to reach Australia was back in the UK many years later to go classic sportscar racing. This is its 1965 livery. (Jim Lowry)

attempt to settle the company's future once and for all. So it was that the impressive Major Timothy Knott became Managing Director of the company in August 1964. Army training (he'd been a Cavalry officer) had left its mark in many ways. Slim and of average height, his immaculate appearance and strong personality were supported by a somewhat stiff upper lip which was resplendently decorated with a handlebar moustache. David Hives remembered how smart he always looked: "He polished his black shoes so brilliantly that you could see your face in them every day!"

Major Knott had previously had some experience in the motor trade, having been a production director at one of the Joseph Lucas factories in Birmingham. But once placed in full charge of Grantura Engineering's busy and often over-stretched production systems, he tended to betray a lack of understanding of both engineering and specialist car manufacturing. Compared to his experience in the Army, the Major also found the need for diplomatic factory labour relations quite unnatural.

THE EARLY YEARS

▲ In the USA Griffiths have become true classics and most have been restored.

▼ Although the Griffith 200 was replaced early in 1965, some examples weren't sold until several months later. This car ended up in Canada. (Tom Beatty)

The Hoo Hill staff didn't always appreciate a sudden warning informing them that the 'guardhouse' awaited them if they didn't act on orders quick sharp! Nor were they particularly amused when, having arrived late for work, they'd have to crawl sheepishly into the Major's office and receive a good ticking-off before being given back their time sheets. His routine was to stand by the time clock at five minutes to eight every morning and then, at two minutes past eight, remove the various offenders' sheets and take them to his office. The guilty men would then be docked at least fifteen minutes' money!

Though the Major's business methods were not ideally suited to a small company (just as Bryan Hopton's hadn't been two years earlier), his intentions were unquestionably honourable. Considering the circumstances, he'd taken on an extremely difficult job. The trouble was, he was too much of a stickler for rules, and it was just unfortunate that many of the Hoo Hill lads could not get on with him. David Hives' view on the situation was more forthright: "Everybody was frightened to death of him!" To a lesser extent, this category included Bernard Williams, who now began showing a tendency to slip away and spend more time on running Grantura Plastics, which of course still made all TVR bodies, including the Griffith ones.

While Bernard was retreating, another new member of the team was the rather grand Ralph Kissack, who was hired by Major Knott as Keith Aitchison's assistant on sales. An ex-Army officer who was about thirty years old, Kissack was from the Isle of Man, where his family was closely connected with Peel Engineering, maker of various bizarre microcars.

THE MONSTER FROM AMERICA

He was a very well-spoken, upright and respectable man whose upper lip displayed a waxed moustache and who more often than not smoked a pipe. A three-quarter length military coat, bowler hat and rolled umbrella were the trademarks of his extra-smart appearance every morning. Ultimately, Kissack would be promoted to sales manager, but sales patter would never be something that he felt completely comfortable with.

Other new recruits hired at this time were a book keeper called Nadine Hoyle and a production manager by the name of Joe Griffiths. Hoyle was soon to be promoted to company secretary, a position that later (at the end of 1965) enabled her to get up to some mischief. A quite amazing coincidence was that the boss of the London freight forwarding agency now being used to ship all the Griffith Series 200s to New York was called Jack Griffith! The latter arrangement was quite stable, but Joe Griffiths' time with TVR was short-lived. Fresh out of the Ford factory at Halewood, he was unaccustomed to the foibles of specialist car making...

It was on his very first day at Hoo Hill that he saw a couple of fitters trying to gently ease out a windscreen from a body because it didn't fit properly (the fibreglass surround would often need trimming to create a good fit). Griffiths considered the problem for a few seconds and told the fitters to let him sort it out. He then crawled into the unfinished car, laid on the centre tunnel, put his feet up against the screen and pushed hard. With that, the screen immediately snapped in two! This instant loss of credibility and other indiscretions led to him being fired within a very short time.

As Arnold Burton had predicted, things at Hoo Hill were once again looking worrying. The honourable Major Knott had marched straight into the sort of stressful scenario that was absolutely typical amongst the Blackpool ranks. Staff numbers had

▼ Difficult to get into, easy to unleash all that explosive power. Around 300bhp in a 1500lb car promised big fun. (Tom Beatty)

THE EARLY YEARS

◀ Built in 1965, this Griffith Series 200 was later imported into the UK to become another restoration job. (Rob Anderson)

been building up towards 100 and during 1964 production was at times running remarkably well, occasionally at up to as many as twelve cars a week (Griffiths *and* a small number of home market Grantura Mk3s). To get the Griffiths to Liverpool docks – a trip that was done every day – the company had been forced to buy a special pick-up truck on to which two cars would just fit. But the fact was that the V8 powered TVR rocket ship was clearly something of a 'special' and still labouring badly, despite all efforts, from under-development. News was regularly filtering back from the USA

▼ This 200 was originally a 1965 car and was restored much later. The American Racing Magnesium Silverstone wheels were Griffith factory options. (Sonny Poarch)

THE MONSTER FROM AMERICA

▲ Those aftermarket American-made wheels are chromed 15in Cragar Supersports. Otherwise it's a very understated car with subtle paint and black leather interior. (Rob Anderson)

▶ The above car's heavily tuned Hi-Po Ford 289 V8 produces a handy 360bhp at the flywheel and 310bhp @ 5400rpm at the rear wheels. (Rob Anderson)

that build quality was still patchy and the cars weren't all they should have been.

All the while, the hard-charging hot rod had continued gaining a hell of a reputation for its electrifying performance on the road. An excellent sales promoter, Jack Griffith had organised blanket advertising and publicity coverage (as already mentioned, the latter not always complimentary!) and it produced results. But he had not provided an advisory and back-up service equal to coping with his regularly wayward monster. To compound matters, American drivers, always notorious for their low driving standards, were not ready to be booted forward with such unbridled venom as the Griffith possessed. Dick Monnich's friend Gerry Sagerman took another view: "Once the customer had bought a Griffith he was on his own. This was no good for the average American because he wasn't too mechanically conscious. When the car refused to go, it would get shouted at and kicked hard, whereas an Englishman might just gently pat it, enjoy the challenge and calmly sort it out!"

Although its on-paper specification looked so sensational and it had by now certainly proved itself as one of the fastest accelerating cars in the world, in practical terms the

Griffith had so far not proved very competent. It had by now learned to stop reasonably effectively and had overcome its general preference for continuing in a straight line despite the existence of corners. But even with its overheating problems under control, its decidedly unscientific creation had left it with minimal ground clearance and inflicted it with excessively loud wind noise at speed. There was also a great tendency for the cockpit to become insufferably hot due to the proximity of the exhaust system to the driver's footwell.

Predictably, these reliability problems reflected strongly enough on operations at Long Island for Jack Griffith to start feeling serious disenchantment with a project he was once overwhelmingly enthusiastic about. Arnold Burton flew across the Atlantic to visit him at one stage. The Chairman's monthly appearances at the Blackpool factory had not kept him entirely in tune with developments in the USA, sometimes by design. He had been led to believe that the trip was a goodwill visit to sort out a few problems and discuss the latest plans for the Italian bodied TVR Trident. Once in Syosett, Arnold was met with the sight of Jack Griffith's expensive, well-staffed, modern factory, but was about to get an earful. "Jack showed me a pile of expensive engines and materials, plus a line of grotty, almost useless cars! It was just too devastating. Everybody must have been losing money hand-over-fist, not the least poor Griffith, who had sometimes paid for ten cars in advance and was angrily demanding that we take them back again!"

The great irony as the growingly unstable saga stumbled along through disruption and disorganisation was that weekly Griffith production at Hoo Hill was showing signs of increasing. More than once at this stage an impressive fifteen cars were built in a week – the most prolific production rate ever achieved for TVRs until much, much later. But Grantura Engineering was never far from serious hassle, as typified by the confusion that often arose through the lack of communication between manufacturer and importer. There was at least one occasion when, astonishingly, Grantura continued to ship cars across the Atlantic despite an angry Jack Griffith's refusal to pay for those he'd already got!

In the midst of all the kerfuffle, it could be argued that some aspects of the Anglo-American project were still looking positive. The Griffith was a hugely entertaining machine and people clearly

▲ Sprint and drag race meets were regular haunts for Griffiths during the mid and late 1960s. This is Tom Trudon's monstrous drag racer at the Connecticut Dragway in 1967. With a modified engine, it consistently ran the quarter-mile in the mid-10 second range.
(Clem Beauchemin)

wanted to buy exceedingly high-performance sports cars at affordable prices. So the news than an updated and much improved TVR bodyshell was under development at Blackpool was greeted with optimism – it looked like another big step forward. Visual changes for the new 'shell were a large, wrap-around rear window and a modern, cut-off Manx tail. There were no changes to the styling ahead of the cabin, but the new rear end gelled nicely and looked much more up-to-date.

With its modernised and more aerodynamic rear bodywork, the new Griffith was to be known as the Series 400 model. Once the whole Griffith operation had been moved into a larger factory at Plainview, Long Island, in December 1964, the Series 400 was scheduled for production in January 1965. The Series 200 model was still being made at this stage and, indeed, would carry on in production for many more weeks, so the two models would share factory space alongside each other. It's believed that well over 60 Series 200s were completed at Plainview during 1965, and they brought the final production total for that model to 192.

The outrageous, explosive, first-generation Griffith had certainly made its mark on the US automotive scene. It had also made a huge impact on TVR's rather inadequate Hoo Hill factory. Let loose amongst the American public, it had stunned enthusiasts with its awesome power, had burnt copious amounts of rubber on the road, been used for competition (mainly drag racing), created a wild and wicked reputation for itself, and thrilled, or scared, every driver who slipped behind its wheel. But there was more to come in 1965 and most of it was bad, very bad, news...

▶ 192 of these stunning Anglo-American hot rods were built. Despite the power of their Ford V8s, almost all Series 200 Griffiths were fitted with MG differentials and halfshafts. Following breakages, some cars later had their diffs replaced by Salisbury or Chevy Corvette units at the Griffith factory. (Sonny Poarch)

Competition in 1964

TVRS HAD BY now gained a much wider reputation for being competitive on track – thanks to their light weight, good performance and fine handling – so more and more drivers wanted to race the cars. During 1963 the factory, keen to encourage motorsport, had set in motion the construction of three lightweight Grantura Mk3s intended specifically for works racing during the coming season. They were bought by Alistair McHardy, Tommy Entwistle and Paddy Gaston.

Alistair's engine for 1964 was a tuned MGB 1800cc unit and it was to bring him plenty of success. First time out this year was at Goodwood on 14th March when he achieved an excellent third in class behind Brian Kendall's Morgan Plus 4 and the winning MGB of John Sharp. Motivated by his love of motor racing, Alistair found regular success through the season, gaining many outright wins and top-three class placings. In a marque scratch race at Aintree in June, he took the flag no less than seven seconds ahead of Ted Worswick's Austin-Healey 3000. At Brands Hatch in August, in another marque race, he had the distinction of taking the honours ahead of 1963 Freddie Dixon Trophy winner Tommy Entwistle, also beating the TVRs of Mike Sargeant and D.E. Gordon.

Despite being a very quick driver, Alistair never won any championships. His good friend Mary Wheeler was also racing a TVR for pleasure. After campaigning her dark green, Coventry Climax powered Grantura Mk1 for four years, in 1964 she upgraded her engine to a tuned 1622cc MGA unit – without any particular change in fortunes. As ever, Firle hillclimb in Sussex was one of her favourite venues, and she was always in action at the annual Brighton Speed Trials in September. In 1964's event she sprinted along the sea front driving her Grantura in the ladies' class against some stiff opposition, which included a Ferrari Berlinetta and a Jaguar D-type. She finished 4th out of the four cars in the class!

After winning the Freddie Dixon Challenge Trophy in 1963, Tommy Entwistle was looking for another successful season in 1964. Driving his works-assisted, MGB 1800 powered Grantura Mk3 lightweight, he had many close battles throughout the year, particularly with Alistair McHardy and Bernard Unett. Tommy performed superbly as usual but saw his efforts ruined by two unfortunate incidents. First he was forced to retire from a race at

▼ Having won the Freddie Dixon Trophy in 1963, Tommy Entwhistle challenged strongly again in 1964 until a heavy crash ruined his efforts. (Ferret Fotographics)

Competition in 1964 cont'd

Peter Simpson's open-mouthed Grantura leads an MGB at Silverstone in 1964. (Ferret Fotographics)

Crystal Palace late in September, due to a broken magnesium wheel, and then he had a major shunt at Brands Hatch the very next day.

Because he'd had to visit Paddy Gaston's garage in Kingston-Upon-Thames to borrow some widened steel wheels, he arrived at Brands too late for practice and had to start the race from the back of the grid. Recalled Tommy: "By the third lap I'd gone right through the field and on the last lap was chasing the leader, Bernard Unett, in his Sunbeam Alpine, when I lost it on a corner. Spinning out of control, I slammed backwards into the bank, which proved rather more substantial than my TVR. I virtually demolished the car and so handed the race series to Bernard. I wasn't a happy man and he went on to win the Dixon Trophy that year."

Like Tommy, John Howard 'Paddy' Gaston flew fighter

▲ Driving the ex-Nick Downie Grantura Mk2A, John Woollon eases past a Rochdale Olympic at Woodcote Bend, Silverstone, during a club race in September 1964.

Competition in 1964 cont'd

planes in the RAF during World War Two. In 1963 he took delivery from the TVR factory of his lightweight Grantura Mk3 with highly tuned MGB power, and gave it the notional number plate PG1. Gaston raced this car – often against Tommy – during the 1963 and '64 seasons without gaining any memorable results. In 1964 he took another Grantura Mk3 abroad for a few international events, including the 3-hours at Spa Francorchamps and the 500km and 1000km races at the Nurburgring in May. In the latter race his TVR was co-driven by Keith Aitchison and Adrian Dence and finished a creditable 48th from 100 starters.

All in all, the list of TVR race drivers for 1964 had substantially increased since the previous year, further names on track including Peter Simpson, Roger Stanger, Mike Sargeant, Charles Saunders and RG Caldicott. John Akers was again braving the bump 'n' thump world of autocross, while blasting up the hills this year were Bob Leach, GP Smith and Geoff Taylor. The latter was well known, not just for his regular successes but for the unusual 1600cc Sunbeam Alpine engine that was under the bonnet of his silver Grantura Mk2A. Usually gaining a top three class placing, he would continue to campaign the car in 1965 and, then, in 1966 would move on to Daimler V8 power in another TVR. As in 1963, TVR's factory entry for a place at Le Mans in 1964 was turned down – maybe a shame this time, because the entry was for a Griffith V8. With proper brakes and a decent water cooling system, it might even have raised a few eyebrows!

NB Competition in 1965 is fully covered in the main text of chapter eleven.

▲ Mike Sargeant corners hard in the ex-John Woolfe Grantura Mk2 at Snetterton in July 1964. (Ferret Fotographics)

CHAPTER NINE

Collapse in 1965

The restyle of TVR's rear bodywork, used for both the Griffith Series 400 and the Mk3 1800S, was a big success, but further trouble was looming with the New York docks strike early in 1965 – just as the revamped Griffith was being launched in the UK. Jack Griffith even put on an impressive five-car display at the New York motor show in April, but it was all too late. After major disagreements between the British and American companies, frustrated Chairman Arnold Burton finally pulled the plug on Grantura Engineering in September. TVR was out of business again!

Wild exaggeration was nothing new for Jack Griffith but, as it happened, the Series 400 badge he'd planned to use for 'his' Trident *did* materialise late in 1964 on a different car, identifying a body update for the Series 200 Griffith. Modernisation of the TVR bodywork's rear end styling – as used on both the Griffith and Grantura – had been on the cards at the Blackpool factory since late 1962 when Dick Monnich had first suggested it, but

▶ Notorious or not, Jack Griffith's Anglo-American hot rods were certainly wild and wonderful. Here's the man with a group of his machines.

it wasn't until autumn 1964 that development work at last began. Working in the Grantura Plastics premises above the brick kilns at Hoo Hill, and using a body taken off the production line, David Hives, Bernard Williams and Keith Aitchison toiled together forming the reshaped rear end by hand and then making a new body mould tool for production. It was the first major change to the 'standard' TVR bodywork for approaching seven years.

Bernard had initially been doubtful about whether the update was needed and whether the company could afford the cost. Keith Aitchison felt it was imperative that

◀ Appearing towards the end of 1964, the Griffith 400's new Manx tail was no doubt influenced by the chopped-off back ends of cars like the Shelby Daytona Coupé, Ferrari 250 GTO and other Italian supercars. (Peter Filby)

▲ The Manx tail was the biggest change yet to the TVR body shape and improved aerodynamic efficiency. Note the radically widened rear wheel arch of this road going racer. (Peter Filby)

the TVR should receive a new image. "Bernard and I talked about it several times and eventually he agreed. I felt we needed to give the car a large, sporty, wrap-around back window, something like the one on the low-production Alfa Romeo Giulia SS coupé. David and Bernard got the ball rolling by working on the new shape during evenings when everybody had gone home. We would then discuss the details and make changes where necessary."

Also influenced by the Ferrari 250GTO and Shelby Daytona Coupé chopped-off rear styling so typical of the era, the new TVR rear end's major change was indeed its vast Perspex rear window sloping down to a new vertical tail panel. It was a great improvement on the old shape, although Arnold Burton had reservations: "With the Trident on the horizon, my view was that we were giving the body its Manx-tailed styling only as a stopgap. Several different ideas were considered at this time and we even looked at developing an opening rear window, which was of course outside the time frame."

Keith Aitchison took credit for designing the new rear window – the shape of which, incidentally, would now be used in unchanged form from this point right through until the end of 1979 when the last Ford V6 powered 3000Ms were built. Said Keith: "Initially I felt we needed to create a visual difference between the models. For someone spending considerably more money, it didn't seem right that the Griffith and the MG powered cars looked the same. However, from a production efficiency point of view it made sense to use the updated body on all cars. Apart from the potential of the body flexing, the main reason we couldn't develop a hatchback was because the fuel tank was in the way and would have needed redesigning. We didn't have time for that."

Below its upturned top lip, the new TVR tail displayed Ford Cortina Mk1 'Ban the Bomb' circular rear light units – obviously the result of an eye well trained for detail design? Well no, not really. Bernard Williams' own Cortina Mk1 had been standing outside at the time and he needed to look no further! One other change brought

▶ TVR's new Manx tail bodywork was also used for the Grantura Mk3 1800, leading to a change of model name to simply Mk3 1800S. Those 'Ban the Bomb' tail lights were from the Ford Cortina Mk1. (Peter Filby)

about by the revised rear end was the spare wheel's new location: instead of being tucked away vertically at the very back of the cabin, it was now bolted down flat on the luggage floor above the final drive unit and fitted with a vinyl cover. It was slightly easier to remove although its new location was of no benefit to the already cramped luggage space!

However, according to the wonderfully eccentric, larger-than-life Bunty Scott-Moncrieff, there was at least one seriously useful benefit from the restyled TVR's greater area behind its seats. Visiting the factory one day, dressed in his classic country tweeds and still limping due to an earlier accident, Bunty spotted one of the new Manx-tailed cars sitting with its door open and its rear deck clear and uncluttered by any spare wheel. Rattling his stick around underneath the rear window, he came out with the immortal words: "Ah, at last a TVR in which you can have a good fuck!"

Surely, the owner would have had to be supremely agile and of supple body to use his car in the way Bunty suggested. Whatever, the significantly improved bodywork went into production late in 1964 and was soon standard for both the Griffith V8s and MG powered cars. For the latter, the letter 'S' was used to denote the update, the Grantura Mk3 1800 becoming known simply as the Mk3 1800S. For a while, both versions of the Mk3 continued to be available, but the 1800S soon started to sell better as a result of its modernised bodywork. Yet the last of the old-style cars would not leave Hoo Hill until mid-1965.

With the thundering American engined TVR causing so much fuss and controversy during 1964, the standard MGB engined car had been left to hold a somewhat crumbling fort in the UK. Because the factory had been so busy shipping Griffiths across the Atlantic and satisfying demand from New York, the V8 supercar wasn't officially available on the home market that year. Although a few left-hand-drive examples were sold to American servicemen customers of Bill Last in East Anglia, it's unlikely that many others slipped through the net. But bearing in mind the huge potential fun factor in a previously mild-mannered little sports car that had metamorphosed into a wild, fire-breathing monster, serious UK interest had mounted steadily in 1964. Fast drivers and serious racers wanted the quickest cars available and many of them were telephoning the factory urgently wanting to buy a machine that could clearly do battle with the Shelby Cobra and clean up on UK circuits.

It must have been extremely frustrating for British enthusiasts to know

▲ This January 1965 ad was the first to promote the Griffith in the UK. Viking Performance was a Bill Last company.

▼ Grantura Engineering's 1965 sales brochure. The Griffith 400 was promoted in Britain as the 200 V8.

COLLAPSE IN 1965

that almost all the Griffiths were heading across the Atlantic. Well over ninety per cent of that year's total production at Hoo Hill was consumed by Jack Griffith – it was just rather unfortunate that at times he'd suffered such severe indigestion on account of them! The small number of cars that didn't cross the big pond went to other countries such as Germany, South Africa and Sweden. In the 'States, although many Series 200 owners had been irritated by their cars' quirkiness, competition events had been a popular way to vent their aggression and the Griffith had proved almost unbeatable in a string of American speed challenges. By the end of 1964 the car had been homologated by the Sports Car Club of America to go track racing in 1965... Shelby Cobras had been warned!

Giving birth to the Griffith monster had been an extremely stressful experience for Jack Griffith. But as if the obsessed and eternally optimistic American entrepreneur hadn't already suffered enough setbacks in his attempts to outgun Carroll Shelby's Cobra, another nasty blow was about to hit – and it was eventually to result in a devastating knockout. Just as he was moving the entire project into a bigger factory at Plainview on Long Island, where the new Series 400 model was due to be made alongside the last sixty or so old-style Series 200s, in December 1964 came a big shock. It was apparent that American dock workers were planning a long strike that would have a drastic effect on the US east coast's import and export business. By January 1965 the strike was much more than a mere threat – it was very real and looking serious, and there didn't appear to be a quick solution to the argument.

▼ The anticipation of what was under that bonnet bulge! Thanks to its early 1965 launch on the UK market, at last British enthusiasts could get their hands on the Griffith! It debuted on the Viking Performance stand at the London Racing Car Show in January 1965. The model is James Bond girl Tania Mallett. (LAT)

Just as the disruption at the docks was beginning to bite, the latest Manx-tailed Griffith at last became officially available on the British market, getting its public launch at the Racing Car Show held at London's Olympia over the second half of January 1965. Its huge performance potential predictably causing a big fuss amongst showgoers, the display car appeared alongside a Mk3 1800S with tuned engine on the stand of Viking Performance Ltd, a company belonging to Bill Last, who had of course been a successful TVR distributor for several years. Griffith power options with the 4.7-litre Ford 289 V8 were still the mild (195bhp at 4400rpm) and wild (271bhp at 7000rpm) versions, and it was stated

201

that an even fiercer 400bhp unit was under development.

While the less powerful Griffith offered a front disc and rear drum braking arrangement as standard, the 271bhp Special Equipment model was now planned to have disc brakes all round. In fact, although this set-up was specified in a Grantura Engineering brochure, it never happened and both versions of the Griffith had disc/drum braking. But the two cars' cooling arrangements *were* different, the 195bhp engined version using a TVR radiator with single Kenlowe electric fan, the 271bhp car getting an advanced Kenlowe Radomatic system with twin fans. The robust Salisbury differential, as used on the E-type Jaguar, was standard equipment for both versions. Ford's all-synchromesh, close-ratio, four-speed gearbox remained as before and a press release stated that an automatic 'box was to be available soon. Both models used 5K x 15in, 72-spoke knock-off wire wheels with 185-section tyres.

Confusingly, the British Griffith's model name was initially TVR Griffith 200 V8 – despite the American market car now being known as the Series 400. Odd, but there must have been some logic there somewhere. What *was* logical for TVR was offering the car to British enthusiasts, because it seemed there would now be drastically reduced sales to the Griffith factory in the USA. Prices in the UK for turn-key Griffiths were from £1620 for the 'mild' model and from £1797 for the 'wild' one.

Customer orders were placed almost immediately after the Racing Car Show, all the early buyers being racing drivers anxious to get behind the wheel of a machine that

Designed by Bob Hallett, this new TVR logo and badge was gradually adopted on paperwork, PR material and bonnets from late 1964 onwards.

Lying in wait at Much Marcle, Herefordshire. Old-fashioned garage, old-fashioned brute power. Very few Griffiths were used solely as road cars. (Peter Filby)

▲ The last Griffith to carry the BFR 400B registration was the first right-hand-drive Series 400 car built by the factory to full production standard. (Peter Filby)

▼ Explosive acceleration was the Griffith's *raison d'etre*. This was the sort of view most other drivers tended to get of the Anglo-American hot rod. This 200 is another road-going racer. (Peter Filby)

was clearly a potential race-winner. One of them was Barnet Motor Company boss and high performance addict Martin Lilley. Martin's ownership of his Griffith, registered MMT 7C, would ultimately inspire an incredible new era in TVR history. This would begin at the end of 1965, but only after yet another major disaster for the marque.

Talking of disasters, TVR suffered a fairly serious one during the Racing Car Show. It concerned the pale blue, right-hand-drive, pre-production Griffith prototype (BFR 400B) built at Hoo Hill in mid-1964 as a 'mule' for development testing. Keith Aitchison had driven it from Blackpool to London to use it as a demonstrator during the show, and he recalled one particular 'demo' run with some horror. "Arnold Burton rang me at my hotel asking if his twin brother Raymond could have a drive. So on a Sunday morning I duly rolled up at this mews property just behind Downing Street and collected Raymond. Because he was a Ferrari Berlinetta owner, I was fairly relaxed about him driving the Griffith. But I did say to him: 'You'll find it quite quick, so keep your eye on the clock'.

"So off we shot, driving out of London and soon reaching the Kingston by-pass. The road was damp but there was good visibility and virtually nothing else around. We were doing about 100mph approaching a slight rise after which the road dipped away just before a speed control area. It was a bridge, I think. Suddenly, for no apparent reason, Raymond slammed on the brakes and everything locked up. We'd just lifted off the rise in the road and the car's weight was probably off the suspension. I think he might have used the brakes because he'd seen the speed limit sign ahead and realised we were doing quite a colossal speed. Anyway, he froze and didn't release the pedal.

"When the Griffith landed back on the road, we were sliding along broadside at about 90mph. Hell! I could see we were heading for a high kerb on the other side of the road, and all of a sudden there

THE EARLY YEARS

was a huge bloody wallop and the car lifted up. When we hit the 30mph speed sign, the passenger door burst open, snapping off the speed sign at ground level! Slowing down now, we then hit a tree and finally came to a grinding halt (mercifully still upright) when the car's rear end was largely demolished after we'd hit a concrete lamp-post. Apart from cuts and bruises we were both OK, but the Griffith was a total write-off, only the engine, gearbox and a few other bits being salvageable. It was a huge and terrifying accident."

With a stunning new, super-quick V8 missile just launched on the home market and a prestige GT coupé (the Trident) waiting in the wings, early 1965 should have been an important and exciting time for Grantura Engineering. On the face of it, despite the roller-coaster ride of 1964 things looked to be full of potential. Indeed, at the end of January it was reported in the motoring press that the company was set to move into a very much larger, ultra-modern factory close to Blackpool Airport. To make full use of the place, production was due to rise from 'the present 500 cars a year' to an incredible 'more than 1250 cars a year by the end of 1965'. Stirring stuff, indeed, but in reality it was a very badly timed media exaggeration created by Arnold Burton and Major Tim Knott. Whereas in previous crises TVR had usually hung on by the skin of its teeth, this time there was to be no escape from the growing storm. Sure enough, the factory move never happened.

But first, regardless of Grantura Engineering's crumbling foundations, the Griffith was about to receive several boosts to its reputation. Early in 1965 the factory carefully assembled a new demonstrator, effectively the first right-hand-drive, Manx-tailed Griffith built to full production standard. Turned out in sparkling medium blue paint, the superb machine was powered by a well tuned version of the 4.7-litre Ford V8 fed by a battery of three Holley twin-choke carburettors, which contributed to raising

▲ This Series 400 was completed at Griffith's Long Island factory in 1965 before being brought some time later back to the UK where its body and chassis were originally built. (Peter Filby)

◀ By the time Series 400 production was under way at the Blackpool factory early in 1965, disruption was already afoot across the Atlantic. The US dock strike was the main culprit and it was to have a shattering effect. (Peter Filby)

▲ The power of publicity. Finished in an amazing tartan-effect paint job, this early Griffith 200 show car is seen in a Griffith dealer's showroom. (Randy Hartigan)

power from the standard 271bhp at 6000rpm to something more like 350bhp at 6500rpm. Ford's four-speed, close-ratio gearbox and a Salisbury diff were in place to make the best of all that energy, and all-round disc brakes were fitted to haul the beast back from speed.

Following the dramatic demise on the Kingston by-pass of the first right-hand-drive Griffith prototype, its registration (BFR 400B) was transferred to the new car before it set out on a series of promotional sorties. One of the first was a trip to the March 1965 Geneva Motor Show, where the long-awaited Trident was finally making its public debut. The new BFR 400B was to be driven to Switzerland by Keith Aitchison, who was going to demonstrate to customers the kind of explosive performance the Trident would have when it reached the market. But the trip couldn't happen until a little problem had been sorted out.

Explained Keith: "Bernard had already raised the question of the new back window possibly popping out when the car was at high speed, but I thought it would be fine. So I set off from the factory, and halfway down the M6 motorway, when I was doing about 70mph and minding my own business, I suddenly thought hell, this is noisy. I then realised I could see daylight through the back – the window had popped out! What had happened was, in our rush to finish building the Griffith we'd forgotten that, by increasing the size of the window and giving it that shape, we'd get vibration and pressure from the air flow in the cabin. So I had to rush back to the factory where Bernard and his men quickly strengthened the aperture and fitted another back window. Everything was then fine, even at 169mph, the speed which Chris Lawrence later achieved in the car during testing at MIRA."

Back to rather grim basics, and it wasn't long before the US dock strike began to take its toll, causing serious cash-flow problems at Hoo Hill. Eating away at the stability of both English and American companies, the strike also created further disagreements between the two. Jack Griffith tried to import several Series 400s into the USA by air, but that simply wasn't economical. Yet, despite the disastrous situation, he still held out hope for his marque's future, taking a large, ambitious (and expensive) stand at the New York motor show in April 1965.

On display at the Coliseum that month were a standard Series 200, a Series 400, a full rolling chassis and a unique 200 painted for publicity purposes in a full tartan

▶ The Griffith company's five-car display at the April 1965 New York motor show included the tartan-effect car (above) and the elegant Apollo GT. The Apollo's presence was intended to generate interest in a forthcoming Griffith model. (Mike Mooney)

THE EARLY YEARS

colour scheme – supposedly the Griffith family tartan. Bizarrely, the car's engine had been painted white! At the earlier Boston auto show, where the extraordinary car had also been displayed, Griffith's entire show stand theme had been tartan and more tartan – involving the brochures, famous racing driver Mark Donohue wearing a tartan racing suit, and the stand's staff, who were all dressed in tartan kilts. And that included Jack Griffith himself!

A stylish 2+2 fastback coupé called the Apollo GT was also shown on the Griffith stand at the New York show, the car being intended as a taster for Griffith's next model, the all-new Series 600 set for launch in 1966. There was apparently no stopping the Griffith model range's expansion, but due to Griffith's growing difficulty with paying for Ford engine supplies, the 600 was scheduled for Chrysler/Plymouth power. The ever-optimistic boss had many friends within the Chrysler Corporation, but they were to be of little help to him – with few cars built, the Series 600 project was to fizzle out by the end of 1966.

While Griffith was clinging on to faint hopes for his troubled marque, BFR 400B, the latest British demonstrator, was seeing lots of action. Testing of the blue 'works' car on local Blackpool roads had by now become quite hilarious – it was a job that everybody loved doing. Often the brutally powerful machine would hammer so fast past a sneakily parked police car that the boys in blue had no time to take the offending registration mark, let alone have any chance of apprehending the car's ecstatic pilot.

The Hoo Hill main entrance was now regularly opened to such greetings as:

▲ Outside the Hoo Hill factory in spring 1965 are four Griffiths, a Grantura and the Trident prototype.

▼ In mid-1965 famous Morgan racing driver and wizard performance tuner Chris Lawrence developed BFR 400B's handling, braking and steering.

COLLAPSE IN 1965

'Aft'noon all, what's been goin' on 'ere then?' The uniformed visitors would always be made most comfortable, given cups of tea and chatted-up enthusiastically. Once softened, they were then commonly known to request the opportunity of experiencing the Griffith's ferocity and being seen – minus blue helmets – beside the test driver enjoying the sheer exhilaration of breaking the law at outrageous speeds!

David Hives even reckoned that he once took Bernard Williams for a test run in BFR 400B and thrashed it to over 170mph on the local Garstang Road, causing Bernard to hold on rather tightly. At slightly lower speed, in May 1965 Keith Aitchison gave the car its first competition outing at Tholt-y-Will hillclimb in the Isle of Man, while further drives took place in the hands of Tommy Entwistle and Chris Lawrence. The latter was a noted specialist car constructor and wizard performance tuning engineer, and over that summer he spent several weeks developing BFR 400B to fine-tune its handling, braking and steering. In an effort to generate publicity, he also drove it at international hillclimb meetings in Switzerland and France (*more on this in chapter eleven*).

Meantime, in the USA it seemed as though the Griffith operation was beginning to fall apart. Chosen because of his knowledge and experience, David Hives had been asked to fly to New York and help the Griffith organisation with development work on the modelling and body moulding of the new Griffith 600 project. Arriving at the Plainview factory in spring 1965, he soon found himself waylaid by mechanics wanting advice on engine bay problems with existing cars. "In fact," recalled David, "everything at Griffith's place seemed to be a mess. There were broken-down cars, fitters who weren't doing their job properly and too many men who appeared to just stand around much of the time! Here was this excellent set-up that was extremely inefficient and staffed by men who weren't producing much at all. It was shocking."

David's brilliant skills were soon proving of great benefit in the Griffith factory. Coincidentally, on one of his rare days off he had an unexpected meeting with Gerry Sagerman. "It was the day of the Vanderbilt Cup race at Roosevelt Raceway on Long

▼ Whilst concentrating hard during 1964 and '65 on building large numbers of Griffiths for the US market, the TVR factory continued to build small numbers of the Mk3 1800S but found little time to promote sales. Pictured in front of Egeskov Castle in Denmark, this example was built in May 1965. (Suzanne Griffin)

Island," he recalled. "I'd gone to enjoy the action and happened to notice one of the ex-Sebring 1962 Granturas being worked on. This chap Sagerman was getting hot and bothered trying to adjust the car's Weber carburettors and failing to get the engine running properly. I offered to show him how to do it, we got the job sorted and he went out and won the race! We became firm friends after that."

Sadly, the sexy looking Griffith Series 600 had little chance of getting unscathed through its creator's current predicament. Lasting more than four months, the dock strike nearly paralysed Griffith Motors Inc and, to make matters worse, at one point Griffith was stuck with a large number of cars that he couldn't remove from New York docks, tying up a large sum of money. At the same time, with only about fifty Series 400s despatched from Blackpool, Grantura Engineering's factory was choked up by another batch of cars in stock awaiting shipment to the 'States, with yet more in the pipeline.

Not surprisingly, the Ford Motor Co was no longer being paid by Griffith for its V8 engines and so pulled the plug on supplies. It was the final straw. The predictable knock-on effect was that about half the 100-strong labour force at Hoo Hill now learnt that they were being laid-off, while the deflated management considered how to urgently revitalise the British market for TVRs. This hadn't been properly promoted for well over a year and had dwindled accordingly, with only a small number (about seven or eight) of MGB powered Mk3 1800S models sold each month and a few Griffiths going to new owners from March onwards.

As for the engine-less Griffiths now marooned at Hoo Hill, there were heated discussions on how to dispose of them. A handful were eventually converted to right-hand-drive and sold in Britain, and a few were exported to Europe. TVR and Lotus dealer David Plumstead of Purley later shifted several examples but some didn't leave the factory at all. It had been a terrible year for Grantura Engineering and the damage had been done; the TVR marque was deep in the mire again.

▼ Paralysing all the docks along the east coast, the US dock strike had a disastrous effect on the Griffith and caused the demise of the project on both sides of the Atlantic. It was much later when this lovely car was imported into the UK. (Andrew Cliffe)

COLLAPSE IN 1965

▶ Most US competition Griffiths of the 1960s wound up on drag strips. This is Jim LoBianco's highly tuned Series 400 car at Connecticut Dragway circa 1968. (Randy Hartigan)

The once 'grrrrreat' Griffith's demise finally happened during the summer of 1965. Talk of impending disaster dominated the situation as Arnold Burton again flew to America in one last effort to repair the damage. Two more disputes had blown up with Jack Griffith, one concerning the money he owed Grantura Engineering, the other over his demands that the TVR Trident be called a Griffith (*another amazing story – see chapter ten*). There was clearly a serious personality clash between the two men, and Arnold made little headway in his discussions with Griffith. As if the dock strike hadn't already done enough damage to both the American and British companies, the upshot of the latest disagreements was that an angry Griffith cancelled his advance orders for Tridents and severed connections with Grantura Engineering altogether.

Totally frustrated by events, Arnold now asked Griffith's old friend Gerry Sagerman to take over the importation of standard MG powered TVRs, but Sagerman could

▶ Many years after they left the factory, Griffiths became extremely desirable collectors' cars. Superbly restored, this high performance Ford 289 engined Series 400 car is in virtually concours condition. (Andrew Cliffe)

209

well have been aware of the imminent collapse of Grantura Engineering because he politely declined. Returning to Blackpool, the Chairman next received the news that an approximate loss of £50 on each car supplied to Jack Griffith had been discovered by the accountants – due to the under-estimating of costings. Coming on top of the large losses already suffered, it was the final, final straw.

Arnold's financial support had already prolonged the unsettled TVR marque's life for nearly three years since the last failure. But now, so fed-up was he with the constant barrage of problems and the huge stress involved that he simply refused to provide any more money to keep the company afloat. One sad day in September 1965 an exasperated and disappointed Chairman held a directors' meeting at the factory (Bernard Williams had resigned shortly before, but Major Timothy Knott, Henry Moulds and Keith Aitchison were still on the board at this time) and announced that he was immediately suspending Grantura Engineering's operations and closing down the Hoo Hill premises. As simple as that. Having lost a huge amount of money – rumoured to be in the region of £200,000! – on an extraordinary automotive dream, Arnold then walked out of the factory for the last time.

▲▼ With wide wire wheels, the Griffith 400 looked menacing and purposeful. Just over 100 examples of this model were made.
(Derek Smith)

▶ Built at Hoo Hill in mid-1965, this car is believed to be the last but one original style Grantura Mk3 supplied for road use. Its first owner lived in Jersey. (Peter Filby)

For the other directors it was all very sudden. Major Knott was mortified and Keith Aitchison rather angry. "Despite all the problems," recalled Keith, "we and the workforce had toiled hard to create a very promising small motor manufacturer, and in many ways we were poised to do very well. I could only suppose that when Arnold saw Jack Griffith was not doing the job right, instead of sending more people over there to sort things out and get the job back on the rails, he got frightened and said 'To hell with it, I can afford to walk away from this'.

"Being totally in control, Arnold didn't come up with a plan B to take the company forward, he just shut it down. True, the Trident had by now swallowed all the money and there wasn't any left, but an extraordinary general meeting should have been held for Arnold to explain his intentions and allow the management (or anybody else) the opportunity to come up with a solution. What he did showed a complete lack of consideration for the entire remaining workforce. It was a great shame."

Amazingly, the TVR marque was out of business again – the third time it had happened in less than seven years – although at this stage some reports curiously said that Grantura Engineering was not actually in liquidation. Indeed, in October it was being claimed that takeover negotiations were taking place with an organisation in London that wished to remain anonymous. While a few 'remnant' cars were still at the factory waiting to be completed, it was also the ignominious end of an adrenaline-charged road for TVR's first big-engined, high performance chariot. The awesome but troublesome Griffith had at least played its part in sensationally establishing for the Blackpool company a tougher, more macho image, unfortunately to the point of notoriety. The TVR name now had a serious reputation thanks to its blindingly quick supercar, although that reputation had clearly already been interpreted in more than one way!

For TVR's unfortunate Trident, the timing of events could not have been worse. After all the earlier delays, the first prototype had attended the Geneva Motor Show and received tremendous acclaim for its beautiful styling. But, as with the Griffith, its immediate destiny was now sealed. Gathering dust in Carrozzeria Fissore's Turin factory, the third and fourth Trident prototypes ordered by Arnold Burton but both unfinished, also looked to be doomed.

Most Griffiths were all thrills and no frills, except when it came to their engines. Ford's 4.7-litre 289 V8 made the Cobra extremely fierce and the lighter Griffith an awesome monster machine! (Peter Filby)

Despite Grantura Engineering's collapse, some unexpected and ill-timed publicity appeared in two motoring magazines in October 1965. The tests could well have taken place in August or September, but both stories were published much too late to reverse the company's fortunes. The report in *Car* commented on the 195bhp Griffith looking its age but having a purposeful air in keeping with its character. The writer also appreciated his test car's brutal performance, stability at high speed, decent ride and direct steering, but unfortunately he was to suffer from something of a shock during the test. Here's how he described it: 'Top speed was purely academic with our TVR, since when we tried urging the reasonably accurate speedometer beyond the 125mph mark, there was a sudden violent explosion which we thought at first could only be the engine blowing up in the biggest possible way. It turned out to be caused by the leading edge of the glassfibre roof coming right away from the windscreen!' Of course, it wasn't the first time this had happened with a Griffith and the fellow was perhaps lucky that the back window didn't blow out too!

Autosport's coverage was rather more positive, but again its timing was mysterious, although it was possible that writer John Bolster simply didn't realise what had happened at Blackpool. The car concerned was Series 400 Griffith BFR 400B and it was lent to Bolster by its then keeper Chris Lawrence, who, after doing much development work on it, possibly hadn't been paid by the now defunct Grantura and had held on to the car in lieu of the money! Whatever, judging from a largely complimentary report, the writer was certainly stunned by the breathtaking performance provided by the tuned Ford V8 with its three twin-choke Holley carburettors.

Many American owners customised their Griffiths. This heavily developed and brutal looking Series 400 car is pictured during a driving test event in southern California. (Randy Hartigan)

COLLAPSE IN 1965

▲ With around 300bhp on tap, the Griffith was an unforgettable beast. But its production lasted only two troubled, turbulent years. (Andrew Cliffe)

▼ Dramatic paint finish for an ex-drag racing Griffith turned road car. (Clem Beauchemin)

Enthused Bolster, 'The sensation of unlimited power is something I shall remember for a long time. Deficient in certain details that would be properly installed in production cars, the test machine was nevertheless an extremely potent instrument. The whole personality of the car is dominated by the marvellous engine that is fitted to it. Over 150mph things become somewhat fraught (aerodynamically). One must either choose a still day or risk becoming one of *Those Magnificent Men In Their Flying Machines*. I think much of the trouble is due to excessive air pressure under the bonnet, for it burst open and rose in front of me, completely blocking my view'.

'Nevertheless,' continued Bolster, 'the car will reach 163mph in a remarkably short distance. It is well balanced on corners; the steering is quick enough to kill any unwanted changes of direction; there is a marked absence of roll; though the ride is not luxurious there is no pitching. The TVR gives racing performance through the gears and splendid flexibility'. On the negative side Bolster found: 'Too much kick-back on the steering wheel over rough roads, too much engine heat in the cockpit, and one could do with more ventilation'. His summing-up said: 'It's a brave man who can keep his foot down for long. As a car for long distance touring, it is utterly effortless and a sheer delight'.

Such positive impressions of a remarkable thunder chariot were all too late for Grantura Engineering, and the company was finally put into liquidation

◀ Griffith imports into the UK increased steadily from the 1990s onwards. This Surrey-based machine is an early Series 200 restored, modified and used for both road and racetrack. (Peter Filby)

early in November 1965. The Griffith era had lasted for two troubled, turbulent years and none of those closely concerned with the brutal machine would ever forget it. Nor would those owners and enthusiasts who'd been lucky enough to experience the savage and exhilarating performance of what was genuinely the fastest production car in the world: an all-thrills and no-frills supercar sensation.

At the end of the day exactly 59 Series 400 Griffiths went through the system of being built to near-complete form at TVR's Blackpool factory and having their engines and gearboxes installed at Jack Griffith's Plainview, Long Island, factory. A further 40 or so examples (the figure could have been as high as 50) are believed to have been built at Blackpool, some of these for customers in Canada, Britain and Europe, and at least one of them going to Australia. Later, in 1966, after a new company, Martin and Arthur Lilley's TVR Engineering Ltd, had resuscitated the marque, a further ten new examples of the Griffith would be built, six of these also being exported. Along with the 192 Series 200 Griffiths that left the Griffith factory in 1964 and '65, the total of all Griffiths built peaked at around 300.

Competition exploits in British Griffiths were braved by several fearless drivers in the monster's latter days of production: Arnold Burton, Malcolm Dungworth, Geoff Wilson, Chris Lawrence and Peter Bolton played their parts on the hills, and Martin Lilley raced his car at several circuits in 1965. Also in Griffith track action that year were David Plumstead, Ted Worswick, Peter Simpson, Doug Hardwick and Dr Euan Paul (*more on all this in chapter eleven*). Also, after two or three TVR outings in 1965 a hugely exciting and quite brilliant driver called Gerry Marshall was to spend much of the '66 racing season entertaining fans with his tremendous, controlled sideways antics in the Lilley car.

◀ After Grantura Engineering's collapse in autumn 1965, TVR dealer David Plumstead of Purley, Surrey, acquired some of the final Griffiths.

Griffith's Final Flourish

FOREVER FULL OF hope and determination, the boundlessly enthusiastic Jack Griffith was one of those individuals who was totally smitten by the dream of building his own car – to the complete detriment of his bank balance! In the spring of 1965, at around the time disagreement began over his wish to call the TVR Trident a Griffith (and following the Trident's debut at the Geneva show in March), Mr Griffith had the first prototype shipped to New York for assessment. He decided against importing the car, feeling it was impractical, too cramped inside, too expensive and not enough car for the money. Yet, even as Grantura Engineering was going through its death throes in September and October that year, the resolute American was still working to keep his own marque alive with another luxury GT car, the Griffith Series 600.

At the New York motor show in April 1965, the large Griffith stand had seen two Series 200s and one Series 400 sharing space with a sleek, steel-bodied 2+2 fastback coupé called the Apollo GT. Using Buick power in a body/chassis unit made in Italy by Frank Reisner's Turin-based Carrozzeria Intermeccanica, it seems most likely that the Apollo GT was displayed as a stopgap while arrangements were being made to design and develop an all-new two-seater coupé initially powered by Ford's 4.7-litre 289 V8. Retaining a front end very much like the Apollo's but featuring a notchback hardtop, this was to be the Griffith 600.

The new car finally came about at the New York International Automobile

▼ Styling-wise, the Griffith 600 was a huge leap forward from the Series 400 TVR body shape. But the project was another disaster for Jack Griffith, only ten examples being made. (Mike Mooney)

Griffith's Final Flourish cont'd

Show in April 1966, where the sleek Griffith coupé was the only all-new car on display. With power now coming from the 4.5-litre Plymouth V8 (the prototype had been 289 Ford engined but there had been problems with engine supplies from Ford – in other words, Ford was no longer prepared to deal with Griffith!), the car's styling was by Robert Cumberford and it was conceived as direct competition for the Corvette Stingray and E-type Jaguar. David Hives had spent some time at the Griffith factory working on the car with Griffith and Cumberford, and at one stage it was even being proposed that TVR's Blackpool factory was to handle production.

Although the first few Griffith 600s had steel bodywork, it was intended to use fibreglass bodies for production examples. Manufacture of the semi-monocoque steel tub was to be by Carrozzeria Intermeccanica. The hopelessly ambitious initial target was to shift 650 cars in 1966 through the large number of Griffith outlets already existing for the Griffith V8 but, as it happened, only a small number (informed sources say it was just ten) of body/chassis units were ever delivered to Griffith's Long Island premises. With Griffith finally running out of cash, the story was all over by the end of 1966, many engine-less cars being unsold and left to gather dust. In further last-ditch attempts to keep alive what looked like a potentially viable up-market sports car, the Series 600 was next offered by another company and called the Omega (thirty of these hit the streets), and then again as the Intermeccanica Italia. Sadly, neither edition enjoyed much success.

CHAPTER TEN

The Trident Dream

With styling that could be traced back to 1958, the Grantura Mk3 was by 1965 sorely in need of more modern bodywork. Revealed at the Geneva motor show in March 1965, TVR's fresh injection of style and prestige came in the form of the strikingly attractive Trident prototype. A beautiful luxury GT car with styling ahead of its time, it looked as though it could take Grantura Engineering up to a new level with ease. But it sadly ended up during the disastrous period of Grantura's closure in autumn 1965 as 'the TVR that got away'.

It was back in 1962 that the Grantura's multi-tubular chassis had first been the subject of discussions about a rebodying exercise. Individual though it was, the TVR shape was looking dated. The possibility of a more exotically styled bodyshell was considered a priority by then Managing Director Bryan Hopton, but the reality was that TVR Cars Ltd simply had no funds to make it happen. Indeed, during October that year the over-stretched Blackpool company plunged into liquidation.

▶ The Trident's gestation period was close on three years but it was well worth the wait. The final result was quite stunning.

THE EARLY YEARS

The final indignity of commercial failure unfortunately happened during the British International Motor Show at Earls Court, where TVR had put on a last-gasp display. Ironically, one notable visitor to the doomed stand was a young British designer called Trevor Frost, who chatted at length with Bernard Williams about an all-new TVR design. Born in Sheffield of an Italian mother and English father, Frost had worked at Standard-Triumph at the age of seventeen, but once he'd graduated into the design business he'd elected to use his exceptional artistic ability to create beautiful cars. For added effect, he also changed his name to Fiore – Italian for flower. This was principally to help him gain entry to the élite group of world-famous Italian car designers, and it worked. Basing his operations in a Paris studio, he soon had a good working relationship with the coachbuilding firm Carrozzeria Fissore of Savigliano, Turin. It was Fissore that put him in touch with TVR.

▲ Stylist Trevor Fiore's early '60s design for a Lea Francis roadster (top) directly inspired his ideas for the TVR Trident roadster. The similarities between the two concepts are very clear.

The origins of what was to become the TVR Trident shape could first be spotted in an earlier Frost project that failed to reach fruition. It was intended to become the Lea Francis Francesca, a restyled version of the bizarre Lea Francis prototype that had appeared at the British motor show in 1960. Frost had designed a 'family' range of 2+2 coupé, four-seater saloon and open roadster models, all along similar lines and all to be built by Fissore. The roadster, complete with its amazing, and potentially dangerous, outside exhaust pipes, was claimed to have attracted an order for a thousand examples from an American distributor. A slightly exaggerated figure, one would imagine, but the car certainly had smooth and very advanced styling for its day. However, work at Fissore never got further than the styling buck stage, for the Lea Francis company ran into financial difficulties and was forced to cancel the project.

Thanks largely to Bernard Williams and a handful of dogged TVR stalwarts, new life was being breathed into the brand early in 1963 and a few more Grantura Mk3s were being made. Bernard and Trevor Fiore were again in contact and it wasn't long before the two men met for lunch at The Derby Arms pub at Treales, Lancashire, not far from Blackpool. Using a felt pen, the designer explained his ideas for a new TVR by drawing them on a table napkin. There were clearly similarities to the earlier Lea Francis designs but the proposed shape had developed and matured.

The problem was that Grantura Engineering was way out of its financial depth in

THE TRIDENT DREAM

even considering a new model at this point. Everyone at the factory was enthusiastic and American importer Dick Monnich was very keen, but for now the plans would have to remain plans. Frustrated, Fiore (as he now preferred to be called) moved on and offered another 'take' on the same styling theme to Elva Cars, maker of the well known Courier and a successful mid-engined sports racer. This time Fiore got a result and styled the beautiful bodywork that Fissore made to clothe three of those Elva sports racer chassis.

Powered by BMW and known as the Elva-BMW GT160, the gorgeous road racer caused a sensation at both the Italian and British motor shows during 1964, though production never progressed any further than the three cars.

Had TVR missed out on a fabulous new model that could have changed its history? Thanks to Arnold Burton, not quite. At last, early in 1964 when Arnold was the financial backer and Chairman of Grantura Engineering, the Fiore proposal for an outstandingly good looking TVR prototype was given the go-ahead. The surprise was that the car was to be a coupé, not a convertible.

Closely involved in the project was Grantura Engineering's Marketing Director Keith Aitchison. "Arnold was exceedingly enthusiastic about the Trident. His view was that we needed something better than the Grantura – a more prestigious car with stunning looks, big performance and more practicality. Arnold was happy to use his own money to fund the car, and originally it was going to be a convertible. Getting the green light for the project meant we were all fired-up for the future. We felt the Trident was the potential key to producing some really grown-up motor cars with beautiful bodies."

But first there was a hurdle to clear. Recalled Keith: "We wanted to make the convertible first, but over in the 'States neither Dick Monnich nor Jack Griffith wanted a soft top despite the Americans' general love of open top motoring. In fact, for some inexplicable reason Griffith would not give me an order for the Griffith V8s unless we agreed to make the Trident a fixed-head coupé. I had to go along with his demands, but I felt we were making a significant mistake. We would have sold a lot

▼ Frustrated by TVR's inability to press ahead with his Trident designs, Trevor Fiore styled the superb GT160 for Elva Cars. Standing only 40in high, it was mid-engined and used 1991cc BMW power. It was capable of 160mph. (Peter Filby)

of convertibles and they would have featured a boot, which wasn't possible with the coupé."

Early 1964 was of course the period when the ultimately disastrous Griffith V8 saga was beginning to rumble into action. Jack Griffith was intent on charging headlong towards what he believed was a great future manufacturing high-performance sports cars, so the Trident had appeared at just the right time. Despite his demand for the coupé version, late in March he took the liberty of issuing a release to prospective dealers describing 'his' two new models, the Griffith Series 400 and 600, both of them to be built at his factory in Syosset, Long Island. Shown in the release as Fiore drawings, these Griffiths were in fact unmistakably the Trident convertible (Series 400) and the Trident coupé (Series 600). The American was in a hurry, as ever.

For added practicality, the new design called for a longer chassis than the existing Grantura Mk3's 7ft 1.5in wheelbase assembly. So chief design and development engineer David Hives stretched a chassis to create a wheelbase of 7ft 6in. This, incidentally, was the first use of the chassis that would eventually become TVR's standard assembly on all cars from late 1968 to early 1972.

Once complete with all suspension and a 4.7-litre Ford V8 engine, the new rolling chassis was airfreighted from Manchester airport to Fissore in Italy. Said Keith Aitchison: "The original plan was for us to trailer the chassis all the way down to Turin, but because of growing pressure to get the finished car to the Geneva motor show in March 1965, we were extremely short on time. Subsequently, Arnold Burton and I drove there together with both our car and a trailer loaded with all the small components needed by Fissore to complete the show Trident. This was early in 1965 and it was already looking like the tightest of schedules to launch the car at Geneva. They were running very late."

In traditional TVR style, the international debut of the company's stunning new prestige GT machine wasn't progressing entirely to plan. Indeed, as the deadline got tighter and tighter, the only solution was for Fissore to deliver the car direct to Geneva. Even then, it wasn't 100% complete or even roadworthy. But it *was* the star of the show...

Finished in light primrose yellow paint and displayed alongside the new mid-engined De Tomaso Vallelunga on Fissore's own stand, the Trident prototype caused

◀ An extended version of the Mk3's chassis was used for the Trident. From a 7ft 1.5in wheelbase assembly, as used for the car shown here, a carefully engineered stretch brought the wheelbase up to 7ft 6in.

THE TRIDENT DREAM

▶ The Trident made its long-awaited public debut on the Fissore stand at the Geneva motor show in March 1965. It was one of the show's stars. Next to it was a De Tomaso Vallelunga. (Keith Aitchison)

▼ This March 1965 ad by TVR shows that somewhat premature marketing of the Trident was already under way.

quite a sensation. Trevor Fiore's superb and smoothly dynamic styling was unquestionably ahead of its time and became one of the major talking points of the show. Outstanding features were the sharply dipping nose, the pop-up headlamps and the great expanse of glass, which included an enormous rear window set at a rakish angle. Whatever angle it was viewed from, the car had amazing presence.

Fashioned mostly in aluminium and including some steel inserts for added structural strength, the Trident's crisply styled body sat atop a Grantura Mk3/Griffith chassis that was standard except for its extra length. Suspension was thus regular but uprated TVR fare – independent all round with unequal length wishbones and coilspring damper units. Under the bonnet was the 271bhp high performance version of Ford's 4.7-litre V8 powerpack with an all-synchromesh, four-speed manual gearbox driving through a Salisbury limited-slip differential. Cooling was looked after by a top-of-the-range Kenlowe radiator with twin fans, while each 6J x 15 Dunlop wire wheel had 72 spokes and was backed by a Girling disc brake – a luxury for the period.

In the luxurious cabin was a left-hand steering wheel, two adjustable bucket seats, a polished wood-panelled dashboard, leather trim, electric windows, deep pile carpets and reasonable luggage space in the rear above the 18-gallon fuel tank. It was truly a prestige package, but Arnold Burton wasn't entirely satisfied. "The original design's headlamps were a major error," he groaned, "because they were below the English legal height and had to be converted to pop-ups. And there was no easy access to the spare wheel, which had to be lifted out from the back of the cabin and over the seats. This was hardly desirable in a luxury car."

The Trident's expected performance was just about everything that could be asked of a V8 powered grand tourer. It was no lightweight (about 20cwt) but acceleration was said to be explosive and a maximum of 150mph quite possible. Just in case anyone doubted these claims, parked in the exhibitor's car park just outside the Geneva show halls was BFR 400B, Grantura

▸ Aluminium bodied with steel strengthening sections incorporated, the sleekly styled Trident was arguably ahead of its time. But why didn't that vast rear window open for access to the luggage deck?

Engineering's latest Manx-tailed 271bhp Griffith V8 demonstrator. A freighter aircraft had flown it from southern Britain to northern France and Keith Aitchison had then driven it non-stop through the night to reach Geneva in time for the show's opening day. The intention was that the Griffith should back up the Trident's launch by demonstrating to customers its potential performance. Keith was in charge: "I demo'd the Griffith many times but was continually pulled over by speed cops. They mostly wanted to know what it was."

Only two TVR men worked on the Fissore stand at Geneva: Keith and Major Timothy Knott. The great buzz generated by the Trident kept them both busy and, not surprisingly, after the show ended the publicity machine started to get out of hand. One announcement stated that Grantura Engineering had somehow received orders worth £150,000, not just for the Trident but also for the Griffith and Mk3 1800S models! There was talk of setting-up a dealer network with outlets in Switzerland, France, Germany, Holland, Belgium and Spain. There were even suggestions, not for the first time, that the company would expand with greatly increased production in a new factory at Blackpool Airport.

Aside of the hype, everybody at TVR was very excited about the fabulous new Trident, and the publicity it generated was indeed massive. All over the world newspapers and motor magazines featured pictures of the car, while an English *Daily Mail* headline read 'The Most Beautiful Car in the World?'. On the back of all this acclaim, Grantura's aim was to fit its prestige coupé into a particular marketing niche –

▾ According to Arnold Burton, the pop-up headlamps came about after a mistake with the height of the original design's fixed headlamps.

THE TRIDENT DREAM

▲ There were small differences between the first two Trident prototypes built by Fissore. The car above, for instance, had shallower side sills than the car below.

▼ TVR's sales manager Ralph Kissack, seen here at the wheel, believed the Trident would move TVR into a more prestige league.

a highly desirable motor car that was extremely fast, more individual and more luxurious than the Jaguar E-type and, with a proposed £3400 price tag, much cheaper to buy than an Aston Martin. Despite the enormity of little TVR challenging the likes of Jaguar, Aston Martin and maybe even Ferrari and Maserati, the Trident seemed to have the potential to make a genuine impact on the top echelons of the international motor industry.

Grantura Engineering's sales manager at this time was Ralph Kissack, and he was certainly a positive believer: "We want to make a name for ourselves for quality and performance. Perhaps in eighteen months we will be accepted in the class of Ferrari and Alfa Romeo." Well, a true salesman would of course be impotent without such starry-eyed self-belief and such a natural ability to exaggerate! About thirty years old, Kissack was yet another of the interesting characters that seemed to thrive at the Hoo Hill works. An 'old school' ex-Army type who was an extremely decent and dignified man, he smoked a pipe and, of course, wasn't lacking in the humour department – always a vital ingredient for anybody working at the TVR factory.

After its triumphant debut at Geneva, the Trident prototype was flown back to Britain to receive its finishing touches at Hoo Hill and be made roadworthy. Its show announcement had made a huge impact but was there a big question mark over what

seemed like an excessively ambitious project for a firm of Grantura Engineering's size and resources? Keith Aitchison was guardedly confident. "The good thing was that we didn't have to start out from a clean piece of paper and design everything from scratch. There was a great deal of upbeat enthusiasm at the factory for what we'd already got, so to step up to a more grown-up car was not a big deal. The chassis and engine were no problem; it was just a rebody job after that. Fissore would have built them, maybe at the rate of approximately 200 per annum."

▲ On a publicity visit to Leighton Hall hillclimb in Lancashire.

Ralph Kissack's naively over-optimistic publicity blurb had suggested that the Trident *could* be in production by June 1965, but first a vital link in the chain had to be secured. Over in the USA, Jack Griffith needed to see the car and give it his approval. Good sales in America were of paramount importance to the whole project. With a second prototype in existence around April or May (it was again a left-hand-drive coupé and had the same mechanical specification as the first car), one example was flown to New York for Griffith to check over.

Bearing in mind that almost twelve months earlier he had confidently trumpeted the sleek, sharp-edged coupé as his forthcoming Series 600 model, Griffith's reaction to the Trident was quite extraordinary, as confirmed by Gerry Sagerman. "Jack saw the car at New York Airport, did not like it and would not accept delivery of it. Any stories about him banging his head on entering the car, and there not being enough headroom inside, were completely wrong because he could *not* get into the car! It was still strapped to the shipping pallet, which didn't allow the door to open fully, and there was also a large package behind the driver's seat prohibiting the seat's rearward movement."

Continued Gerry: "The next thing that happened was that Arnold Burton called me, asked me to collect the Trident from the airport and suggested I should look after it and display it to interested parties at my convenience. Although I showed it off at several racing circuits, the car was not displayed at the New York show, as originally intended, and was never offered for sale in the USA. It was eventually shipped back to Blackpool late in 1965 at the request of Arthur Lilley, the new owner of TVR."

With Jack Griffith's support crumbling, the Trident's future appeared to need fresh impetus. It was early summer 1965 and already financial nightmares were being caused at Hoo Hill by the mess surrounding

▼ TVR's brochure for 1965 offered a terrific range: the Mk3 1800S, Griffith and Trident. It was a great shame that the company went bust in September that year.

THE TRIDENT DREAM

the Griffith V8 after the US dock strike had so badly disrupted production. Nevertheless, the Trident now appeared as part of the TVR range in a new brochure and was offered in both left-hand and right-hand-drive versions. Despite ominous warning signs, there was apparently still some confidence in the boardroom at Grantura Engineering. Indeed, Arnold Burton now authorised the building by Fissore of two more Tridents of unchanged mechanical specification, again using 7ft 6in wheelbase TVR chassis which were flown out to Turin. One of these cars was the first convertible roadster, the other being another coupé, both of them being right-hand-drive. It seemed that 'the most beautiful car in the world' and its modest British manufacturer were apparently still hopeful of some sort of future.

In truth, there was no hope. There were several reasons for this, the key one being that neither Griffith Motors nor Grantura Engineering were anywhere near financially strong enough to emerge unscathed from the disastrous effects of the US dock strike. Both factories were struggling badly over the way the Griffith V8's bubble had burst, and they'd both lost a lot of money.

In Blackpool, Trident production had *not* yet been organised and was looking extremely unlikely for 1965. In Long Island, New York, Jack Griffith had made known his views on the Trident and had gone off at a tangent by getting involved in the development of the new Bob Cumberford-designed Griffith 600. Disagreement between the English and American companies over calling the Trident a Griffith had

▼ The third Trident prototype appeared after TVR's demise in September 1965 and was displayed in unfinished form on the Fissore stand at the Turin motor show in November. It wasn't fully completed until 25 years later! (Peter Filby)

already compounded matters, and then came the final blow. Having endured something of a nightmare with his car-making attempts so far, Griffith angrily pulled the plug on all his connections with Grantura Engineering. It was the end of a turbulent relationship that had initially been so full of promise.

Things at Blackpool were now desperately bleak and lasted only until September, when Arnold Burton closed down Grantura Engineering. Trident development costs to date were alleged to have hit the £30,000 mark, but of course that was only a fraction of what Arnold had lost overall on funding the company. Two casualties of the sad situation were the third and fourth Tridents being built by Carrozzeria Fissore. With no further payments forthcoming, the Italian coachbuilder halted work and put the two incomplete cars into storage. It was the ignominious end to a brilliantly styled prestige car that just *could* have transformed TVR's future. Sadly, the Trident dream was over.

Trident Tribulations

WHEN GRANTURA ENGINEERING went down the pan in September 1965, the highly acclaimed TVR Trident went down too. Its only hope of being revived, and possibly reaching production status, was if the TVR name, assets and production rights were to be bought by a new company. After all, the Trident was surely an extremely desirable part of those assets.

Both Trevor Fiore and Carrozzeria Fissore were owed significant sums of money upon Grantura's collapse. With the Trident project halted and in limbo, Fiore no doubt felt the design rights still belonged to him. Possibly assuming that a TVR resurrection was unlikely, he had little to lose by meeting a trio of TVR people who'd come up with a surreptitious scheme to 'acquire' the Trident while its existence was shrouded in doubt and disarray. Members of the trio were TVR's long-time East Anglia dealer Bill Last, the Coventry dealer Peter Simpson and one Nadine Hoyle, a close friend of Simpson's and, until the collapse, Grantura's company secretary.

To say that Last, Simpson and Hoyle's intentions weren't entirely honourable wouldn't be far from the truth. Though there was clearly some doubt over ownership of the Trident design rights, the Fissore executive who dealt with the tricky trio could be forgiven for being led to believe by Bill Last that he was representing TVR interests on an official basis. The result was that a deal was done, Last commissioning the construction at Fissore of his own completely new Trident, a convertible roadster based on an archaic Austin-Healey 3000 chassis. Power was to be Ford's 4.7-litre 289 V8, as used by TVR's Tridents.

Under the murky cover of Grantura Engineering's liquidation, the Trident had stealthily slipped into new hands. Finished in metallic light blue, Last's new prototype first showed its face to the world in January 1966 at the Racing Car Show in London, being shamelessly displayed by his company Trident Cars Ltd. With slightly longer and wider bodywork, it looked very similar to the TVR version but featured some detail restyling (by Fiore) that did it no favours. The front end, for instance, displayed a revised headlamp arrangement which recessed the lights into unattractive cut-outs in the bonnet's leading edge. Also distinguishing the revived Trident were two chunky, and rather clumsy, hot air outlets in each body side panel ahead of the doors.

Whatever question marks there were over who owned the rights to the genuine TVR Trident, Bill Last had seen his opportunity, moved sharply and taken advantage of a confused situation. But progress with his new acquisition was to be slow and unstable. A 2+2 fixed-head coupé Trident called the Clipper V8 GT was at last offered to the public in kit form late in 1966. Incredibly, Grantura Plastics at Hoo Hill made the first few glassfibre bodies for that version. The next ten years, however, were to see the Trident struggle to exist through model name changes, engine and chassis changes and different companies. None of them ever did justice to what had started out as a brilliantly fresh and extremely desirable luxury sports car.

◀ Bill Last's revised Trident roadster made its debut at the London Racing Car Show in January 1966. It was easily identified by its recessed headlamps and chunky hot air outlets behind the front wheels.

CHAPTER ELEVEN

1965 - Racing for Survival

1965 was a disastrous year for TVR maker Grantura Engineering. Not only did the troublesome Griffith V8 reach the end of the line but the lovely Trident was 'lost' to another company. September saw Grantura's operations grind to a halt and, indeed, the Blackpool sports car appeared to be dead. But bursting with energy during this gloomy period and keeping the TVR name alive was the marque's increasingly active racing fraternity, amongst which were key names such as Tommy Entwistle, John Wingfield, Martin Lilley and Gerry Marshall.

Spending all their funds, time and resources trying to sort out the troublesome Griffith V8 and get the Trident project under way, the directors and workforce of Grantura Engineering were chasing lost causes during 1965. Without the New York dock strike early in the year, maybe, just maybe,

▼ Martin Lilley's first involvement with TVR came via his early 1965 purchase of a Griffith Series 400. Car and owner are seen here in race action at Brands Hatch early in the '65 season.

◀ Though it was somewhat neglected by TVR's marketing and sales people during 1965, the Mk3 1800S continued to be made in limited numbers. (Peter Filby)

Grantura might have survived and stabilised. Any dreams of prosperity during that summer were, however, completely academic – between them, the wayward Anglo-American hooligan and the expensive Anglo-Italian seductress really knocked the stuffing out of the Blackpool company.

Home market cars in production in 1965 were the MGB engined Mk3 1800S, which had now lost the Grantura part of its name, and limited numbers of the Griffith V8, both models adorned with the Manx-tailed bodywork first introduced on production cars late in 1964. Whilst concentrating on making the Griffith and furthering development of the Trident, the men of Grantura Engineering had unwisely neglected the 1800S and sales had dwindled as a result – a great shame as it was an extremely competent sports car. Indeed, it was ever so slightly more competent when during 1965 its engine gained a power increase from 94 to 98bhp at 5400rpm, allowing marginally improved performance.

Continued motor trade support for TVR cars saw most of the company's established dealers and distributors still trying hard to keep home sales moving at this difficult time. East Anglia dealer Bill Last had launched the British market Griffith on his Viking Performance stand at the January 1965 Racing Car Show in London, and was signing-up new customers (mostly racing drivers) whenever he could. Also promoting the brand at the Racing Car Show had been Grantura Engineering's own stand displaying a Mk3 1800S, and James Bond girl Tania Mallett was there to help promote the TVR name. Laughed Keith Aitchison: "She looked amazing in a thin white trouser suit, but she was a stroppy bag!"

▼ Racing driver Paddy Gaston had taken over London's TVR Centre by early 1965 and was running it from his garage in Kingston, Surrey.

1965 – RACING FOR SURVIVAL

Further efforts to help keep the TVR name alive during 1965 were coming from Peter Simpson's Coventry garage and a sports car dealer called David Plumstead, who had garage premises in Purley, Surrey, and had been a TVR specialist since spring 1964. There had been changes at the London TVR Centre (as run by James Boothby), which hadn't sold many cars and was no longer an 'official' factory-supported organisation: since October 1964 this honour had been transferred to a reformed centre at the Kingston upon Thames, Surrey, garage run by TVR racing driver Paddy Gaston. And then there was Martin Lilley, whose Barnet Motor Company became a TVR dealer in spring 1965. But through the long, hard summer of 1965 none of these people were finding it at all easy to sell TVRs.

Over the years the entry-level TVR had matured nicely and had become a civilised, entertaining and well-mannered machine. But compared to the brilliant Lotus Elan, the stunningly styled Marcos 1800 and even mass-production sports cars such as the MGB and Triumph Spitfire, the Mk3 1800S was showing a few wrinkles – even with its latest Manx tail. Its main charms were its individuality, exuberance and personality, while its overall character was truly stoical. This had always given the marque a loyal band of supporters, some of whom had reformed the sometime defunct TVR Car Club at a meeting on Bill Last's stand at the January 1965 Racing Car Show.

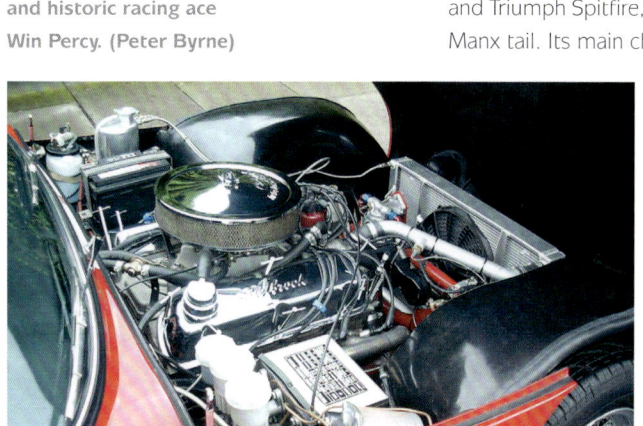

▼ This Griffith 400 was built in 1965 at the time when things were beginning to look bleak for Grantura Engineering. With a fully tuned Ford V8 producing over 350bhp, it was later owned by Le Mans winner and historic racing ace Win Percy. (Peter Byrne)

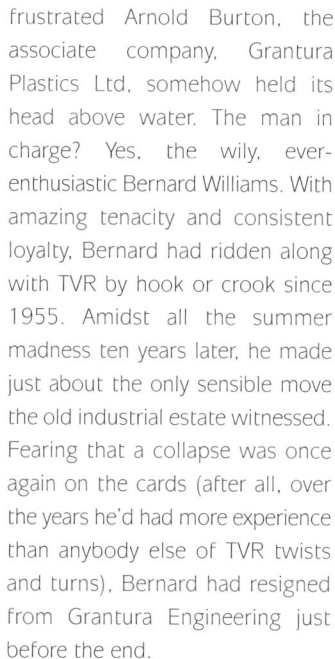

Last kindly made space for the club to promote itself for the duration of the show, an effort which enrolled many new members from around the country. With TVR dealer and racing driver Peter Simpson acting as Chairman, the club became RAC registered the following September, by which time a rough total of 900 TVRs and derivatives had been built. Now, in August 1965, it sadly seemed that the magic total of 1000 might never be reached. But, as ever, there was one small ray of hope...

While the senior company responsible for producing TVRs had its operations suspended in September by a totally frustrated Arnold Burton, the associate company, Grantura Plastics Ltd, somehow held its head above water. The man in charge? Yes, the wily, ever-enthusiastic Bernard Williams. With amazing tenacity and consistent loyalty, Bernard had ridden along with TVR by hook or crook since 1955. Amidst all the summer madness ten years later, he made just about the only sensible move the old industrial estate witnessed. Fearing that a collapse was once again on the cards (after all, over the years he'd had more experience than anybody else of TVR twists and turns), Bernard had resigned from Grantura Engineering just before the end.

This wasn't really a terminal loss

229

THE EARLY YEARS

◀ TVR racing was going strong in 1965. This is John Woollon's ex-Nick Downie Grantura Mk2A in a club event at Brands Hatch in March. (Ferret Fotographics)

for him because Grantura Plastics had possession of the vital TVR body mould tools and had for some time been making and supplying all the various fibreglass sections and panels which made up the cars' bodywork. Under the circumstances it was a position of some strength despite Bernard's shortage of working capital. Also in his company's grip were a small number of Mk3 1800S and Griffith bodies (which, of course, hadn't been paid for by Grantura Engineering) along with several chassis. And there were engines, too, a stock of them being held at a storage premises at nearby Broughton in a rather dilapidated barn rented not long before by Arnold Burton. There was, no doubt, a serious question mark concerning ownership of the engines, but to a man of Bernard's guile and durability things didn't look so bleak.

Although the Hoo Hill production line was now motionless, the overall situation at the old industrial estate seemed to suggest that at least a handful more TVRs could be completed by Grantura Plastics. Grantura Engineering was clearly out of the picture, but maybe there was still some form of life left for the now well known marque? There had certainly been masses of activity on the racing circuits that year, and it played a solid role in helping to keep the TVR name alive.

Earlier in 1965, as the competition season opened for business, the TVR club racing fraternity had set out to show they were absolutely bursting with energy. Well known drivers who were active on the tracks and hills during the

▼ The Grantura's short wheelbase gave it excellent manoeuvrability for autocross events. John Akers was the best known TVR mud slinger during the mid-1960s.

1965 – RACING FOR SURVIVAL

year included Tommy Entwistle, Ted Worswick, Arnold Burton, Peter Simpson, Alistair McHardy, David Plumstead, Nick Downie, Mary Wheeler, Doug Hardwick, John Woollon, Stuart Hemley, James Boothby, Roger Stanger, Godfrey Binks and sprint and hillclimb specialists, Malcolm Dungworth and Geoff Wilson.

John Wingfield, the new owner of Paddy Gaston's ex-works Grantura Mk3 lightweight (now carrying the XPG 1 plate), was another 'regular' this season. Unusually, Wingfield always raced without shoes. Owing to his large feet, he reckoned that wearing just socks gave him better pedal control. There seemed to be some truth in that because, first time out, his new steed was placed third in the GT race at Goodwood's season opener in March.

After more good early-season placings in club events, Wingfield took the Mk3 to Belgium in May to compete in the international 500km race at Spa-Francorchamps. Starting from the back of the grid following qualifying problems, he drove the whole distance himself, completing twenty-nine laps of the thirty-six lap race to finish seventeenth overall from twenty-seven starters. However, there was better news: his lightweight machine gained a fine third in the up-to-2000cc class for GT cars, getting the bonus of a point in the 1965 World Sports Car Championship – the only time a TVR ever achieved this.

Wingfield gained another satisfying bonus in the race by finishing ahead of a Porsche Carrera. He'd made a pit stop, managing to grab twelve gallons of fuel, one pint of oil and a clean windscreen, all in 11.5 seconds. The over-confident Porsche driver had done the necessaries and then also downed a refreshing can of Coke during his stop. Charging off to try and catch the TVR, he later admitted to feeling very angry at his failure to make up for his added drinking time!

Cheshire decorating contractor John Akers was again giving his MGB 1800 powered car rough treatment in the uneven world of autocross and usually being rewarded with class placings (mostly firsts), but the most outstanding of the TVR competition bunch in 1965 was again Tommy Entwistle. After his heavy crash at Brands Hatch in September 1964, his lightweight Mk3 1800 works racer was given a new body of standard fibreglass lay-up and so became more of a middleweight. It was a customer's body taken from the production line – mainly because there was a rush to get the racer ready for the new 1965 season.

The rebuilt Entwistle racer, finished in white with green sides, was again a fully works supported car, and its final assembly was still continuing throughout the night before its first race. Chief mechanic David Hives, assisted by Graham Wallwark and others, found sustenance during the job

▼ 1965 was the year brilliant TVR driver Tommy Entwistle won the Freddie Dixon Challenge Trophy for the second time. Better still, he would go on to win the Dixon series for the third time in 1966.

THE EARLY YEARS

with a crate of beer bought from a local pub, and the car was finally finished at around 7am. And that included an engine rebuild! At 7.30am the racer was loaded on to its trailer, hitched up to Tommy's Vauxhall Wyvern tow car and taken to Oulton Park. Without having turned a wheel before practice that day, the TVR was driven to victory by a delighted Tommy – a superb result for a new car first time out.

Tommy was, as ever, very grateful for David Hives' exceptional skills in the rebuilding of his racer's engine. David had coaxed great power – about 150bhp – from the unit, a bored-out 1850cc MGB engine with an HRG crossflow head and twin Webers. Despite its power, the engine was quite flexible, and Tommy mostly drove the car on the road to each meeting with wife Sylvia in the passenger seat. On the track he was dynamic, grabbing enough firsts and class placings through the 1965 season to win the Freddie Dixon Challenge Trophy for the second time in his career. It was the first time in the history of this competition that a driver had won it twice – another fine achievement for the TVR marque.

While Tommy was now probably the best known of all TVR racers, Alistair McHardy had made a name for himself in 1964 successfully campaigning his white lightweight Mk3 1800, and he was again up for the challenge in 1965. His results this year weren't so good but enjoyment was still the name of his game, and the season saw him competing in a total of sixteen races and one hillclimb – at Firle in Sussex. Unfortunately, due to losing money on a bad business investment, funds for racing were becoming tight, and an engine blow-up at Brands Hatch on 27th September was the last straw. Making his usual quick getaway off the line, Alistair had immediately stormed off into a commanding lead when, on lap two, his MGB engine decided to start disintegrating. Short, sharp and expensive, it was Alistair's last race in the Grantura.

Two extremely significant new names made their track debuts in TVRs during 1965: Martin Lilley and, later on in the season, the great Gerry Marshall. Martin had taken delivery of his British Racing Green Griffith, with Ford's 271bhp high performance engine, early in the year and

◀ Selling TVRs wasn't the easiest job during 1965, but ex-TVR racing driver Paddy Gaston gave it his best effort.

▼ Martin Lilley's 271bhp Griffith rounds Druids bend at Brands Hatch ahead of a Diva GT. Although it's not displaying a registration plate, this TVR was the famous MMT 7C.

▲ Like Martin Lilley, Malcolm Dungworth was amongst the earliest owners of a right-hand-drive Griffith V8 in 1965. He concentrated on sprints and hillclimbs, and is seen here spinning the car at Harewood's Quarry corner in June that year.

planned to use it as a dual-purpose road racer. That intent became a shade more track-biased when MMT 7C, as it was registered, was returned to the Blackpool factory for servicing and the fitting of some high-performance extras. At the same time its green paint was adorned with a white, nose-to-tail racing stripe.

Martin's first competitive event with his freshly liveried Griffith was in April at Brands Hatch in a GT race held in dreadful, blizzard-like conditions. David Plumstead's Griffith, soon to become known as the Mongoose, was battling through the same awful weather and, in fact, made a superb start to snatch the lead. But with John Miles' Diva having edged by, Plumstead's great efforts to fight back resulted in his Griffith having a mighty spin at Druids bend. After further enlivening proceedings and entertaining the fans, the car finally retired with a burst water hose. Over to Martin: "Throughout the race I was having a right old dice with Jerry Amato in his extremely well sorted Jaguar E-type. We were neck and neck, having a brilliant race, and the crowd were loving it. Somehow I overtook him for the last time on the finishing straight of the last lap – in fact, right on the line – and got first in class."

The Lilley Griffith was in action several times on the tracks early that summer at venues such as Brands Hatch, Mallory Park, Lydden Hill and Snetterton. Martin drove well and always enjoyed a great blast of exhilaration without achieving anything special in the way of results. The car was looked after by Barnet Motor Company, the Lotus agency and sports car sales business set up by Martin the previous year. By April '65 BarMoCo, as it came to be known, had signed as a TVR dealer, further developing the relationship between Martin and the men at the Hoo Hill factory.

In mid-June the wickedly powerful MMT 7C bared its fangs rather fiercely during practice for another race at Brands Hatch. Martin received something of a shock as the car suddenly started revolving wildly after a halfshaft broke and a wheel came off halfway round Paddock bend and continued down the track on its own. Meantime, with brakes that weren't able to cope, the Griffith three-wheeler maintained its gyrations down Paddock Hill until it hit a marshal's post at the bottom, badly damaging its rear bodywork. Returned to Grantura Plastics at Blackpool for repair, MMT 7C was repainted in silver with a dark blue roof – Barnet Motor Company's new team colours. Although the crash reduced Martin's enthusiasm for piloting the fearsome V8 thundercar again, racing was going to be taken more seriously from now on... with a new man behind the wheel.

At the same Brands Hatch meeting where Martin crashed MMT 7C, an important new name entered the TVR racing fray. Already a successful Mini racer – he'd started campaigning a 998cc Cooper in 1964 – 24-year-old Gerry Marshall enjoyed his first bash in a TVR in mid-June behind the wheel of John Wingfield's ex-Paddy Gaston lightweight Grantura Mk3 1800 (XPG 1). It was a round in the Redex GT Championship, and while John Miles' all-conquering 1650cc Ford engined Diva took the honours, Gerry charged around in great style, always sliding on the edge of the Grantura's handling abilities, and making a memorable TVR debut. His final placings were third

THE EARLY YEARS

Malcolm Dungworth's Griffith prepares to rocket off the start line at Harewood hillclimb in 1965. Over the next five years he became the best known and most successful TVR hillclimb driver.

overall and second in class, and it was the first time one of the Blackpool bombers had lapped the Kent circuit in less than sixty seconds. Martin was impressed (and brave!) enough to suggest letting Gerry loose in his repaired Griffith.

In August 1965 it was announced in the motoring press that the Barnet Motor Company team was to start entering MMT 7C for Gerry Marshall to drive and a factory built, 1650cc engined Lotus Elan 26R racer for Martin to drive. Gerry, it seems, did most of the driving in both cars. Accordingly, followers of TVR racing exploits were to hear much, much more of the portly entertainer from St Neots, Huntingdon, over the next eighteen months, especially with regard to the Griffith.

Indeed, Gerry bagged his first competition drive in the V8 big-banger when he got behind the wheel of MMT 7C at an Eelmore Plain sprint meeting taking place near Aldershot, Hampshire, early in September. Predictably enough, he won his class that day although didn't receive the honours for pure driving style. They went to Martin, as described by *Autosport*: 'Second was the same car driven by Martin Lilley, who looked very spectacular as he unleashed this very rapid machine up Eelmore's short straights'.

Over just five months MMT 7C had certainly issued due warning of the Griffith V8's raucous and explosive intentions. But another trailblazing Griffith delivered in Britain early in 1965 was

▼ Another early Griffith racer was TVR dealer Peter Simpson, seen here in the Martini Trophy race at Silverstone in July 1965. He came last!
(Ferret Fotographics)

234

1965 – RACING FOR SURVIVAL

Malcolm Dungworth's car. February 11th was the date when Malcolm met Bernard Williams at the Blackpool factory and agreed to purchase his 271bhp Griffith, the car being finished in white with red interior trim. Malcolm, who worked for his family's transport business in Sheffield, had already built a Grantura Mk2A but, due to various breakages, had been very disappointed with the car and part-exchanged it for a Jaguar XK150.

After spending 1964 behind the wheel of an Allard J2 in sprints and hillclimbs, Malcolm took delivery of his Griffith late in March 1965 – it would become his competition chariot for six years' worth of sprints and hillclimbs. Unlike his Mk2A, the Griffith would be a 'happy' car for Malcolm and he was to become arguably the best known TVR hillclimb driver between 1965 and 1970 – out of sixty-nine events entered, he was to achieve fifty-four class placings, including twenty-seven firsts, seventeen seconds and ten thirds.

Untamed handful though it was to drive, the Griffith's combination of explosive power and monstrous fun tempted more and more race drivers as word of its unique character spread during 1965. TVR dealer Peter Simpson's example was in action several times through the second half of the year, though one result he might have preferred to forget was his twentieth (and last) place after forty laps of the Martini Trophy race at Silverstone in July.

Like Peter Simpson, Malcolm Dungworth and David Plumstead, ex-Elva man Dr Euan Paul and ex-Lotus Seven racer Ted Worswick were also amongst the earliest British owners of Manx-tailed Griffiths. The Worswick car was a special lightweight example finished in red with a white nose-to-tail stripe that widened at the nose. Supplied as a full kit with a 4.7-litre high-performance V8 engine, it was built at the family business's works in Rochdale and used on both road and race track. First time out on a track was at Oulton Park in April, and throughout a twelve-race season

▼ Dr Euan Paul's BRG Griffith wasn't ready to race until the second half of the 1965 season. The fearsome projectile is shown here at Brands Hatch in July with a stonking 370bhp coming from its works Shelby Ford V8. (Ferret Fotographics)

THE EARLY YEARS

conducted exclusively at Oulton and Aintree circuits in the north of England, Ted enjoyed plenty of entertaining battles against the E-types and Elans of the day.

At the other end of the country, London based GP Dr Euan Paul's super-powerful Griffith racer was seen mainly at southern circuits and then only from mid-year onwards. Along with several other high-performance addicts, Dr Paul had been tempted into Griffith ownership by the example displayed on Bill Last's stand at the January 1965 Racing Car Show in London. Built up from a rolling body/chassis unit and completed at Alan Mann's workshops in Woking, Surrey, the Griffith was fitted with a fully tuned, works Shelby Ford 4.7-litre V8 producing a whopping 370bhp. Finished in British Racing Green, it was raced several times over the second half of 1965, often suffering development problems – like screeching along the bottom straight at Brands Hatch in June minus a complete offside rear suspension assembly!

▲ Arnold Burton powers up Harewood hillclimb in a lightweight Griffith in 1965.

▼ David Plumstead's Griffith shows the first signs of drastic body modifications at Brands Hatch in June 1965. (Ferret Fotographics)

After gaining moderate success over about ten races during 1965, Dr Paul's last time out with his fiery beast was in the Guards 1000 event at Brands Hatch in May 1966. It ran beautifully in 3rd place behind Roy Salvadori and Jack Sears, and ahead of all the other works entries, until its radiator burst after thirty-two laps due to the increased demands made on it. The monster obviously still required further taming, something that would now become the responsibility of the car's new owner, Maurice Gates, who would go on to race it for several more years.

TUM 1 was the special registration plate of another notable Griffith reaching British roads during 1965 (in July, in fact), the owner being TVR Chairman Arnold Burton, who also used the dark blue lightweight car for the occasional hillclimb and sprint meeting. Yet another name on the Griffith racing scene this year was Doug Hardwick, a good friend of Peter Simpson. Hardwick had bought his car, a 197bhp example finished in white, from Simpson around spring time, tried it out at several sprint meetings and then turned his hand to circuit racing. One of his first recorded races was a seven-

236

1965 – RACING FOR SURVIVAL

▶ By July 1965 the Plumstead Griffith had taken on a more monstrous appearance with wide Borrani wire wheels, huge wheel arches and a dark blue paint job with white stripe. Now known as the Mongoose (after an argument with TVR), the beast is pictured here at Brands Hatch in July. (Ferret Fotographics)

lapper at Silverstone late in September, where he came third behind Bill Nicholson's MGB and Ted Bunce's winning Tornado Talisman. Indeed, despite its dubious reputation in the USA, the brutal Anglo-American hot rod was rapidly becoming a popular choice with intrepid British racers.

David Plumstead's car had started life in March 1965 as a standard Griffith finished in white, but it soon became known as the Mongoose GT, mainly because its creator believed it capable of eating up Cobras – but also because he had a serious argument with TVR's management over monies owed and subsequently refused to call his car a TVR. And this was despite the fact that he ran the TVR Centre in Purley, Surrey! This Griffith first raced early in April at Brands Hatch in the Redex Trophy, when it finished a creditable fourth.

Its bodywork much modified, by July the car had been repainted in Plumstead's racing colours of dark blue with a nose-to-tail white stripe. Power was a largely standard high performance 4.7-litre Ford 289 V8 and the aggressive looking machine was notable for its extra-wide Borrani wire wheels all round (8.5in wide at the back), behind all four of which were disc brakes. The modified nose looked lower than standard, and the wheels were kept legal by radically widened wheel arches (particularly at the rear) that naturally enhanced the beastly look. Yes, this Griffith special didn't look particularly friendly – certainly not to other drivers.

The trouble was, it had the capacity to break halfshafts as easily as any other Griffith, an ability it demonstrated at Brands Hatch during the St John Trophy meeting early in August. Storming through Paddock bend (scene of Martin Lilley's similar disaster not long before), Plumstead's Mongoose launched one of its rear wheels high into the air, causing many onlookers to take rapid avoiding action. Following right behind, Euan Paul's car had to do the same thing, a move which he performed successfully, allowing him to carry on racing until... a halfshaft broke and his Griffith lost a wheel too! It was hardly surprising that the big V8 powered TVRs had already gained real notoriety for their wayward antics.

◀ Keith Aitchison behind the wheel of the works development Griffith at Tholt-y-Will hillclimb in the Isle of Man in May 1965. Keith finished with a 2nd in class. This car was later raced by famous Morgan driver Chris Lawrence.

Another Griffith seen in action occasionally in 1965 was BFR 400B, the blue Manx-tailed works development car built at Hoo Hill early in 1965. The company wanted more competition airings for the marque, and the car's first outing was in May at the Isle of Man's Tholt-y-Will hillclimb with Keith Aitchison at the wheel. Keith remembered the Griffith being very quick in practice despite being all over the place on the bends. "In the event proper I came second in class by a gnat's whisker to Phil Scragg's lightweight E-type, and I reckon he'd been practising there for the best part of a week! Still, it gave TVR some useful publicity."

In June BFR 400B was raced by Tommy Entwistle at Goodwood before passing into the hands of Chris Lawrence, the expert tuner and specialist car builder famous for his exploits at Le Mans with Deep Sandersons and Morgans. The plan was for Chris to further develop the Griffith particularly in the areas of handling, steering and braking,

◀ After three years of competition driving, Roger Stanger's trusty Grantura Mk1 was still in racetrack action in September 1965. This is Woodcote bend at Silverstone with the little TVR being gobbled up by a 5.3-litre Attila sports racer.

1965 – RACING FOR SURVIVAL

▲ Two minutes before the start of a sports car race at Oulton Park in 1965. Tommy Entwhistle's Mk3 has pole position on the far right next to Alistair McHardy's similar car.

and he was to borrow the car several times over the second half of 1965 and well into 1966. He often went testing and at MIRA one day, while attempting to discover its ultimate safe speed, he saw an incredible 169mph on the clock.

Chris also competed with the ferociously powerful BFR 400B at a handful of national and international hillclimb meetings. The first of these was at Harewood hillclimb in Yorkshire on 20th June, the car taking first place in class. More success came in August at the St Ursanne-Les Rangiers hillclimb near Basle in Switzerland, where Chris again won his class. Continuing his short continental tour, Chris also blasted the Griffith up the hills at Villars in Switzerland and Chamrousse in France before returning home for a Silverstone club race in October in which the car didn't distinguish itself.

A TVR with something different in the way of power units was hillclimb specialist Geoff Taylor's silver Grantura Mk2A, which had a 1600cc Sunbeam Alpine engine under its bonnet. Geoff had started campaigning the car in 1964, occasionally doing sprints but mostly charging up the hills at all the well known venues. There was more of the same for Geoff in 1965, a typical result being his best time in class at Great Auclum hillclimb at Burghfield Common, near Reading, in August that year. Generally outstanding at its job, the Rootes powered Grantura usually finished in the top three places in class and became a well known competition TVR.

Back on the club racing scene, an enjoyable outing to the 750MC's Birkett Six-hour Relay race at Silverstone in August finished with an excellent third place overall going

▶ Atrocious conditions at Castle Combe for a sports car race in October 1965, with Roger Stanger's Grantura Mk1 leading a Triumph Spitfire.

▲ Powering through a long curve at Castle Combe in July 1965, Peter Simpson's Griffith resists a challenger. It was racing exploits like Simpson's that helped keep the TVR name alive during a year when the company was inexorably sliding towards disaster. (Ferret Fotographics)

to the TVR team of Tommy Entwistle (Mk3 1850), Peter Simpson (in his 271bhp Griffith) and Arthur Mallock (in John Wingfield's ex-works lightweight Grantura Mk3 1800). Despite eventually blowing the head gasket of the Wingfield car's engine, Mallock drove the greatest mileage in the race – on account of the long-range fuel tank fitted in the car.

Early the next day Wingfield appeared at the Silverstone pits to retrieve his Mk3 for a meeting at Lydden Hill, only to discover, of course, that his engine now had a useless cylinder head. After trailering the car to the Kent circuit, the answer was a bit of skulduggery: John lurked in Lydden's paddock ready to pounce on the first private MG-powered TVR to drive in... then, after some friendly persuasion, commandeered its cylinder head, repaired his car and went on to compete in two races that day, winning the first and coming second in the other. All so typical of the great spirit amongst TVR owners at the time.

Few problems with TVRs in competition, then – apart from overheating, halfshafts breaking and wheels falling off! As for Grantura Engineering itself, the whole awful wheel of TVR misfortune had turned a complete revolution yet again. In only three years, a small, admittedly struggling but potentially growing outfit had become a large, unwieldy and debt-ridden behemoth. Only about ninety examples of the neglected but excellent Mk3 1800S had been built and Arnold Burton, the perennial saviour, had gone for good. In October 1965 the situation at Hoo Hill seemed extremely bleak.

Only Grantura Engineering's liquidator had a true sense of direction and purpose. His main task was to find a brave, somewhat daredevil risk-taker to buy a problem-plagued business that had a remarkably turbulent history and an extremely uncertain future. In trying to clear up a horrible mess, he was at least getting some help – Henry Moulds, Stan Kilcoyne, Nadine Hoyle and others such as Brian Murphy and Graham Wallwark were all temporarily employed to look after his interests. The main job involved putting old TVR stock into lots, labelling them and preparing them for sale.

Wallwark had been the company's parts buyer for some time but had just recently been thrown out of his digs and was facing one of life's low points. Wages from the liquidator weren't much, so for the sake of economy he'd parked his Austin A50 saloon outside the factory and had taken to sleeping in it. He did this for no less than three weeks, doing his washing and taking his baths in a sink in the factory!

As the days passed and no brave businessman came forward to sweep the dust from the silent TVR production area and bring life back to the marque, Bernard Williams' Grantura Plastics Ltd, now with David Hives and John Ward helping out, was enduring its own hard times. Money was extremely tight, but somehow the ever-resourceful Bernard managed to acquire a quantity of components that enabled him, David and John to complete and sell three engine-less Mk3 1800S kits. Assistance with this project came from a perhaps predictable source, as David remembered: "As fast as the liquidator was trying to sort out and count all the parts, that wicked Stanley Kilcoyne was knocking them off and bringing them up to our workshops – despite him being there to help the liquidator!"

One further rolling body/chassis unit handled by Grantura Plastics during this period was a lightweight 1800S assembly that started life with MGB power and was initially campaigned in hillclimbs and sprints in that form by owner/builder Brian Alexander from Cheltenham. Ultimately, for the latter part of the 1968 season the car would receive tuned suspension and the fitment of an American Buick 3.5-litre V8, while all four wheel arches were flared to accommodate wider wheels. Personally driving both versions of his TVR to most meetings and keeping the car in full road trim, Alexander notched-up many class wins and records over his years storming up the hills.

Late in 1965 Bernard and team also found themselves an interesting sideline: a main BMC agent in Plymouth, Devon, wanted fibreglass hardtops for the Mini-Mokes it was selling. But little money was brought in by the project as only about six hardtops were supplied. Clearly, Grantura's future income would best lie in supplying TVR bodywork for crash repairs or to a new production company – should anybody be so rash as to want to make the car again.

▼ Well over thirty TVR drivers, not all of them well known, were involved in various forms of motorsport and promoting the TVR image during 1965. This is D.Gordon's Grantura Mk3 at Brands Hatch in May. (Ferret Fotographics)

A group of men who would have loved the opportunity to make more TVRs were the stalwarts who'd been with the company several years and were almost addicted to the marque. Amongst them were Stan Kilcoyne, David Hives, Brian Murphy and Graham Wallwark. Recounted Graham: "After it finished, this group of us were still going in – somebody had the necessary factory keys. We were having a brew, chatting and trying to dream up a way of buying the company and taking the place over. Bernard was involved, too, but the scheme was financially beyond our reach."

Through all its many TVR years, the old brickworks at Hoo Hill, Layton, Blackpool, had certainly witnessed some extraordinary events. And still they continued. The Trident's incredibly turbulent first year of life was a fine example of typical TVR trouble. But what of the genuine TVR sports car's future? If a sale of rights and assets were to be made to someone with the right money, the brave buyer would certainly inherit some extras he might prefer to go without. Not the least of them would be the company's muddled, depressing and almost embarrassing history.

The fact that a separate company, Grantura Plastics, had possession of all the vital body moulds wasn't exactly heart-warming. Then there was TVR's commercial reputation. After going out of business three times and suffering several near-misses, the companies responsible for making the cars seemed to have reached the final, undisputed end of the road. Indeed, most people from the motor industry and motoring press, general enthusiasts included, could now be excused for having little clue whether or not the Blackpool sports car was dead or alive.

The extraordinary existence of TVR had no parallel in recent motoring history. Now, in November 1965, would its always resolute and gritty British character become obsolete altogether? Or was there any way – could answers be found – for the car to live on? The numbers of TVR competition drivers were growing by the year and the marque's on-track reputation was spreading wide, but maybe the challenge of reviving production at Blackpool was simply too daunting? Yet there was one name very much in the picture – that of TVR enthusiast and Griffith V8 racing driver Martin Lilley. His company, Barnet Motor Co, was a TVR dealer and although still a young man, Martin harboured a strong ambition to be a sports car manufacturer...

◀ Apart from racing his early Griffith in 1965, Martin Lilley also found time to run his small car sales business in Barnet. However, selling TVRs wasn't easy at the time.

THE STORY CONTINUES...

The amazing roller-coaster saga of the TVR sports car continues in *TVR Volume Two*, also written by Peter Filby.
Please see **www.tvrbooks.com** for more details.

TIMELINE 1956 - 1965

The next few pages show the evolution of the 'classic' TVR shape from 1956 over the next ten years. Starting with the 'open sports' (this car never had a proper model name), these are all the limited and full production TVRs that were designed and styled in-house during those ten years. Hence not included are the first three TVR one-off specials or the series of twenty chassis that were built between 1953 and 1954 and bodied with various glassfibre 'shells made by other companies. Nor have the four Trident prototypes built by Carrozzeria Fissore been included.

Also provided in this section are specifications and details that weren't necessarily included in the relevant chapters. This information refers to the cars at the time of their introduction. Regular development took place with most models, meaning that some specifications may have changed during production.

TVR OPEN SPORTS

Manufactured: Summer 1956 to summer 1957
Total built: Three or four are believed to have been built, one of them being exported to the USA, where it was known as a Jomar.
Chassis: Multi-tubular backbone using mostly 1.5in diameter 16-gauge round tubing, with outriggers.
Bodywork: All glassfibre, bonded to chassis.
Suspension: Independent all round by trailing arms and laminated transverse torsion bars of VW Beetle origin. Telescopic shock absorbers all round.
Engine used: 1098cc Coventry Climax FWA **Gearbox:** MGA 4-speed **Steering:** Worm and peg, Ford 100E-type.
Brakes: 11in Girling drums front and rear. **Wheels:** 15in diameter Dunlop 48-spoke wires.
Wheelbase: 7ft **Track:** 4ft 4in front, 4ft 4in rear **Overall dimensions:** Length 11ft 6in, width 5ft 4in, height N/A.
Fuel tank: N/A **Kerb weight:** N/A

NOTES: Aside of the three one-off TVR specials of 1949-1951, the Open Sports was the company's first attempt at making its own bodywork – albeit by using two slightly modified Microplas Mistral bonnets, one for the front and one for the back! Under those simple glassfibre panels was an example of the latest backbone chassis (with VW Beetle based suspension) which the company had started making in 1955 and which was initially sold mostly to Ray Saidel in the USA.

Although its styling had cut a few corners, the Open Sports turned out to be an attractive sports racer, and its front and rear bodywork marked the very beginning of what became the 'classic' TVR shape. The last Open Sports to be made was used at the factory to develop the first TVR Coupé.

TVR COUPÉ

Manufactured: Summer 1957 to end of 1957
Total built: Seven are believed to have been made, of which four were exported to the USA, where they were called Jomars.
Chassis: Multi-tubular backbone using mostly 1.5in diameter 16-gauge round tubing, with outriggers.
Bodywork: All glassfibre, bonded to chassis.
Suspension: Independent all round by trailing arms and laminated transverse torsion bars of VW Beetle origin. Telescopic shock absorbers all round.
Engines used: 1172cc Ford 100E side-valve with optional Shorrock supercharger, 1098cc Coventry Climax FWA, 1489cc MGA (BMC).
Gearbox: Ford 3-speed with Ford engine, MGA 4-speed with Climax and MG engines.
Steering: Worm and peg, Ford 100E-type.   **Brakes:** 11in Girling drums front and rear.
Wheels: 15in diameter Dunlop 48-spoke wires   **Wheelbase:** 7ft   Track: 4ft 4in front, 4ft 4in rear
Overall dimensions: Length 11ft 6in, width 5ft 4in, height 4ft.   **Fuel tank:** 8.75 gallons   **Kerb weight:** Approx 12-13 cwt
Claimed performance: Supercharged Ford version – 110mph maximum; Coventry Climax version – 125mph max.

NOTES: Using an unchanged chassis, the Coupé's bodywork was created by adding a simple hardtop to the last example of the earlier Open Sports model. The Coupé was generally referred to as the 'notchback' and showed how the 'classic' TVR shape was beginning to evolve. After the first four examples were ordered by USA importer Ray Saidel, the first British customer to buy a kit took delivery in August 1957.

The Coupé was not publicly announced in Britain until January 1958, but although prices were quoted as starting at £990 for a turn-key 1172cc Ford side-valve engined car, no more examples were built. In fact, the last body/chassis unit was modified during 1958 to create the prototype TVR (Grantura) Mk1. All four US export Coupés still survive, while one car still exists in Britain.

GRANTURA Mk1

Manufactured: Early 1958 to mid-1960.
Total built: 100 are believed to have been made, of which some (about 25) were exported to the USA.
Chassis: Multi-tubular backbone using mostly 1.5in diameter 16-gauge round tubing, with outriggers.
Bodywork: All glassfibre, bonded to chassis.
Suspension: Independent all round by trailing arms and laminated transverse torsion bars of VW Beetle origin. Telescopic shock absorbers all round.
Engines used: 1172cc Ford 100E side-valve (optional supercharger), 1098cc Coventry Climax FWA, 1489cc MGA, 1216cc Coventry Climax FWE.   **Gearbox:** Ford and MG   **Steering:** Worm and peg, Ford 100E-type.
Brakes: 11in Girling drums all round, as used for Austin-Healey 100-Six.
Wheels: 15in diameter Dunlop 48-spoke wires.   **Wheelbase:** 7ft   **Track:** 4ft 4in front, 4ft 4in rear.
Overall dimensions: Length 11ft 6in, width 5ft 4in, height 4ft   **Fuel tank:** 8.75 gallons   **Kerb weight:** 13cwt approx

NOTES: The Mk1 was the first TVR with styling done entirely in-house. Initially it was made solely for the USA market, where it was called the Jomar Coupé. Very few cars were built during 1958, and the Mk1 wasn't available in the UK until early 1959, at which point the Grantura name began to apply.

Most UK cars were sold in kit form at prices from £660 to £950 depending on engine. The Shorrock supercharger was an option with the Ford 100E engine, boosting power from 35bhp to 56bhp at 4600rpm. Three stages of tune were offered for the Climax engines, while some later kits were supplied with the 997cc Ford 105E engine.

Each kit was supplied to individual customer specifications and optional extras included a ZF close-ratio gearbox, front disc brakes, a heater/demister unit, screen washer and racing clutch. A laminated windscreen and leather upholstery were also offered, although these were standard on the Climax powered models.

GRANTURA Mk2 & 2A

Manufactured: Mk2 – June 1960 to early 1961. Mk 2A – Early 1961 to September 1962.
Total built: About 400 of both models, some 150 thought to be exported.
Chassis: Multi-tubular backbone using mostly 1.5in diameter 16-gauge round tubing, with outriggers.
Bodywork: All glassfibre, bonded to chassis.
Suspension: Independent all round by trailing arms and laminated transverse torsion bars of VW Beetle origin. Telescopic shock absorbers all round.
Engines used: 1489cc MGA, 1588cc MGA, 1622cc MGA, all with 4-speed MG gearbox.
Power output: 1489cc – 68bhp; 1588cc – 79bhp @ 5600rpm; 1622cc – 90bhp.
Engine options: 997cc Ford 105E, 1216cc Coventry Climax FWE. **Steering:** Worm and peg, Ford 100E-type.
Brakes: Mk2 – 11in Girling drums all round, as for Austin-Healey 100-Six. Mk2A – 11in discs at front, 11in Girling drums at rear.
Wheels: 15in diameter Dunlop 48-spoke wires. **Wheelbase:** 7ft **Track:** 4ft 4in front, 4ft 4in rear.
Overall dimensions: Length 11ft 6in, width 5ft 4in, height 4ft. **Fuel tank:** 8.75 gallons **Kerb weight:** 13cwt approx.

NOTES: Little more than a lightly modified Mk1, the Grantura Mk2 was easily identified by its extended tail fins carrying the rear lights, its rear wheel arch flares and its front indicator lights mounted on the bonnet close to each headlamp. The bodywork was bonded to the chassis, which remained unchanged. Stronger disc brakes at the front were the identification point for the otherwise identical Mk2A.

Supplied to UK customers mostly in kit form, the Mk2's introductory prices were £880 with MG 1588cc power and £1045 with 1216cc Climax power. Key options for the Climax cars were a 4-speed ZF close-ratio gearbox and rack and pinion steering sourced from the Morris Minor. Also on the extras list were various performance tuning parts, a heater/demister unit, wood rim steering wheel and external spare wheel mountings. Standard for the Climax cars, but optional for the MG and Ford cars, were leather upholstery and a laminated windscreen.

Twin vents for extra cooling air, set in the bonnet just below the indicators, were initially intended for Ford powered cars but only until they were requested for MG and Climax cars too. Several lightweight body/chassis units were made available for racing.

GRANTURA Mk3 & Mk3 1800

Manufactured: Mk3 – Launched in April 1962, made from around June until October that year. Production then restarted late in 1962 and continued until August 1963. Mk3 1800 – September 1963 to mid-1965.
Total built: About 90, many of which were exported.
Chassis: Multi-tubular backbone using mostly 1.5in diameter 16-gauge tubing, with outriggers.
Bodywork: All glassfibre, bonded to chassis.
Suspension: Independent all round by unequal length double wishbones and coil springs with shock absorbers. The front upper wishbones were made by the TVR factory, the lower ones being of Triumph Herald type. The front uprights were also Herald type; front anti-roll bar as standard. The whole rear suspension was of TVR design and manufacture.
Engines used: 1622cc MGA (90bhp) in Mk3; 1798cc MGB (95bhp) in Mk3 1800, both with 4-speed MG gearbox
Steering: Modified Triumph Herald-type rack and pinion.
Brakes: Girling 10.75in front discs and 9in rear drums, all sourced from the Triumph TR4.
Wheels: 15in diameter steel disc wheels stated as standard fitment, though most cars used 15in diameter 48-spoke wires.
Wheelbase: 7ft 1.5in   **Track:** Front 4ft 3in; rear 4ft 4in.   **Overall dimensions:** Length 11ft 6in, width 5ft 4in, height 4ft.
Fuel tank: 10 gallons (45.5 litres)   **Kerb weight:** 14cwt (1800lbs)

NOTES: A hugely improved car over the Mk2s. Main identification point for the Mk3 was its restyled nose with raised and more upright air intake aperture with indicators placed at each side. Later cars also featured a raised plinth to carry their rear number plates. Under the skin, all cars featured a much improved chassis (with 1½in extra wheelbase) designed by John Thurner. Integral front inner wheel arches were another improvement.

At the beginning of Mk3 production, the 1216cc Climax FWE and 1340cc Ford 109E Classic engines were offered, but only while stocks lasted. Most UK Mk3s were sold as kits, introductory prices being £862 for the 1622cc MG version (£1182 fully built) and £872 for the 1798cc MG model (£1054 fully built). Wire wheels were listed as extras but were fitted to almost all cars. Other extras included a 4-speed ZF close-ratio gearbox, servo assisted brakes and performance items such as an HRG light alloy crossflow cylinder head and twin Weber DCOE carburettors. For added practicality and style, customers could choose from a laminated windscreen, heater/demister, screen washer, wood rim steering wheel, alloy wheels and leather upholstery. Lightweight body/chassis units were also available for competition use.

GRIFFITH SERIES 200

Manufactured: April 1964 to approximately mid-1965. **Total built:** 192
Chassis: Multi-tubular backbone, 1.5in diameter 16-gauge round tubing, with outriggers. Very similar to Mk3 chassis but modified at front to accept the Ford V8 engine and gearbox. All suspension pick-up points strengthened.
Bodywork: All glassfibre, bonded to chassis.
Suspension: Independent all round by unequal length double wishbones and coil springs with shock absorbers. The front upper wishbones were made by the TVR factory, the lower ones being of Triumph Herald type. The front uprights were also of Herald type; front anti-roll bar as standard. The whole rear suspension was of TVR design and manufacture and included a second coil spring/damper unit at each side.
Engines used: 4.7-litre Ford 289 V8 in 195bhp (standard) and 271bhp (SE) stages of tune. Both versions with Ford's all-synchromesh 4-speed gearbox and MG differentials. **Steering:** Modified Triumph Herald-type rack and pinion.
Brakes: Girling 10.75in front discs and 9in rear drums, all servo-assisted and sourced from the Triumph TR4.
Wheels: 5K x 15in diameter Dunlop 72-spoke wires. **Wheelbase:** 7ft 1.5in **Track:** Front 4ft 4.5in; rear 4ft 5.5in.
Overall dimensions: Length 11ft 6in, width 5ft 4in, height 4ft 1.5in **Fuel tank:** 17 gallons **Kerb weight:** 17cwt

NOTES: Launched on the US market in April 1964, the Griffith 200 was effectively a Grantura Mk3 with a beefed-up chassis and a Ford small-block V8 shoehorned under its bonnet. It was the brainchild of American motor dealer and racing team owner Jack Griffith, who wanted a lightweight, high performance car that could outgun the Shelby Cobra. The left-hand-drive Griffith was an instant hit in the USA, and such was demand that it immediately dominated TVR's production facilities at its Blackpool factory. As such, the car wasn't offered for sale in the UK.

For its day, the Griffith had massive acceleration – the 195bhp version reached 60mph in 6 secs, the 271bhp version shaving that time to 5 secs. Maximum speeds were 140mph and 160mph respectively. Torque was extremely impressive too – 282lb ft @ 2400rpm and 314lb ft @ 3400rpm respectively.

Distinguishing the Griffith from the Grantura Mk3 were the big central bulge in its bonnet and the twin exhaust tail pipes under its rear end. All Griffith 200s were built at Blackpool as fully painted, trimmed and wired cars and then shipped to New York for the installation of their Ford V8s and gearboxes in the Griffith Motors factory. Almost all 200s were fitted by TVR with BMC/MG final drive units – despite their V8 power. Optional extras included two-speed wipers, a Kenlowe twin-fan Radomatic radiator and a reversing light, although cars supplied with 271bhp engines were said to have these features fitted as standard.

GRIFFITH SERIES 400

Manufactured: January 1965 to September 1965. After Martin Lilley's company TVR Engineering had taken over the business at the very end of 1965, more cars were built between April 1966 and January 1967.
Total built: Exactly 59 examples left the Griffith factory in New York before the end of 1965. Somewhere between 40 and 50 further 400s are thought to have been built at TVR's Blackpool factory for customers in Canada, Britain and Europe. Of these, ten were built by TVR Engineering in 1966, six of them being exported.
Chassis: Multi-tubular backbone, 1.5in diameter 16-gauge tubing, with outriggers. Very similar to the Griffith 200 chassis.
Bodywork: All glassfibre, bonded to chassis.
Suspension: Independent all round by unequal length double wishbones and coil springs with shock absorbers. The front upper wishbones were made by the TVR factory, the lower ones being of Triumph Herald type. The front uprights were also of Herald type; front anti-roll bar as standard. The whole rear suspension was of TVR design and manufacture and included a second coil spring/damper unit at each side.
Engines used: 4.7-litre Ford 289 V8 in 195bhp (standard) and 271bhp (SE) stages of tune. Torque was 282lb ft @ 2400rpm and 314lb ft @ 3400rpm respectively. Both versions with Ford's all-synchromesh 4-speed gearbox and Salisbury differentials.
Steering: Modified Triumph Herald-type rack and pinion.
Brakes: Girling 10.75in front discs and 9in rear drums, all servo-assisted and sourced from the Triumph TR4.
Wheels: 5K x 15in diameter Dunlop 72-spoke wires.   **Wheelbase:** 7ft 1.5in   **Track:** Front 4ft 4.5in; rear 4ft 5.5in
Overall dimensions: Length 11ft 6in, width 5ft 4in, height 4ft 1.5in.   **Fuel tank:** 17 gallons   **Kerb weight:** 17cwt

NOTES: On sale in the USA early in January 1965, the Griffith 400 was launched on the UK market at the London Racing Car Show in late January that year. What distinguished it from its earlier Griffith 200 sisters was its cut-off Manx-tailed rear bodywork with Ford Cortina Mk1 'Ban the Bomb' tail lights and huge new rear window. To start with, left-hand-drive cars were all but completed at Blackpool, leaving just their V8 engines and gearboxes to be fitted by Griffith Motors in New York. But the long US dock strike of early 1965 badly affected shipments, so the 400 was immediately offered to British customers.

The 195bhp engined 400 was sold in Britain as a kit at £1342 or as a fully complete car at prices from £1620. For the 271bhp model, prices were £1488 and £1797 respectively. There was no shortage of racing drivers who wanted the blistering performance both versions enjoyed – 6 secs to 60mph and a maximum of 140mph for the 195bhp version, and 5 secs and 160mph for the 271bhp car. Many examples had their engines tuned for even greater power. All 400s used Salisbury differentials, as fitted to the E-type Jaguar.

Mk3 1800S

Manufactured: November 1964 to September 1965. Then January 1966 to June 1966 by TVR Engineering.
Total built: About 130, 35 of which were in 1966.
Chassis: Multi-tubular backbone, 1.5in diameter 16-gauge tubing, with outriggers.
Bodywork: All glassfibre, bonded to chassis.
Suspension: Independent all round by unequal length double wishbones and coil springs with shock absorbers. The front upper wishbones were made by the TVR factory, the lower ones being of Triumph Herald type. The front uprights were also from the Herald; front anti-roll bar as standard. The whole rear suspension was of TVR design and manufacture.
Engine used: 1798cc MGB with 4-speed MG gearbox.
Steering: Modified Triumph Herald-type rack and pinion.
Brakes: Girling 10.75in front discs and 9in rear drums, all sourced from the Triumph TR4.
Wheels: 5K x 15in diameter Dunlop 72-spoke wires.
Wheelbase: 7ft 1.5in   **Track:** Front 4ft 4.5in; rear 4ft 5.5in.
Overall dimensions: Length 11ft 6in, width 5ft 4in, height 4ft.
Fuel tank capacity: 10 gallons (45.5 litres)   **Kerb weight:** 14cwt (1800lbs)

NOTES: The Mk3 1800S was built by Grantura Engineering until the company went bust in October 1965, then by TVR Engineering after it had taken over in November that year. The 'S' in its model name denoted the new Manx-tailed bodywork first introduced in November 1964 and featuring Ford Cortina Mk1 'Ban the Bomb' tail lights and a huge new rear window. Apart from the bonnet, the 1800S's body was the same as that used for the Griffith 400.

It was all the commotion surrounding the Griffith 400 that badly curtailed production of the Mk3 1800S, which was an extremely competent sports car. Power from the MGB engine was 98bhp @ 5400rpm, providing performance of 0-60mph in 10 seconds and a 110mph maximum.

Among extras listed were a close-ratio gearbox, Pow-lock differential, oil cooler, brake servo, laminated windscreen, chrome luggage rack, heater/demister, two-speed wipers, electric screen washers and performance tuning gear.

ABOUT THE AUTHOR

Born in Plymouth, Devon, Peter Filby was brought up in a farming environment in north Norfolk before his family moved to a rather more suburban existence in Croydon, Surrey. He was educated at the Trinity School of John Whitgift, then located in the centre of the town. Realising it was much too crowded in Croydon, Peter accepted his first 'proper' job as a junior officer at sea with Union Castle Lines, making several trips to South Africa. However, while most people worked for promotion, Peter happily moved *down* the ladder to travel around the world on a P & O Orient Lines ship – as a night telephonist!

Next came a few years being stuck in a sports shop working in the family business, followed by a short time on open-air tennis courts trying unsuccessfully to coach unruly children how to become mini-Roger Federers. Not the easiest challenge. Then came the final solution to what had so far been a somewhat haphazard career. It arrived in the form of a hugely entertaining rear-engined Unipower GT, which left Peter smitten with hand-built specialist sports cars and then turning his hand to writing about them. Magazines to which he contributed included *Hot Car*, *Motor*, *Autocar*, *Classic Car* and *Auto Enthusiast*.

Books came next, Peter being responsible for writing such memorable titles as *The Amazing Sports Car Journal*, *The Fun Car Explosion*, *Roadsters, Replicas and Fun Cars*, *Specialist Sports Cars*, *Success Against the Odds*, *Amazing Mini* and even a brief history of MG. In 1979 he created and published a radically different car magazine called *Alternative Cars* and then added to his portfolio other successful titles such as *Kit Cars* and *Which Kit?* There was also *Carrera*, arguably the first men's glossy lifestyle magazine, but unfortunately this one lasted only three issues!

Apart from writing his own books, Peter is particularly proud to have edited and published five other books: *Three-Wheelers*, *TVR Muscle and Curves*, *Classic Kit Cars*, *Performance Roadsters* and *Cobra Replicas*. But it was *Success Against The Odds*, the first-ever book about TVR, that really made his name as an accomplished and highly entertaining author. Amongst the many specialist sports cars he has owned are one of the three Elva-BMW GT160s, masses of Lotus Seven-style chariots, several Cobra replicas, two Trident Venturers, a V8 powered Marcos and two TVRs, a 1980s Tasmin Convertible and a late '90s Chimaera. Assuming *TVR The Early Years* is a success, a pristine 1965 Griffith V8 would be nice, but thanks to the passage of time, Peter now struggles a bit getting through those tiny doors!

THANKS TO ALL...

Enthusiasm and generosity amongst TVR buffs for every aspect of this book has been nothing less than fantastic. I've enjoyed terrific support, encouragement and assistance whenever I've needed it. Whether I've wanted to spend time with ex-TVR racing drivers from the 1960s and '70s or pepper mature ex-employees with questions about company history, everybody has been wonderfully patient and helpful. Owners of individual cars have been brilliant too, by supplying excellent photographs or making their cars available for my own ancient camera. Thank you so much, everybody.

People who I've chased many times in the course of my research (and always been welcomed) include Jim Lowry, Steve Reid, Ian Massey-Crosse, Richard Carter, John Mleczek, Graham Wallwark, Bruno Meier, John Bailie and, of course, Martin Lilley. The lovely people of the TVR Car Club have been great too, in particular Richard Sails, John Lowey, Ralph Dodds and Mandy O'Neale, editor of *Sprint*. And there are no doubt others I've forgotten to mention – apologies if you're one of them.

This book would never have been so comprehensive without the superb support I've received from across the Atlantic Ocean. So a huge thank you to Alex Saidel, Randy Hartigan, Marshall Moore (President of the TVR CC North America), Mike Mooney, Gerry Sagerman and others. All those photographs and information have been more than gratefully received. Thanks a million, guys.

I probably spent more time discussing pre-1966 history with TVR's ex-general manager David Hives (below right) and ex-shareholder/director Keith Aitchison (centre) than anybody else. I can't tell you how grateful I am for all your help, chaps. A big thankyou also goes to Sally Mitchell (below left), with whom I worked for many years on my own magazines and car show organisation and who has done all the typing and computer work for this book. As I'm a caveman, things could have been rather tricky without Sally's brilliant efforts. A real rock during production was graphic designer James Mansell, a very patient and tolerant man. Thanks for that, mate! And finally I must give huge credit to my partner Jane, who has unselfishly supported and encouraged me throughout the rather excessive time I have spent working on this book.

Peter Filby

COMING NEXT ...

As already described in the introduction to this book, I became so enthusiastic and involved with writing about TVRs that a second volume has already been completed! Covering the marque's history from late 1965, when Arthur and Martin Lilley took over, to late 1981, when Martin gave 'the keys' to the late Peter Wheeler, volume two is written in the same style and has more chapters and more pages. That means more previously untold history, more photographs and more amusing anecdotes.

If you enjoyed this first volume, you'll not regret reading the second, I promise. All being well, publication is in October 2010 and further details are available on my website - www.tvrbooks.com . When it's ready, you can order your copy of *TVR Volume Two* in the following ways:

Website: www.tvrbooks.com
Email: sales@tvrbooks.com
Telephone: Autocraft Books on 01737 222336 (11am – 6pm, Monday – Friday)

ALSO PLANNED ...

TVR in Competition – During my research for the first two volumes of TVR history, I acquired a vast amount of additional information from the many racing drivers I contacted about their various TVR motor sport activities: track racing, sprinting, hillclimbing and autocrossing. Indeed, so much so that plans are afoot to produce a book covering TVRs in competition from the 1960s to the present day. The drivers, their cars, their thoughts and anecdotes will all be part of the package, and it will be profusely illustrated of course.

At the time of writing, nothing has yet been set in stone but work on this further TVR volume is ongoing and publication *could* take place in 2011 or, perhaps more likely, 2012. There's plenty of time, then, for TVR competition drivers to contact me and have their cars and stories featured in the book. Whether it's more 1960s or '70s racing, Tuscan racing or historic/classic car racing, I'd love to hear from you all. Contact details are above or you can write to me at *Autocraft Books, 1 Howard Road, Reigate, Surrey RH2 7JE*.

Marcos – With all research already done, this book was originally going to be published before *TVR Volume One*, but strong encouragement from certain quarters persuaded me to switch to TVR. Another amazing and remarkable story full of highs and lows and entertaining anecdotes, the history of Marcos and my work on it will trundle along through to 2011 and *could* be published towards the end of that year.

TVR 1982 to 2006 – A final TVR volume charting the last 24 years of an incredible marque's history could and *should* become reality. Yes, having got this far, it's a logical thing to do and would complete an absolutely comprehensive four-volume history of one of the specialist sports car industry's greatest names.

Of course, I'd be delighted to be the one responsible for wrapping-up this amazing story. It would help to hear your views on this, so if you'd like to see it happen, please let me know. If the demand is there and all the right contacts can be made, I'll happily tackle the job.

Peter Filby